RACIST VIOLENCE IN EUROPE

SEVEN DAY LOAN

This book is to be returned on
or before the date stamped below

UNIVERSITY OF PLYMOUTH

PLYMOUTH LIBRARY

Tel: (01752) 232323
This book is subject to recall if required by another reader
Books may be renewed by phone
CHARGES WILL BE MADE FOR OVERDUE BOOKS

Racist Violence
in Europe

Edited by

Tore Björgo
Research Fellow
Norwegian Institute of International Affairs
Oslo, Norway

and

Rob Witte
Researcher
Willem Pompe Institute for Criminal Law
University of Utrecht, the Netherlands

M
St. Martin's Press

First published in Great Britain 1993 by
THE MACMILLAN PRESS LTD
Houndmills, Basingstoke, Hampshire RG21 2XS
and London
Companies and representatives
throughout the world

A catalogue record for this book is available
from the British Library.

ISBN 0–333–60101–7 hardcover
ISBN 0–333–60102–5 paperback

Printed in Great Britain by
Antony Rowe Ltd, Chippenham, Wiltshire

Reprinted 1994

First published in the United States of America 1993 by
Scholarly and Reference Division,
ST. MARTIN'S PRESS, INC.,
175 Fifth Avenue,
New York, N.Y. 10010

ISBN 0–312–10297–6

Library of Congress Cataloging-in-Publication Data
Racist violence in Europe / edited by Tore Björgo and Rob Witte.
p. cm.
Includes bibliographical references and index.
ISBN 0–312–10297–6
1. Europe—Race relations. 2. Europe—Ethnic relations.
3. Racism—Europe—History—20th century. 4. Violence—Europe–
–History—20th century. 5. Minorities—Europe—Crimes against–
–History—20th century. I. Bjørgo, Tore. II. Witte, Rob.
D1056,R34 1993
305.80094—dc20   93–8717
                                                           CIP

Contents

v

Contents

Preface

This book is based on contributions from fifteen leading experts in the field of racism and racist violence from various European countries. They were each invited to write a chapter on a topic specified by the editors of this volume. The contributors met at a workshop at the Norwegian Institute of International Affairs in Oslo, 22–24 January 1993, to discuss and improve their contributions before final publication. However, the analysis and views expressed in the individual chapters remain the responsibility of each author.

The workshop and the book project *Racist Violence in Europe* were made possible by economic support from governmental and non-governmental sponsors, to whom we would hereby express our appreciation: *from Norway:* the Ministry of Foreign Affairs, the Ministry of Justice, the Ministry of Labour and Local Administration, the Directorate of Immigration, the Norwegian Research Council for Applied Social Science (NORAS), the local action group 'Brumunddal on New Paths', and the Norwegian Institute of International Affairs; and *from the Netherlands:* the Dutch Ministry of Justice, the Ministry of Welfare, Health and Culture, and the Willem Pompe Institute of Criminal Law at the University of Utrecht.

We want to thank the participants of the workshop for their contributions, discussions and constructive criticism. We also appreciated the pleasant cooperation with our editor at Macmillan, Clare Wace. A special thank to Tone Strand Muss at the Norwegian Institute of International Affairs for her invaluable assistance during the organisation of the workshop and the editorial process. Thanks as well to Keith Povey and Eilert Struksnes for editorial assistance. Finally, we would also like to thank our wives, Tone and Marja, for forbearance and support.

Oslo   TORE BJÖRGO
Utrecht   ROB WITTE

vii

Notes on the Contributors

Tore Björgo is Research Fellow at the Norwegian Institute of International Affairs, and a guest researcher at the Centre for the Study of Social Conflicts at the University of Leiden in the Netherlands. Trained as a social anthropologist, he is currently doing research on right-wing violence and terrorism in Scandinavia. He has published on the Israeli–Palestinian conflict, political communication, terrorism, racist violence and right-wing extremism.

Rob Witte is a political scientist at the Criminology Section of the Willem Pompe Institute for Criminal Law, University of Utrecht in the Netherlands. He is completing his doctoral dissertation on state response to racist violence in France, Britain and the Netherlands. He has published a study on the 1990 local elections in the Netherlands with respect to the results of the extreme right parties.

Graeme Atkinson is European Editor of *Searchlight Magazine*. He was a Special Adviser to the European Parliament, Committee of Inquiry into Racism and Xenophobia in Europe (1990). He has published extensively on racism, Fascism and right-wing extremism.

Benjamin Bowling is Senior Research Officer in the Home Office Research and Planning Unit. A former action-research project (with William Saulsbury) developed a locally coordinated response to racial harassment in East London. He is writing his PhD at the London School of Economics, studying the emergence of violent racism as a social problem in Britain, and political, policy and practical responses to it.

Jaap van Donselaar is a cultural anthropologist at the Leiden Institute of Social Scientific Research, University of Leiden. He has published several books and articles on right-wing extremism, among them his doctoral dissertation 'Fout na de Oorlog' (1991) on fascist and racist organisations in the Netherlands, 1950–90. He is continuing research on right-wing extremism in the Netherlands and Western Europe.

Paul Gordon was a researcher at the Runnymede Trust, London, from 1980 until 1993. He has written extensively on problems of racism and racial discrimination including *White Law: Racism in the Police Courts and Prisons* (1983), *Fortress Europe? The Meaning of 1992* (1989), and *Racial Violence and Harassment* (1990). He is now a practising psychotherapist.

Wilhelm Heitmeyer is Professor in Socialisation Research at the University of Bielefeld in Germany. He heads a research project on violence in the Special Research Unit on Prevention and Intervention in Childhood and Adolescence. He has published extensively on problems of right-wing extremism, violence and adolescence. He is the author of the influential *Rechtsextremistische Orientierungen bei Jugendlichen* (4th edn. 1992), and editor of publications in the field of adolescence.

Christopher T. Husbands is Reader in Sociology and Internal Academic Audit Officer at the London School of Economics and Political Science. He has published widely on extreme-right politics and on immigration policy in Western Europe, with special focus on Belgium, the Federal Republic of Germany, France, the Netherlands and the United Kingdom.

Erik Jensen is a historian working for a PhD on xenophobia and Nazism in Denmark at the University of Copenhagen. He is also the editor of the anti-fascist monthly *Demos Nyhedsbrev*.

John D. Klier is Corob Reader in Modern Jewish History at the Department of Hebrew and Jewish Studies, University College of London. He is the author of *Russia Gathers Her Jews: The Origins of the Jewish Question in Russia, 1772–1825* (1986) and editor, with S. Lambroza, of *Pogroms: Anti-Jewish Violence in Modern Russian History* (1992).

Cathie Lloyd is Research Fellow at the Centre for Research in Ethnic Relations at the University of Warwick, England. She is working on anti-racist movements and strategies in Europe and is currently completing her doctoral thesis on anti-racism in France. She has published widely on anti-racism in the context of the history of ideas, and public order. Prior to this, she worked as head of research at the Commission for Racial Equality.

Heléne Lööw is Research Fellow at the Department of History, Gothenburg. Her present fields of study are national socialism, racism, state response, nationalism, and national socialist women. She is the author of *Hakkorset och Wasakärven: En studie av national-socialismen i Sverige 1924–1950* (doctoral dissertation, Gothenburg, 1990).

Katrin Reemtsma is an ethnologist. From 1981 to 1987 she was in charge of the work with Sinti and Roma ('Gypsies') at the minority rights organisation, *Gesellschaft für bedrohte Völker*. She is now doing freelance research and writes for newspapers, magazines and books, particularly on the situation of the Roma in South Eastern Europe. She is also providing expertise in asylum and criminal cases.

William Saulsbury is at present Assistant Director of the Police Foundation in London. He has been a consultant to the Research and Planning Unit and the Police Department of the British Home Office. Prior to this, he administered research and development programmes on policing for the National Institute of Justice, the research arm of the US Department of Justice. He started his career as a police officer in Washington, DC.

Yücel Yeşilgöz is a researcher at the Criminology Section of the Willem Pompe Institute for Criminal Law, University of Utrecht, the Netherlands. He is working on a doctoral thesis on the communicative interaction between Dutch Criminal Law representatives and Turkish clients of the justice system. He has published several articles on this subject, and on the human rights situation in Turkey, where he was a leading lawyer defending oppositional activists and organisations. He is now a political refugee.

1 Introduction

Tore Björgo and Rob Witte

Racist violence has reached alarming levels all over Europe. By the early 1990s, many groups of people have had to face racist violence and harassment as a threatening part of everyday life. This is the situation in a Europe characterised by rapid economic, social, demographical, political and ideological changes and by increasing instability – especially since the fall of the Communist systems in Eastern Europe.

The growing number of racist violent attacks is aimed particularly at immigrants and their descendants, asylum-seekers and refugees. But also minorities who have lived in Europe for generations, such as Jews and Roma, are the targets of racist violence and the threat of it. This violence is aimed at people not as individuals, but as members of minority groups in the population – on the basis of skin colour, religion, and ethnic, cultural or national origin.

THE EUROPEAN CONTEXT

Racism and racist violence are nothing new in European history. Both have a long history – in connection with European imperialism in earlier centuries, with the pogroms in Russia during the late nineteenth and early twentieth century (see Chapter 9 by Klier), and with the Holocaust during the Second World War. However, racism has also undergone changes due to socioeconomic, demographical, political and ideological developments.[1]

The 1980s and 1990s have been characterised by a process of increasingly interwoven economic and political relations across Europe, especially with respect to the European Community (EC). 'Europe 1992' was proclaimed as a turning-point in history with respect to the development of 'a strong and united Europe'. At first this integration was seen primarily as an economic and to some extent political unity – the EC as a strong and united bloc against the USA and Japan. Increasingly this idea came to include a strong unity against people who would seek to enter the EC territory. Forecasts of 'floods' and 'waves' of immigrants from the South (Africa) and the East (Asia) were

1

increasingly presented as threats, as the causes for problems, competition, cultural conflicts, economic burdens and possibly crime and disorder. These forecasts became more and more prominent on the European political agenda after the changes in Eastern Europe. Often these views were presented in close connection with already existing and worsening social problems of unemployment, deprivation, criminality and inner-city conditions.

The idea of an economically strong and united Europe increasingly became linked with the idea of 'Fortress Europe'. Significant in this respect was the Schengen Agreement in connection with the abolition of border controls between the signatory states (France, Germany, the Netherlands, Belgium and Luxembourg) because it may serve as a blueprint of that 'Fortress'. The agreement envisages the harmonisation of national policies on visas, immigration and asylum laws, as well as coordinated crime prevention and search operations. In December 1989, the European Parliament passed a resolution stating that the Schengen Agreement could lead to discriminatory police actions, with detrimental effects on the rights of refugees and migrant workers and endangering legal protection and the privacy of individuals (Bunyan, 1991).

These and similar developments will have implications not only for 'new' immigrants, asylum-seekers and refugees in the 1990s, but also for their families and for ethnic minorities already settled in Europe as naturalised citizens. A move from external border controls to internal controls will have a massive influence on daily life for non-white ethnic minorities.

The same time-period, the 1980s and early 1990s, has seen the emergence in Europe of an increasing nationalism, ethnocentrism and racism. This has found expression in racist and nationalist movements (see Chapters 5 and 6 by Lööw and Jensen) as well as in 'everyday racism' (see Chapters 2, 3, 12 and 15 by Heitmeyer, Björgo, Gordon and Lloyd). Neo-Nazi, fascist and far right xenophobic groups and political parties are on the increase within democratic systems all over Europe. Among the more successful political parties are *Front National* in France, *Vlaams Blok* in Belgium, *Die Republikaner* in Germany, *Centrumdemocraten* in the Netherlands, the *Freiheitliches Partei Österreich* in Austria, the *Movimento Sociale Italiano* and the *Lega Nord* in Italy. In some European countries, a threatening situation has emerged in which respectable well-established right-wing and/or left-wing parties respond to these trends by adapting parts of their rhetoric and programme to woo voters of the extreme Right. More and more, socioeconomic problems like unemployment, poor housing, crime and deprivation, are portrayed in close – if not directly causal – connection with the presence of ethnic and cultural minorities and with the growing numbers of asylum-seekers and refugees. The continuing marginalisation and criminalisation of minorities is apparent in several European countries, a tendency which seems no longer to be the monopoly of neo-Nazi and right-wing extremist movements and parties.

It is within this context that racist violence is occurring frequently all over Europe. Some violent racist incidents have attracted international attention: here we may mention the desecration of Jewish graves in Carpentras, France (1990), the violence against African street vendors in Florence, Italy (1990), and in Germany the racist attacks against asylum-seekers in Hoyerswerda (1991) and Rostock (1992) and the racist murder of three Turkish women in Mölln (1992). Most racist incidents, however, receive neither international nor even national attention. The majority of racist attacks against people, their property or places of worship occur without any mass media publicity or political attention throughout Europe – from Sweden to Italy, from Britain to Russia.

PATTERNS OF VIOLENCE

The patterns of racist violence are far from uniform across the continent (see Chapter 8, by Husbands). Recent years have seen a significant increase in this violence – in terms both of numbers of incidents and seriousness – in countries like Germany, Sweden, France, Britain, the Netherlands, Spain and Switzerland, although to differing degrees. Elsewhere, as in Norway, Denmark and Belgium, the level of racist violence seems to have remained relatively stable and low in comparison with other countries. Racist violence tends to come in waves – as in 1973 and 1982 in France, during May and June 1990 in Sweden, during the Gulf War (1991) in Britain and France, during 1991–2 in Germany, and during the first half of 1992 in the Netherlands. Sudden news items, media coverage and 'moral panics' (Cohen, 1980), often in close connection with the presence of minorities, may contribute to provoke these waves. 'Copycat' actions may produce a contagion effect, with sudden surges of racist violence in 'new' localities (see Chapters 3 and 7 by Björgo).

Various types of racist violence exist with different levels of severity. One category is *terrorist attacks*, in the form of bombings, arson (including Molotov cocktails), shootings and other armed attacks. A second category is *street violence*, including premeditated assaults as well as more spontaneous violence. Less lethal, but nevertheless potentially highly intimidating, are *vandalism of property*, *threats*, and *verbal abuse and gestures*. The severity of this violence and harassment should be perceived in a relative sense. Incidents which attract mass media publicity tend to be individual attacks of a life-threatening kind – mostly involving the more spectacular forms of violence. Racist violence should not be seen merely as isolated incidents, however: in most cases it consists of a series of repeated incidents which is properly understood as a process (Bowling, 1990). Each single incident in this process may be perceived as being less serious, but the process as a whole may have a very serious and threatening impact on the everyday lives of the potential victims.

There are also differences among several European countries in terms of the attention and media publicity given to racist violence. In some countries, racist violence constitutes a first-order topic for the mass media and for public, political and academic attention; while in others hardly any notice may be taken (see Chapters 7 and 10, by Björgo and Witte). Nor is there any direct relation between the degree of this attention and the level of racist violence in the country concerned.

The scale and intensity of racist violence differ as well. Statistical comparison is difficult, however. Although there may exist statistics on racist violence in some countries, these tend to be based on different labelling practices and/or definitions. The British Home Office estimated (Home Office, 1981) that there were about 7000 racial incidents a year in England and Wales. Their definition included all incidents or alleged offences (including all kinds of harassment) in which victims and perpetrators belonged to different 'racial' groups and where there were indications of racial motives. In a report issued ten years later by the Inter-Departmental Racial Attacks Group (Home Office, 1991b)[2] only racially-motivated incidents reported to the police were counted. This showed an increase of the number of incidents from 4383 in 1988 to 7793 in 1992.

The German security service, *Verfassungsschutz*, in their statistics of right-wing extremist violence, include all kinds of physical violence; they conclude that there were 1483 violent attacks in 1991 (of which 383 were cases of arson and bombings with explosives). Preliminary figures for 1992 are 2506 attacks (712 were cases of arson and bombing) Björgo's statistics from Scandinavia (see Chapter 3) include only instances of what he defines as 'terrorist attacks'; this does not include street violence, which is a more common form of racist violence. In 1992 there were forty of these terrorist attacks in Sweden, four in Denmark and four in Norway. Needless to say, the enormous variation in statistics and definitions makes it impossible to compare the situations between various European countries directly.

A related problem is that much racist violence never gets reported at all, not in the media nor to the police, nor is it often registered specifically as racist. Within one country, some local police stations may register racist violence, while others may put similar cases in other categories. In 1988 the Swedish National Police Authority asked its 118 local police departments to report all cases with a racist aspect during the period 1984-7. Although 2039 cases were reported, some departments in larger cities claimed that there had been not one single case to report from their area – even if these were areas where many incidents of racist violence are known to have taken place. Such lopsided reporting is probably caused by a lack of agreement within the police with respect to defining 'racist crime' (Rikspolisstyrelsen, 1988, p. 14). For instance, some police officers may rule out racist motives if a violent action was carried out under the influence of alcohol, or if perpetrators were not directly connected to racist organisations. A study of police compliance with guidelines on reporting complaints of discrimination in the Netherlands yielded similar findings (WODC, 1993). These findings on police reporting practices in individual countries point to the difficulties of comparison on a European level.

Not only do patterns and types of racist violence differ, but also target groups are different from country to country. In some countries people from former colonies constitute the main targets of racist violence, like people of Algerian origin in France and people of Asian and Afro-Caribbean origin in Britain. Immigrants and their descendants from the Mediterranean area and the Middle East are under frequent attack in other countries, like people of Turkish origin in Germany and people of Moroccan origin in Belgium. The 1990s have seen asylum-seekers and refugees from Africa and Eastern Europe increasingly confronted with racist violence – in countries like Italy, Spain, Germany and Sweden. In former Communist countries, minorities of ethnic or national origin are among the main targets of racist violence. Sometimes these minorities originated from a neighbouring country, like the Hungarians in the Slovakian republic and Romania, and the Romanians in Hungary. All over Europe, certain religious minorities are frequent victims. The devastating history of anti-Jewish persecution did not end in 1945. In the early 1990s, anti-Semitism again seems to be on the rise. Also Muslim minorities have been among the main targets of racism since the 1980s. In many European countries, Roma and Sinti ('Gypsies') have a history similar to that of the Jewish people with respect to being targets of racist violence in both the past and present – especially in Eastern European countries like Hungary, Romania and Poland, but also in, for instance, Spain and Germany (see Chapter 14 by Reemtsma).

Not only does the situation vary from country to country, there are also several ways in which this violent phenomenon is labelled and defined. Commonly used labels are: *racist violence, racial violence, right-wing extremist violence, anti-Semitic violence, anti-immigrant violence, violence against foreigners.* Some may even claim that racist violence is just plain violence like any other criminal violence and refuse to put it in any special category or to give it any special status. In this volume various labels are used according to the various definitions of the contributors or according to the main labels and definitions used in the country in focus. Labels and definitions may point to the potential victims, like 'anti-immigrant violence', 'violence against foreigners' and 'anti-Semitic violence'. They also may point to the perpetrators and their motives, like 'racist violence' and 'right-wing extremist violence'. The label 'racial violence' (meaning 'inter-racial violence') points to both.

We have as editors chosen the label *racist violence*, defined as *any violence in which victims are selected because of their ethnic, 'racial', religious, cultural or national origin. The victims are attacked not in their capacities as individuals, but as representatives of such groups which are normally minorities in terms of numbers as well as in terms of power. Buildings, properties and institutions may also be attacked because they represent these groups or their interests.*

This definition of racist violence allows for compounded motives and does not require perpetrators to have any elaborated 'racist ideologies'. Under the terms of this definition, victims may be foreigners, asylum-seekers or immigrants, but they may also have been a part of society for generations and may hold the same nationality as the perpetrators. In general, perpetrators of racist violence define their potential victims as 'them' who are distinguished from 'us' on the basis of skin colour, religion, cultural, ethnic or national origin. Often the presence of 'them' is experienced and portrayed as a threat to 'our' culture, life style, welfare, 'race', etc. 'They' should be excluded from various aspects of life, to varying degrees: from social services, jobs, housing, to living at all in the same country. The most extreme expression of this racist exclusionism is found in racist violence.

EXPLANATIONS OF RACIST VIOLENCE

Many explanations – of a popular or more scientific character – have been presented in the public debate concerning the emergence of racism and racist violence and why it may increase or decrease in some societies:

✳   1.   The level of racist violence is seen as directly linked to the size (or increase) of certain minority populations, such as immigrants or asylum-seekers. According to this popular explanation, there is a 'natural threshold' to the number of 'foreigners' a society can absorb. Once the limit is passed, conflicts will erupt – whether that is due to economic competition or to 'cultural' clashes.

The experience of some countries may seem to support this argument, such as Germany compared with the rest of Europe, or Sweden compared with Norway and Denmark. But there are also numerous cases where the existence of relatively large minority populations has *not* coincided with a high level of violence. The Netherlands, Britain and France have about the same level of minority populations, but very different levels of racist violence. When the Republic of Indonesia became independent, 300 000 people came to the Netherlands during the early 1950s – without any serious violent reaction. On the other hand, sometimes the arrival of just a few individual 'foreigners' in a local community may be perceived as a dreadful threat to some by the locals, who respond with violence.

Another aspect of the line of explanation described above is expressed in the assumption that political measures to limit or to reduce the presence of the minority populations in question would lead to a decline in racist violence. However, in many cases racist violence has increased dramatically shortly *after* the government or other leading politicians have implemented or propagated measures to restrict immigration and asylum policies. In Sweden, a wave of racist attacks started in May 1990, five months after the Social Democratic Government tightened up its traditionally liberal asylum policy (see Chapter 3 by Björgo). In Germany, racist attacks and riots intensified dramatically after the CDU-led Government in the summer 1991 opened the so-called 'Asylum Debate', concerning the intended amendment to the Constitution in order to limit the numbers of asylum-seekers coming to Germany (see Atkinson's contribution in this volume).

2. The level of racist violence is often explained as being directly linked with socioeconomic factors and circumstances. In particular, racist organisations and racist violence are supposed to flourish in times of economic recession and crisis. According to this line of argument, 'less well-off' sections of the majority population perceive minorities and 'foreigners' as unwelcome competitors for scarce resources. People show their resentment of this by using violence.

Few researchers in the field would dispute that there is a connection between social and economic crisis on the one hand, and a rise in racism and racist violence on the other. However, the link between unemployment and racism is not as direct as the popular argument might have us believe. Studies in Scandinavia, for instance, have shown that unemployed people do not have particularly negative attitudes toward immigrants – although there may be a correlation between low socioeconomic status and developing negative attitudes towards immigrants. The level of education was found to be the strongest explanatory variable. This was related to having a high degree of control over one's own destiny and positive economic prospects (e.g. Hernes and Knudsen, 1990, pp. 97–128). Several studies of elections and party affiliation have also failed to show any clear and direct correlation between unemployment and support for racist parties (e.g. Witte, 1991). The example of Denmark – which has had a high level of unemployment throughout most of the 1980s – has shown a relatively low level of racist violence. Thus, socioeconomic factors such as education level and social security systems, may be more important than unemployment as such. The relation between socioeconomic circumstances and racist violence is therefore far more complex than generally perceived. Heitmeyer (Chapter 2) expounds on several of the influences of socioeconomic circumstances on individual behaviour in connection with racist violence.

Racist activists, politicians and ordinary people themselves often establish a link between the perceived 'wave of refugees' and the economic hardship and unemployment experienced in daily life. Although an increase in the influx of asylum-seekers and an economic recession are two separate processes, people sometimes come to believe that there is a direct, causal relationship between the two. When there is a concurrence in time, such relationships are assumed to exist. Racist organisations and parties are always quick to take advantage of such situations to channel public discontent and frustration towards 'convenient' objects of hate.

3. A widespread explanation of the emergence of racist violence focuses on the alleged cultural or national traits attributed to the perpetrators of the violence – or to the victims of the violence. A high level of racist violence in a particular country is often explained in terms of 'national character'. For instance, the violent attacks in Hoyerswerda and Rostock in Germany were sometimes interpreted by other Europeans as showing a re-emergence of 'the true German' or as 'the Germans are showing their real face'. Similarly racist violence in Eastern European countries and the Balkans is explained by referring to the assumption that the people there are violence-prone, because of 'hot blood', 'violent traditions', or their 'innate irrationality'.

In its direct and general form, explanations like these may represent in themselves an ethnocentric or racist way of thinking. This does not mean, however, that historical legacies and political culture may not play a role. But it probably operates more on the level of subculture, where some sections of a society may embrace certain violent or racist traditions while others distance themselves from these tendencies.

A variation of the 'national character' type of explanation is that it is sometimes also used to explain relatively low levels of racist violence. The Netherlands is perceived to be a very tolerant country. A relatively low level of racist incidents is sometimes presented as a consequence of the 'national character'. This sometimes leads to a situation in which the perception of reality is adjusted to fit this self-image. Racist incidents are often claimed not to be racist – because there is allegedly no racism in the Netherlands.

The 'national character' line of argument is also frequently used to explain why certain groups, such as Jews and Roma people, are victimised by racist violence. Thus 'blaming the victim' by assuming that a specific minority group is made up of notorious thieves, rapists or greedy exploiters has been standard procedure in justifying pogroms, genocide and more recent racist violent attacks in Europe.

4. While most types of explanations so far have focused on the macro level, we need to analyse individual motives and group dynamics in order to get a better understanding of why people decide to carry out violent attacks. Contributions in this volume by Heitmeyer, Björgo and Lööw (Chapters 2, 3, 5 and 7) address this issue. They focus on processes of identity formation and the search for 'belonging' which some young people find in close-knit, racist groups. Motives for violent

behaviour against minorities are often a combination of political and private ones.

Although this approach does have a considerably explanatory value on the individual and group level, it is also useful to link it with other types of factors on the national level. This Heitmeyer does (in Chapter 2) when he describes the general process of individualisation in the social and economic system, where social status and identity are no longer 'givens' but have to be achieved through personal effort with a great risk of failure – particularly in times of social and economic crisis. The trend among many young Germans to define their identity in terms of such 'natural characteristics' as 'race' and nationality may be seen as an attempt to solve this dilemma.

5.   One popular type of explanation of racist violence is that it is merely the work of 'drunken pranks', not at all linked with racism. This explanation may in part be based on a correct observation, but it is a mistaken interpretation. Many (possibly most) racist attacks are in fact carried out under the influence of alcohol. This, however, does not mean that racist elements in the violence may be ruled out. As several authors in this volume point out, it is a *typical* trait of racist violent behaviour to be preceded by heavy consumption of alcohol. In contexts as different as the anti-Jewish pogroms in Russia at the turn of the century (see Klier, pp. 133, 135), riots against Italian immigrants in France during the 1890s (see Lloyd, p. 204), and present-day fire-bombings of asylum-centres in Scandinavia (see Björgo, pp. 35–6, 41–2), the authors find alcohol consumption to be a recurrent component in the patterns of events. Alcohol appears to be not only a way to overcome inhibitions when the situation arises, but also a way to muster the necessary courage and bravado for planned racist attacks (see Husbands, in Chapter 8). Thus, even if an act of violence is perpetrated under the influence of alcohol, this certainly does not mean that it may not also be influenced by racist motives.

6.   Another set of explanations concerns the influence of the response of authorities to racist violence – or the lack of it. Whether or not politicians and other national and local authorities respond – and how they respond – may influence the occurrence and development of racist violence. Especially, lack of police response to racist violence tends to lead to an increase in the violence; conversely, certain types of responses towards the perpetrators generally reduce the violence.

In this volume, the contributions of Bowling and Saulsbury, Klier, Reemtsma, Yeşilgöz, Atkinson, Witte, Lloyd and Gordon (Chapters 9–16) all discuss responses by specific authorities in several situations and countries across Europe. A main finding here is that police passivity towards racist violence leads to a continuation and increase in such violence. The response of the authorities is also of central importance with respect to feelings of insecurity among groups of potential victims. People not (yet) victims, but belonging to these groups, will feel more insecure when authorities fail to respond adequately to racist incidents.

7. Related explanations of the emergence of racist violence concern the impact of state response to racist organisations. Some explain the emergence of racist violence by the oppression of the political extreme Right. If this group is deprived of the chance to express itself through the regular political channels, with no opportunity to 'let off steam', this may lead to an explosion of violence, being the only alternative left (e.g. Frigaard, 1989, p. 50). On the other hand, others argue that the emergence of racist violence is the result of parties and organisations of the extreme Right being able to propagate their racist message unhindered, even having it legitimised by being represented in parliament and other public offices. Violent groups, it is argued, just carry things a bit further than the politicians.

Examples can easily be found to support both lines of arguments. So far there has been no systematic testing of these hypotheses on a comparative basis. Van Donselaar, in Chapter 4, reports a striking relationship between an increase in the number of racist incidents and the rising support of racist political parties in the Netherlands. The same co-variation can be observed in Germany, France and other European countries. However, whether an increase of racist violence is influenced by the success of racist parties, or whether both are independent results of a more general tendency towards xenophobia in parts of public opinion, is an issue which needs more research.

8. Another set of explanations involving far-right organisations holds that racist violence takes place because it is organised and perpetrated by extremist groups. This is based on the assumption that violence is not 'racist' if it cannot be linked to racist organisations or persons with outspoken racist convictions. Unorganised and spontaneous violence is then often brushed aside as 'boyish tricks and drunken pranks' and as 'plain vandalism' – in effect denying the racist character of the act.

A major finding in this volume is that most of the racist violence is perpetrated by youth gangs or individuals who are *not* affiliated to political organisations. Sometimes the perpetrator may belong to a racist organisation but is apparently acting on his own initiative, or he may belong to the fringes of a youth gang where influential members are involved with extremist politics (see Björgo, van Donselaar, Lööw, Jensen, Husbands, Klier, Chapters 3–9). Of course, organised groups are directly involved in a significant proportion of racist attacks, but the notion that racist violence is as a rule perpetrated by such groups is definitely not correct.

9. Many explanatory statements of racism and racist violence emphasise the responsibility of the state. Measures in a state's immigration policy and its policies towards minorities are perceived as forms of institutional racism and as creating an atmosphere in which racist violence can flourish. Moreover, state agencies may themselves be directly involved in racist violence as perpetrators.

Several contributions in this volume point to state policies and political initiatives on immigration and minority issues which pave the way for racist violence (Witte, Lloyd, Klier, Reemtsma, Atkinson, Yeşilgöz, Chapters 10, 15, 9, 14, 11 and 13). State agencies have been found to play a role as active perpetrators of racist violence, especially the police (Gordon, Lloyd, Reemtsma, Chapters 12, 15 and 14). Yeşilgöz's discussion of the specific situation of Turkey sheds a special light on the role of the state. On the one hand the Turkish state has condemned racist violence perpetrated against minorities of Turkish origin in several European countries. On the other hand, this same state has a double standard concerning racist violence against minorities within Turkey itself.

10. Explanations are also directed at the role of anti-racist organisations. It is often claimed that the way in which these organisations operate influences the way racist violence develops. One line of argument holds that if anti-racist organisations resort to force and violence themselves to prevent racist and neo-Nazi groups from assembling in public, these racist groups will become more violent as well, seeing their violence as justified counter-violence. Others see the far Right as inherently violent, and attribute the emergence of racist violence to the weakness of the anti-racist movement, which is unable to keep the racists off the streets. Some explain the violence of certain anti-racist or minority groups as a consequence of the lack of response to racist violence by various sectors in society, especially the authorities.

The role of anti-racist action is the topic of heated discussion in several countries. This is also reflected in several contributions in this volume. In Chapter 15, Lloyd addresses the way anti-racists respond to racist violence, while Witte (Chapter 10) considers how anti-racist action can contribute to bring racism on the public agenda. From a different perspective, in Chapter 5 Lööw discusses the influence of certain types of anti-racist action on the world-view of some racist groups.

11. Another set of explanations focuses on the role of the media. In the public debate, there are conflicting claims about whether media coverage of racist violence serves to increase the violence and support of racist groups, or to curtail it. One common claim is that media coverage of racist violence inspires others to carry out similar actions ('copycatting'), often motivated by a desire to get attention themselves. Others, however, claim that we need a penetrating searchlight from the media on the seriousness of the issue in order to expose violent groups and bring the problem to the attention of political authorities and the police.

Most of the contributions in this volume mention the role of the media only briefly. In Chapter 7 Björgo discusses the role of the media in greater detail, and examines and evaluates a number of different effects – both facilitating and inhibiting – in relation to racist violence.

A RESEARCH AGENDA

Although much academic research has been carried out with respect to racism and extreme right organisations, there has been surprisingly little research focused explicitly on the violent aspect. Studies and books which analyse racist violence specifically often take up one single racist incident or only one specific aspect of the violence. The vast majority of these analyses concern the situation in one country (e.g. Björgo, 1989; Gordon, 1990) or in one local community (Bowling, 1994). On the international level, racist violence hardly constitutes a topic which is studied and analysed in depth, not to speak of any comparative perspective. The only report to deal specifically with racist violence on a European level, the work of Robin Oakley at the request of the Council of Europe (1991), describes the situation in six countries – the UK, France, Germany, Italy, the Netherlands and Sweden. This report, however, is rather descriptive without much analysis. Almost all other studies of the phenomenon on an international or European level tend to discuss racism, right-wing extremism and Fascism in general without specifically analysing racist violence as such (e.g. European Parliament, 1990; Hainsworth, 1992; Butterwegge and Jäger, 1992; Elbers and Fennema, 1993).

It was this situation that convinced the editors of this volume of the need to bring together a group of selected researchers to exchange findings and insights in this specific field. They were invited to a workshop at the Norwegian Institute of International Affairs in Oslo in January 1993 to discuss and revise their contributions to the book. They were asked to write about one specified aspect of racist violence within their field of expertise. Contributors have different views and perspectives – and it was not our goal to have the book appear as being written by a single individual. None the less, the book will show there was a high degree of accordance between many of their findings and conclusions.

Although it would have been highly desirable to have made comparative studies of the situation in several countries, very few of the individual researchers have carried out such studies at this stage. As a first step towards developing international comparative research on racist violence, our goal was to cover the most important and relevant aspects of racist violence through different analytical approaches, and at the same time to cover as many parts of Europe as possible – in particular those countries most exposed to racist violence. This goal has been almost impossible to accomplish within the framework of one single volume. First, with more than thirty European countries, not every one can be covered if there is to be some in-depth analysis. Second, while academic and governmental research has been conducted into phenomena like racism and racist violence for a long time in some countries – particularly in Germany and Britain – other countries lack such a research tradition. Especially in Eastern and Southern Europe it has been very difficult to find researchers able to deliver a contribution on racist violence in these countries. For this reason, as well as the fact that our research networks are concentrated in Western and Northern Europe, the present volume is somewhat under-represented on the situation in Southern and Eastern Europe.

Some aspects of racist violence, such as the state response and the motivations of perpetrators, are dealt with by several contributors. Other aspects are not covered to the same extent. This does not mean that aspects of racist violence which are not taken up or are scarcely touched on in this volume are unimportant. On the contrary, aspects such as the victimisation process are of utmost importance. This aspect is well-covered by British research on racist harassment (Bowling, 1992; Gordon, 1990, and others). In organising the workshop and the present volume, choices had to be made according to the goals mentioned. This has led to a situation in which certain aspects of racist violence had to be left out, because the only research which was known related to countries already reported on by several other contributors. We did not want to have the vast majority of the contributors and their chapters represent only two or three European countries.

On principle, the concept of racist violence covers a wide range of phenomena – from genocide and large-scale ethnic conflict to harassment on a local level, for instance against shopkeepers. We decided to limit the scope of the book and to avoid bringing in too many phenomena with only a few traits in common. Therefore, large-scale ethnic conflicts like the civil war in former Yugoslavia or the civil war between Muslims and Armenians in Nagorno-Karabakh were not included – although these conflicts clearly involve aspects of racism and racist violence. For similar reasons, the Holocaust against the Jews and the 'Gypsies' during the Second World War is not discussed separately in this volume – although it is incorporated as part of the historic background in some of the contributions (Chapters 14 and 15 by Reemtsma, Lloyd respectively). In the USA, the term 'hate crime' (see Hamm, 1994) is used to describe both racist violence, violence against homosexuals, and against other types of hate objects. Violence against homosexuals is a 'hidden' problem also in Europe, and often carried out by the same groups that commit racist violence (see Lööw, Chapter 5, pp. 72–4). However, violence against homosexuals is not discussed specifically within this book on racist violence. One difficulty with the concept of hate crime is that it tends to widen the scope so much that the specific features of racist violence may get neglected.

Comparative international research is necessary in order to develop and improve our insight into the problem of racist violence. Such research should deal with the differences as well as with the similarities in various countries. A precondition for such research is the existence of international contact, cooperation and exchange of knowledge, facts, theories, findings and methods of research in the field. Despite the recent increase in organised workshops and conferences in Europe concerning issues like migration, racism and discrimination, little has been done in the field of racist violence. This book may be seen as a first step towards developing international comparative research on racist violence.

At the same time, we believe that this book presents – in an accessible form – insights which may be of interest and use to anti-racist organisations, government agencies, minority organisations, students and others who are concerned with the problem of racist violence.

NOTES

1. See, e.g., Barker (1981), Miles (1989).
2. British Home Secretary Kenneth Baker stated that these figures do not fully indicate the scale of the problem (Home Office, 1991b, p. 1).

2 Hostility and Violence towards Foreigners in Germany

Wilhelm Heitmeyer[1]

Racism, hostility towards foreigners, ethnocentrism, fear of deviance from the norm and privileges for local residents are phenomena that have now been present in European societies for many years, in many aspects and to a varying extent. They are based on ideologies of inequality, non-equivalence and unequal treatment of human beings. When such ideas become linked to violence, extreme right-wing orientations and behaviours result.

A tendency that has been developing for many years (see the studies on racism of the European Parliament, 1985, 1990) has now expanded in a threatening manner. It adopted dramatic forms in Germany in 1991 and 1992. This growth in hostility towards foreigners is based on the following process (see Heitmeyer, 1991):

1. At first, *feelings of estrangement* from others appear as a mass social phenomenon. This is usually expressed as an attitude of *distance* that scarcely differentiates between tolerance and *contempt*, which is revealed through stereotypes and prejudices.
2. In *fear of foreigners*, this distanced attitude is overshadowed by a *competitive* stance fuelled by economic and/or cultural considerations. The balance between tolerance and devaluation is lost: tolerance is limited to those small areas that lie outside 'personal' spaces, positions, rights and so forth. Disparagement is linked to a *defensiveness* that is expressed partly in political concepts (e.g. ethnopluralism: 'Stay right where you are.') and partly through political action (e.g. neighbourhood protests against plans to construct housing for political 'refugees').
3. *Hatred of foreigners* is a further stage in which tolerance disappears completely. In its place, and building on distanced and competitive stances, a *hostility* arises that aims to introduce 'clarity' by making

17

fundamental distinctions between friends, the 'natives', and foes, the foreigners. This helps to justify an offensive *struggle* ('If you don't get out, something's going to happen') in which all the above-mentioned variants of xenophobia are drawn upon and exploited.

Politically motivated forms of action start from politically unobtrusive, subtle and overt disparagements of foreigners which, because of their broad social dissemination, can readily be used to make this kind of prejudice sound reasonable and legitimate: 'Since most people think this way . . . ' This provides a basis on which the defensive struggle against material (housing, jobs, etc.) and cultural competition (the danger of being 'overrun' by foreigners) can build, so that, ultimately, even violent, offensive acts seem justified.

Against this background, hostility towards foreigners is not to be understood primarily as a personality trait but rather as a social and political 'tide' whose ebb and flow can be influenced politically and limited by the activity of social groups and government authorities and their definitions of violence. Fighting foreigners with various forms of violence, whether by right-wing organisations, unorganised groups, or 'normal citizens', is therefore inseparable from the mass phenomenon of unresolved feelings of estrangement and the accompanying distanced attitude. It is precisely on this basis that hatred of foreigners builds its legitimation, calculating that those who are inclined towards a distanced attitude will not intervene when advocates of hatred shift to the offensive.

GERMANY AFTER UNIFICATION – A SITUATION REPORT

First, I will describe the phenomena that are the outcome of such a process. It should be noted that in the political reunification of the German state there is hardly any correspondence in economic, social, and individual areas, so that we have to talk about two societies that rub against one another institutionally and, above all, in terms of socialisation.

West Germany is dominated by a society with individualisation processes, while East Germany used to be dominated by repressive and authoritarian processes that are now being superseded by new demands. East German citizens have to rearrange their previous life course and completely re-evaluate their previous biography. Initially, this complicated process in Germany has to be taken into account in any description. However, it simultaneously already forms one aspect of the explanation of these events.

Until now, the latest peak was the outbreak of violence in the East German city of Rostock in August 1992. This was accompanied by numerous follow-up activities not only against political refugees and their housing but also against other foreigners. This outbreak was no surprise, as 250 acts of violence against foreigners had already been registered in the monthly statistics for the first six months of 1992.

Parallel to this, public opinion polls have shown the following changes in the first half of 1992:

1. In June, acceptance of foreigners had changed slightly in West Germany and strongly in East Germany; and in both cases, in a negative direction. Compared with 60 per cent in May, 57 per cent of West Germans still considered that it was right for a lot of foreigners to live in Germany; 40 per cent thought that it was not right, compared with 35 per cent in May. In East Germany, in contrast, only 39 per cent still accepted foreigners in their country compared with 51 per cent in May; while 60 per cent were opposed to foreigners compared with 49 per cent in May.[2]

2. Public sympathy towards 'extreme right-wing tendencies because of the problem with foreigners'[3] increased from 24 per cent in December 1991 to 37 per cent in April 1992 in both parts of Germany. This trend has to be related, in turn, to the increasing numbers of political refugees and the calculated political discussion directed towards preventing them from remaining in Germany.

3. None the less, this violence was publicly ignored during the first half of 1992, mostly because of the lack of coverage in the majority of mass media. The public gained the impression that the wave of violence in Autumn 1991 had been only a one-off event. The outbreak at that time was linked to 'Hoyerswerda', although, again in statistical terms, acts of violence had increased successively throughout 1991.[4] They increased discontinuously from thirty-nine in January 1991 to sixty-four in May, 102 in August, 313 in September, and 964 in October. In November, they dropped to 422; and in December, to 221. The age structure of investigated and suspected persons showed that 32 per cent were younger than 18 years old, 78 per cent were younger than 22, and 90 per cent were younger than 26.

4. The background in Autumn once more reflects a process of growth in xenophobic orientations and an acceptance of violence among

adolescents. However, this process can only be plotted in West Germany as such studies were not permitted in the German Democratic Republic (GDR).

In a study of West German 16- to 17-year-olds carried out in the mid-1980s, we were able to show that 40 per cent agreed with authoritarian, nationalistic perspectives, that is, they advocated parts of ideologies of inequality, while approximately 16 per cent allied these positions to an acceptance of violence, that is, tended towards an extreme right-wing orientation (Heitmeyer, 1992a).

THE MAIN THESIS

Explanations for the problem of hostility towards foreigners are diverse and complex. They cannot be dealt with in detail here. Instead, I shall proceed from the following assumption: the more strongly that social, occupational and political processes of disintegration develop in a society to which foreigners migrate, the greater the problems that these migrants will face in their integration. The present analysis is limited in two ways: first, it concentrates on adolescents, although it must be noted that it is not merely an adolescent problem, as the outcomes of the public opinion polls mentioned above have shown. Second, the analysis focuses particularly on socialisation processes, that is, on experiences, their subjective processing and the political affinities towards extreme right-wing orientations that result. As already mentioned above, this analysis has to be carried out for both German societies.

ATTEMPTS AT AN EXPLANATION FOR THE WESTERN PART

The characteristic conditions of life and socialisation in today's highly industrialised West German society are grouped around the process of *individualisation*. This should not just be associated with an increase in liberty and in no way with a decrease in social inequality. An increase in the scope to shape one's own path through life is also tied to the dissolution of self-evident membership of social living contexts of family, class and so forth. Individuals not only can but also *must* shape their own path through life; in the final analysis, they have to bear the risks of failure alone. Anxiety engendered by the risk of failure and isolation as a result of increased individual competition is a major source of feelings of estrangement.

Feelings of estrangement can also be associated with economically fuelled modernisation processes that are 'mixing up' persons because of open borders and possibilities (but also constraints) of mobility. *New opportunities* are directly tied to new *'confrontations'* with other cultures and languages, which, at least at present, can be dealt with most successfully by those who are highly qualified and flexible and who do not immediately need to fear an existence-threatening social declassification in each new confrontation.

The mixing-up mechanisms currently favour this group because migration movements on their level of qualification occur only one by one, thus rarely eliciting significant competition. If anything, members of this group merely express certain reservations about 'excessive' numbers of foreigners. However, even they are prone to xenophobic hostility when their social status is endangered. For example, affluent citizens in a major German city paid skinheads to attack a home for political refugees that had been built at the end of their residential street.

In contrast, these mixing mechanisms increase the pressure on those who are already socially disadvantaged because of the relatively large movements of unskilled and semi-skilled workers. And these people have minimal financial or other resources to fall back on when migratory movements and unemployment increase.

Hidden behind this mixing-up, lurk certain *ambivalent* social individualisation processes. An important characteristic of these is the acquisition and solidification of social status through individual achievement. The high rate of technological development makes the job carousel turn increasingly faster, creating centrifugal forces that an individual can only counter through a high degree of flexibility. For example, in Germany, the competition from East German migrants and German-born children of migrant workers who are now entering the labour market can change existing feelings of estrangement into outright *anxiety*. This increases even further when it is unclear under which conditions, in which region and with what status one will once more find a place on the job carousel. Discrepancies between job offers and the availability of housing are an additional aggravating factor. The fears fuelled by feelings of estrangement are not simply products of subjective prejudices but are real, just as fear is real the moment somebody says that he or she is afraid. Therefore, there is no way to control the fear of other persons. It cannot be argued away, and any such attempts are not necessarily a sign of humane social policy.

On the social level, these mixing-up processes and increased achievement pressures have produced not only a loss of traditions (the disappearance of traditional career biographies, life stations, customs, etc.) but also an isolation that is increasingly perceived as a burden by a part of the population, as the possibility for stable social integration seems to be increasingly beyond the reach of individuals. At the same time, foreigners are perceived as belonging to a group. Under these conditions, feelings of estrangement, and anxiety, fuelled by a sense of having been abandoned, can turn into subjective fears of threat that release feelings of hatred. Simultaneously, these feelings trigger a search for 'compensatory' integration possibilities that cannot be wrenched away from the individual: this has been experienced in the erosion of family, clan, neighbourhood and social class. Nationalist orientations thus regain a particular significance as a means of binding society. The traditional nationalism of the nation state, which was also always accompanied by violence towards the exterior, is now being replaced by a new 'materialistic' nationalism that is easy to manipulate for domestic political purposes. It is based on the rapid processes of modernisation accompanied by material and cultural trends. At present, these are not being countered by social policies aimed, for example, at alleviating competitive situations, but are being accelerated politically to satisfy predominantly economic interests.

If we use this background to consider the situation of *adolescents* who are approaching a socially recognised adult status, the accelerated modernisation processes can worsen the problems caused by the ambivalent individualisation process. The positive development of expanded individual freedoms is accompanied directly by the loss of feelings of security that formerly arose from 'natural' membership of social groups – memberships that seem to be disappearing more and more.

Natural membership has been replaced by achievement-dependent access. This also means that the rigorous dissemination of the competition principle amounts to a forced choice between either cutting oneself off from others or running the risk of existential punishment. The resulting isolation can become stressful: individuals are exposed to increasingly complex social demands. They are without protection, because they can no longer link their own fate to any larger group, and there is no social milieu to help to provide social and political orientation. Our own empirical research (Heitmeyer, 1992a) has shown that this has led to a marked increase in orientation problems, particularly among adolescents on the threshold of adult society. On the one hand, they are increasingly thrown back on themselves and their individual achievements and, as a result of individualisation, they are exposed to the collective fate of isolation. On the other hand, they are expected to resolve socially generated contradictions that are completely impossible to solve on an individual level.

This constellation can lead to problems when adolescents increasingly gain the impression that they are losing control over their own lives, since they believe that they are unable to cope with their *powerlessness, isolation* and *uncertainties* about how to shape their future careers.

These are everyday economic and social experiences that have a strong impact on the lives of many individuals. How are they processed? How are they transformed politically? How do extreme right-wing ideas tie in with these experiences?

Uncertainties about what to do can be traced back to the dissolution of the normal career and to status anxieties. As the chance of successfully plotting any sort of life plan diminishes, pressure to behave flexibly increases. Thus, although today's adolescents are free to make more decisions than earlier generations of adolescents, they are also compelled to make more decisions – despite the fact that it is often unclear to them precisely how they should decide.

Adolescents deal with these issues in a variety of ways, and there are no iron laws. A flexible type of approach, a handicraft mentality, is particularly necessary to cope with these demands. At the same time, adolescents are often forced to make a lot of 'provisional' decisions. They cannot establish firm orientations and forms of action because this would impair a flexible response to rapidly changing offers of the culture industry as well as the demands of the career system.

Some adolescents attempt to regulate their dealings with these opaque situations by searching for certainties in order to achieve behavioural security. These certainties include reference to unambiguous norm systems; total identification with symbols and rituals that promise strength; integration into 'natural' hierarchies; and membership of powerful institutions, under whose protection the individual's strength and self-confidence can develop. This particularly includes the attachment to seemingly 'natural', and thus unavoidable and unchangeable, principles that clarify the situation and, in part, also relieve the individual's burden of responsibility. One of these clear principles is the belief that 'the strongest always wins'.

The potential for political problems is the ready acceptance of political concepts which articulate social prejudices towards those who purportedly threaten one's own status. Concepts promising to re-establish the 'old order' (whatever that was) and thus reduce status anxieties have an increasing chance of gaining adherents. Xenophobia can function here as a political tool if 'natural' privileges and hierarchies seem to be a 'meaningful' political means of (re)estab-lishing social stability. The key lies in transforming the individual's unresolved, economically rooted fears of estrangement into the fear that society is being overrun by excessive numbers of foreigners.

Experiences of powerlessness can be traced back to individuals' overpowering experiences of competition that threaten their social status and expose the isolated individual to the experience that 'the strongest always wins'. As powerlessness narrows down an individual's alternatives, violence can become a subjectively meaningful means or even an end in itself, because it achieves clarity in unclear situations. It is at least a momentarily effective (self-)demonstration that power-lessness can be overcome. It guarantees attention from others that could not be obtained through other means. It creates (at least in the short term) partial solidarities or functions as a clearly recognisable test of solidarity. On the basis of socialisation experiences, it proves to be a successful model for action.

As violence always requires justification, political programmes offering this will inevitably prove attractive. This is particularly true for extreme right-wing concepts, because they assert that processes in both nature and society are ultimately settled by force.

The potential for political problems is the endorsement of political concepts that attempt to transform the everyday experience that 'the strongest always wins' into the political maxim that 'the strongest *should* always win'. One's own suffering is transformed and gains direction once one discovers others who are even more powerless. This transformation takes place all the more easily the more completely that society's public sphere is saturated by a 'normalised' ideology of inequality that can be used to legitimise subtle and overt forms of violence towards rightless foreigners or anyone who thinks differently.

Experiences of isolation can be traced back to the dissolution of social milieux, so that natural membership of social groups, which can provide stability particularly in critical and disoriented times, can no longer be taken for granted. However, when it is unclear to which social groups an individual can feel a sense of belonging, then group categories based on 'natural' characteristics, or ones that can be understood as such, gain in importance. This particularly means skin colour, 'race' and nationality. These are attributes that nobody can take away from the individual and which cannot be disposed of. Their validity is independent of individual principles of achievement or competition. The experiences of natural membership, dependability, and community that have become dispersed in everyday life are replaced by feelings of belonging to a nation. Nationalist feelings replace whatever seems to be missing from the individual's immediate environment.

The potential for political problems lies in the acceptance of political concepts that propagate nationalistic positions and also always carry notions of inequality.

ATTEMPTS AT AN EXPLANATION FOR THE EASTERN PART

Growing up in the society of the former GDR was characterised by authoritarian socialisation, that is, a rigidly structured life course had to be followed. Deviations were directed back to the functional path in an authoritarian manner.[5]

Adolescents in the East German states now have to cope with a twofold transformation process: the first is the transfer from the planned to the individualised society. The second (and included in the first) is the transformation of the adolescent phase from an automatic, functional adjustment with an ambivalent role of repression and externally controlled security into an autonomous adolescent life-phase for which the adolescents are forced to take active responsibility with all its consequences. This revaluation of new opportunities has to be coordinated with the threats of a devaluation of prior biographical achievements. It requires an increased effort to interpret new situations that are, above all, characterised by a previously unknown measure of potential economic and social disintegration – until new possibilities of reintegration are achieved.

In a causal analysis, three major sources have to be differentiated. These are GDR-specific historical and political sources as well as specific West German ones:

1.   The historical sources are that antifascism in the former GDR did not involve a critical examination of history, but rather a ritualised process that was never internalised. If one belongs to the victorious party *per se*, critical examination is superfluous.

2. The main sources certainly lie in the specific authoritarian and repressive conditions under which individuals grew up and lived in the GDR with their accompanying feelings of inferiority and distress. This was allied to an education towards simple friend–foe images of 'good' communist and 'wicked' capitalist systems.

Under such conditions, individuals can live in a socially inconspicuous way as long as they remain in clearly structured situations. They 'function' without being exposed to personal pressure. If deviations from this pattern occur, relationships consequently become opaque and everyday life becomes alien. Massive anxieties and insecurities are triggered.

Current changes, as well as abrupt disintegrations of life contexts, have led to increased occupational uncertainty, experiences of powerlessness in, for example, new competitive situations, and experiences of estrangement through the dissolution of family milieux or working relationships. These experiences have to be processed, as in West Germany, but none the less under extremely more difficult conditions.

3. The third source is not one of the causes; instead it contributes to escalation. Two circumstances have to be pointed out here: first, escalation is reinforced when West German policy directed towards exclusively economic goals contributes massively to the destruction of life contexts. This particularly concerns company closures. In everyday life in the GDR, companies made a greater contribution to social integration than in West Germany. Hence, closure means more than just the loss of a work place, which would already be hard enough.

Second, the demonstrative superiority of West Germans greatly hinders a development towards more self-confidence in mastering problems without tending to shift blame onto others. Hence, individual inferiority, towards West Germans, among others, is transformed into 'German' superiority. Nationalistic feelings now become a particularly appropriate means of social integration. In addition, opportunities are sought to demonstrate one's own superiority. For these reasons, some groups, such as skinheads, particularly like to attack individual foreigners or, in any case, inferiors.

These three sources can also help to explain why there is more overt gang violence in East Germany; why violence thus appears to be out of control. The following relationship provides a plausible reason for this lack of control: the more strongly authoritarian education and state repression grows which cannot be cushioned in social 'niches', the less can self-responsibility develop. If social bonds also weaken, less and less consideration is given to consequences for others. If everyday experience and official presentation then diverge, explosive situations result. They require interpretations and balancing acts that are particularly beyond the ability of persons with an authoritarian disposition, so that their internal burdens increase even more. When external guidance and controls fall away, hardly any internal orientations, such as meaningful and credible moral stances, are present. An anomic situation with a lack of standards and rules arises, so that anxiety and uncertainty easily give way to violence.

This brutalisation is achieved – without personal feelings of guilt – even more easily the more overtly political justifications are proposed in public. It becomes particularly explosive when democratically elected politicians spread the message that 'We will not allow fundamental changes to our society's racial composition'.[6] Such utterances increase the normality of extreme right-wing positions – and thus lower the violence threshold even further.

On the other hand, neo-Nazi groups are able to break through the violence dilemma because they can now view themselves as a mouthpiece for a segment of the population that is still afraid to act because of the risk to their normal external status. The danger here is that it enables neo-Nazi groups to view themselves as an élite. This can be reinforced additionally by under-reactions and inconsistency in the police.

CONCLUSION

There is a very real risk that social, occupational, or political *processes of disintegration* will increase. They will lead to increasing violence because, when social responsibility and integration dissolve, individuals no longer consider the consequences that their actions will have for others. They completely disregard the consequences for those who are, in any case, dealt with instrumentally – and this includes foreigners. The violence threshold lowers. When natural social membership and acceptance disintegrate to such an extent that only the certainty of being German remains, then violence is given a direction.

On the one hand, a more careful examination of the social dimension of rapid economically and technically fuelled modernisation is required. It is necessary to estimate the impact of technology on the social environment as well as the natural environment, because drawbacks in the form of the destruction of *life contexts* attack the very core of identity formation. Hence, there is a need for simultaneous and far-reaching sociopolitical measures to prevent any expansion in the use of nationalism as a means of countering social, occupational and political disintegration.

NOTES

1. This article is based on several publications that have appeared in Germany. I wish to thank Jonathan Harrow at Bielefeld University for producing the present translation.
2. Political barometer of the second German public television channel (ZDF), taken from *Süddeutsche Zeitung*, 140, 1992, p. 10.
3. Emnid survey, taken from *Der Spiegel*, 18, 1992, p. 61.
4. Official 1991 statistics from the Federal Criminal Police Office. These statistics must be viewed very cautiously and can be evaluated as only a very rough indicator. Different registration procedures in each state criminal police office or, in part, a complete lack of registrations in East German states because of a lack of structures have to be taken into account. Figures for 1992 are unofficial statistics from the Federal Criminal Police Office.
5. The description of the situation in East Germany is taken from Heitmeyer (1992b).
6. This is a translation of a public statement by the Bavarian minister E. Stoiber.

3 Terrorist Violence against Immigrants and Refugees in Scandinavia: Patterns and Motives

Tore Björgo

The disturbing rise in bombings, Molotov cocktail attacks and other terrorist violence against immigrants, refugees and asylum-seekers have given rise to two contrasting interpretations:

1. Anti-racist activists have often claimed that these attacks are nothing but an expression of clear-cut racism – and that racist and neo-Nazi organisations are behind them.
2. The other interpretation – often held by the police – is that the attacks are just 'boyish tricks and drunken pranks', having nothing to do with politics or racism.

This chapter, which examines recent trends of terrorist violence against refugees, immigrants and non-indigenous ethnic minorities in Norway, Sweden and Denmark, provides a basis for evaluating and modifying these interpretations. The chapter examines the patterns of these violent acts, the perpetrators, and the rather mixed motives behind their actions. Although at least some of the bombings have been perpetrated by political activists, the primary concern of this chapter is the question of how seemingly apolitical youth gangs become involved in political or racist violence, and how their acts take on political dimensions.[1] The study thus focuses on the less organised forms of racist terrorism, and on groups whose ideological and political consciousness is not very articulated.

The present study focuses on terrorist-type attacks, that is to say, bombings, arson and shootings. Other types of violence, such as street violence, riots and vandalism, are not covered in this inquiry. It must be noted that from the point of view of the victim, the daily harassment in terms of racist remarks, threats, damage to property and low-scale violence may be just as terrible and terrorising as suddenly getting a firebomb through the window. A focus on the more spectacular acts of violence may take attention away from this more everyday process of harassment. However, since we here wish to analyse the motivations of the perpetrators rather than effects on the victims, it is useful to focus the examination on terrorist events.

Terrorism may be defined as the use of violence and destruction – or threats of such – aimed at creating a state of fear, directing attention to a cause, forcing someone to give in to specific demands, and to achieve an effect on others besides the direct victim or target of the violence. It is common to reserve the concept of terrorism to organised political groups which over a period of time conduct a systematic campaign of violence. We may, however, also use the term 'terrorist violence' to describe specific kinds of sporadic violent acts, even if they are perpetrated by persons who do not belong to organised political groups.

It has been generally observed that 'right-wing terrorist groups' tend to be less ideologically motivated, less structured and more decentralised than militant groups on the left (Crenshaw, 1991, p. 78). Members and sympathisers of racist organisations tend to act more or less on their own. However, my examination of groups which have carried out terrorist-type attacks against immigrants and asylum-seekers in Scandinavia revealed a wide variety of organisational levels. At the highest level we find formal political organisations and parties or their armed wings. At the lowest level of organisation are youth gangs or groups of friends with no formal structure, no ideology and no political orientation above a general hostility towards 'foreigners'. Between these extremes we find youth gangs and informal youth movements with more defined group identities, shared symbols and slogans, some racist ideology, and sometimes with ties to right-wing political organisations. Typical examples are some skinhead gangs and other 'White Power' groups which may be described as part of youth subcultures. However, even the more apolitical youth gangs have played significant roles in what appear as campaigns or waves of terrorist violence against immigrants or asylum-seekers. This makes it of particular interest to examine the patterns of violence, how these violent events evolve, what motivates youth gangs to carry out such actions, and under which circumstances the decisions to act are taken. In Chapter 7 I will analyse in more detail the role played by the media in relation to these waves of violence.

Acts of violence where the victims are selected because of their status as refugees, immigrants or members of ethnic minorities are racist in terms of our definition. However, when studying the actual motivations of the perpetrators behind violent attacks on 'foreigners', it is premature to apply the label 'racist violence' at an early stage in the investigation of individual attacks. This may close the search for possible motivations, which may turn out to be more complex than mere 'racism'.

THE PATTERNS OF VIOLENCE[2]

The use of terrorist violence against immigrants and asylum-seekers in Scandinavia was to some extent pioneered by political activists from right-wing organisations. Particularly in Norway and Sweden, neo-Nazi or 'nationalist' organisations have served as trail-blazers for terrorism by establishing a tradition of using bombs and Molotovs against immigrant targets. However, during the past few years, most of the terrorist acts appear to have been perpetrated by members of various youth gangs, often persons with criminal records. Although they may hold strongly anti-immigrant or racist views, they are normally not affiliated with political groups. But these groups have often been exposed to propaganda, and seem to have taken over the arguments, targets and terrorist methods from right-wing, anti-immigrant organisations. The patterns and types of terrorist violence against immigrants, refugees and asylum-seekers are displayed in Figure 3.1 and Table 3.1.

The higher number of terrorist actions in Sweden may in part be explained by the fact that Sweden has a population roughly twice the size of either Norway or Denmark, and a higher proportion of

Table 3.1 Types of terrorist violence against immigrants, refugees and asylum-seekers in the period 1982–2. Number of incidents. For sources and code rules, see note.[3]

	Norway	*Sweden*	*Denmark*	*Total*
Explosives	13	17	4	34
Arson	12	77	14	103
Armed attacks	7	10	3	20
Other	1	7	3	11
Total	33	111	24	168

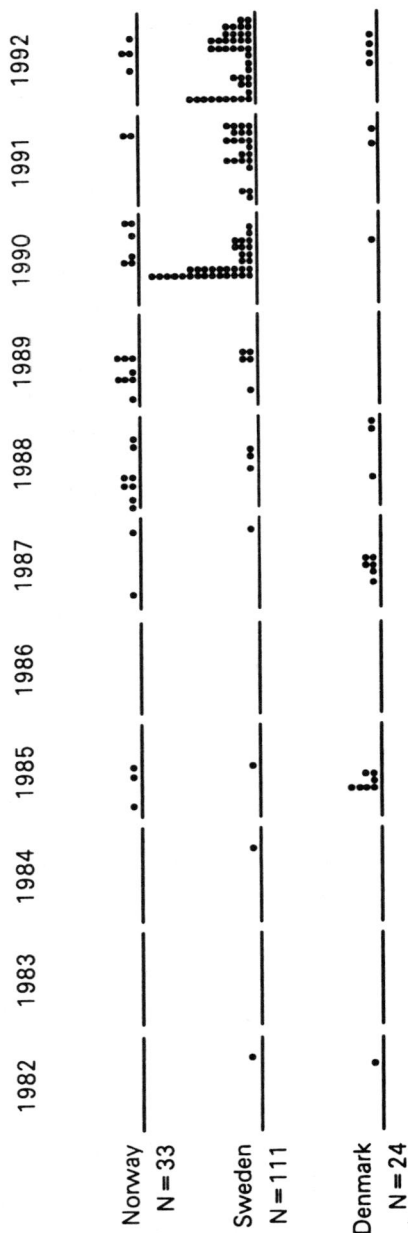

Figure 3.1a Time–axis: Cases of bombing, arson, shooting and other terrorist-type action against refugees, immigrants and ethnic minorities in Scandinavia during the period 1982–2. Several cases within the same calendar month are marked as a bar (Total = 168).

immigrants in the population.[4] However, even in relative terms there has been a significantly higher level of racist violence in Sweden than in the rest of Scandinavia since the wave of attacks on asylum reception centres escalated in May 1990 (Figure 3.1).[5] There has also been an alarming tendency towards more lethal violence in Sweden. During a five-month period in 1991–2, eleven immigrants were shot by the so-called 'Laser man'. He used a rifle with a laser sight and a pistol to shoot dark-skinned foreigners. One died, several were seriously injured. A suspected perpetrator was subsequently arrested. He was apparently a loner who hated foreigners, and spent much time in South Africa because he liked the apartheid system. He has been indicted for one murder, ten cases of attempted murder, and other crimes.

The sharp increase in attacks in 1990 cannot be explained primarily by socioeconomic factors such as unemployment. The 'wave' of attacks began *before* the economic recession of 1991 which brought increased unemployment to Sweden. Until then Sweden had had the lowest unemployment rate in Scandinavia. By comparison, Denmark, for several decades, had by far the highest level of unemployment but nevertheless a relatively low level of racist violence. It is, however, worth noting that the increase in violence came *after* the Government restricted Sweden's liberal immigration policy in December 1989. It may be argued that this change in policy legitimised the arguments of the anti-immigration activists, who at this time intensified their propaganda activities.

Even in Norway there has been an increased tendency towards the use of (shot)guns against the houses of refugees, but so far apparently only with the intention to scare rather than to kill or injure. The use of explosives has been relatively more common in Norway than elsewhere. This may to some extent be explained in terms of a 'dynamite tradition' established by right-wing and neo-Nazi activists, who used bombs on several occasions in 1979 and 1985. In Sweden and Denmark, as well as in Germany, the use of firebombs has been the dominant method. In Sweden the *Riksaktionsgruppen* (National Action Group, RAG) of the neo-Nazi *Nordiska Rikspartiet* was among the pioneers, committing three firebomb attacks in 1985. One of these cases was against the apartment of an immigrant family. This may have contributed to establish Molotov attacks and arson as the favoured method against such targets in Sweden.

In Denmark, racist street violence has been a more serious problem than terrorist-type violence, especially in the 1980s. A White Power-inspired subculture of so-called 'Green Jackets' became active during the mid-1980s. These highly criminal youth gangs committed a series of violent acts, mainly street violence. More organised right-wing or neo-Nazi groups have so far not been firmly linked to terrorist violence against immigrants or asylum-seekers in Denmark.

The dominant *modus operandi* is 'hit and run' attacks by a single or a few individuals under the cover of darkness. This mode of operation may be seen as an indication of a relative lack of public support. However, in all three countries there have also been a few cases of riots where large mobs have attacked refugee centres, particularly in Sweden during the late 1980s. Scandinavian right-wing extremists are generally not strong enough to take over control of the streets, as happened in German cities like Hoyerswerda and Rostock. There is, however, reason for concern in some local communities, and particularly about the growth of militant racist groups in Sweden (see Lööw, Chapter 5).

In Sweden and Norway, most of the attacks (about three-quarters of the cases) have taken place in smaller towns and local communities, although the majority of immigrants and asylum-seekers live in more urban areas. However, because of a decentralised integration policy, and a wish to avoid the formation of 'immigrant ghettos' in the cities, many newly arrived refugees tend to be sent to refugee centres in smaller local communities. Here, where the local population is small and not very used to foreigners, the sudden arrival of, say, ten to fifteen Somalis or Tamils is rather noticeable, amounting to something of a culture shock on both sides. Although many local communities are very receptive, others turn out to be inhospitable to the new inhabitants. Stories of small conflicts and nuisances tend to spread rapidly and are blown up out of proportion.

PERPETRATORS – ORGANISED OR UNORGANISED?

Of the 168 terrorist-type actions against immigrants, refugees and asylum-seekers recorded in my Scandinavian database for the period 1982–92, the perpetrators were known and apprehended in about a third of the cases (including several important cases which have not yet been tried in court, and where the outcome is uncertain).[6] According to information available, it may be estimated that organised political activists have been found to be perpetrators in fifteen to twenty-five of sixty to seventy-five solved cases of such violence (depending on the definition of 'political activist' and the level of organisational involvement). In several of these cases members of organisations appear to have acted on their own initiative. Some convicted perpetrators manage to keep their organisational affiliation hidden from the police and the prosecutors, who at times even fail to ask about the defendants' connections with right-wing organisations. Such ties are sometimes known to observers of the right-wing scene, or are revealed at a later stage. The majority of the solved actions were perpetrated by unorganised, generally apolitical youth gangs who were often feared and despised in their local communities for their arbitrary violence and criminality. There is also ample reason to believe that a number of the *unsolved* cases were perpetrated by organised political groups, or by persons who were active in right-wing groups but acting on their own. At least fifteen to twenty of the unsolved cases contained evidence or clues pointing in such a direction. The fact that cases remain unsolved may also in itself indicate a higher level of planning, preparation and professionalism. Nevertheless, most of the unsolved cases were carried out in ways which indicate that local youngsters were responsible.

It is most likely that the *majority* of the terrorist-type actions against immigrants and asylum-seekers have been perpetrated by youth gangs without any articulated political ideology, with only few and simple political thoughts, and in most cases no formal connections with political organisations have been found (Säkerhetspolisen, 1993). They do, however, often use symbols, slogans and arguments 'borrowed' from organisations of the far right. Many actions appear to be inspired by media accounts of similar actions in other localities – what I in Chapter 7 call *the contagion effect*. In some cases, however, it is known that they have had informal contacts with anti-immigrant leaders and activists, and received anti-immigrant propaganda before they carried out actions. More commonly, however, right-wing or anti-immigrant activists have moved in to try to recruit or organise these youngsters *after* their violent actions against immigrants and asylum-seekers.

A common pattern is that the group consists of a hard core of a few individuals with racist convictions and (sometimes) connections with racist organisations. The larger circle of followers and hangers-on have not really absorbed these racist attitudes. It is significant, however, that they may nevertheless express racist views when they are among their peers in the gang. As will be shown in more detail, these marginal members are sometimes liable to carry out acts of violence against immigrants and asylum-seekers in order to win acceptance and status within the group.

Another striking fact is that in most solved cases the actions turned out to be conceived and/or executed under the influence of alcohol.

This was true even in some of the cases where the perpetrators were organised political activists. The use of alcohol in connection with 'political' actions has in fact been a very hot and controversial topic in right-wing organisations, sometimes causing organisational splits (see Lööw, Chapter 5).

Typically, the idea of throwing a bomb or a Molotov cocktail at a refugee centre or an immigrant shop was conceived during a drinking party. This finding suggests that the influence of alcohol may have been underestimated as a relevant triggering factor in right-wing or anti-immigrant political violence. A well-known effect of alcohol is that it reduces self-restraint and inhibition, 'allowing' people to do things they would not have done in a sober state. Another interpretation is that they drink 'to get courage'.

The events leading up to a bombing or Molotov attack generally follow a very stereotyped pattern. The following case, described in a Danish newspaper,[7] is typical:

> Five young racists were yesterday sentenced to prison (from 9 to 15 months) for having firebombed an Indian-owned shop in Copenhagen. During a private party April 14 [1987] the five had several drinks. Late at night they started to discuss 'how many privileges guest workers and refugees are granted in Denmark', and 'that they are trampling on the Danes'. They talked about going to a hotel they knew was inhabited by 'blacks' in order to start a fight. They decided not to, however, because 'it was too big'. Instead they went to a night kiosk . . . which they knew was owned by an Indian. On their way they prepared bombs made of cola bottles and petrol they bought for this purpose. They agreed on who should smash the window so that the others could throw the bombs into the shop . . . They ran off after having made sure the shop was ablaze.

Seen in isolation, a case like this may not seem to be particularly alarming. The use of the label 'terrorism' may appear to be an overstatement when drunken youngsters with few and superficial political ideas throw a bottle full of petrol at a shop which is owned by an immigrant. The problem is, however, that these cases are part of a consistent pattern, and the violence tends to terrorise a large number of people who belong to the minority which is the object of their hate.

Nevertheless, the police often emphasise the non-political elements: the role of alcohol, the lack of explicit ideology or affiliation to political organisations, and the perpetrators' past record of petty crime, violence and vandalism. Consequently, the police have tended to ignore any element of racist and political motive or content that these attacks against immigrants or asylum-seekers may have. One example: a few days after two young men exploded half a kilo of TNT outside a reception centre for asylum-seekers in Norway, a local police officer characterised the event as 'boyish tricks and drunken pranks'. The statement aroused public controversy because it appeared to belittle the seriousness of the act. In another case, a Pakistani-owned shop had been the target of repeated vandalism, racist graffiti, arson and several bombings. The head of the local police still claimed that it was probably just a matter of coincidence, and doubted whether it was a result of racism.

There might be valid arguments for playing down the political aspect of these acts in order to deny the perpetrators the prestige and status they often try to gain from their actions. This should, however, be balanced against other important considerations, like taking effective actions against the violence and mobilising support for the victims. And law-enforcers should certainly not abstain from examining the political significance and the motives behind these actions if there are any indications of such.

WHAT MAKES THESE ACTS 'POLITICAL'?

Despite the fact that the majority of the solved bombings and cases of arson against immigrants and asylum-seekers were committed by unorganised, non-ideological youth gangs there are a number of factors which give these acts a political aspect.

1. In the cases recorded in this study, the victims were selected *because* they were immigrants or asylum-seekers. Alternatively, the targets were institutions or buildings which represent these groups, and were selected for that reason. In other words, the victims were not attacked primarily as individuals but as representatives of a group. This can often be recognised by the graffiti left on the scene of the crime, or by the perpetrators' explanations given to the police or the media. The 'victim-chosen-as-representative' is a characteristic of most terrorist acts, as opposed to random terrorism (which is relatively rare) and assassinations (which are directed against a specific individual). The terrorist tries to make the victim symbolise what he is fighting against – in this case immigration – by selecting a target which is 'part of' the problem/enemy. The scapegoat syndrome is often prominent.

2. Anti-immigrant organisations and activists have been particularly active – and often successful – in propagating their views on foreigners towards underprivileged social groups, blaming the immigrants and asylum-seekers for their grievances: unemployment, lack of housing, the presence of drugs and AIDS, and even failure to get girl-friends are explained as consequences of immigration. Such arguments have gained a certain credibility among those marginalised sections of the population which have been affected by these social misfortunes. Thus, the main role of the anti-immigrant organisations in relation to the perpetrators of violence has been played in the field of propaganda, by creating an atmosphere of anxiety and crises,[8] objects of hate, and political justifications for violence. This may be termed 'scapegoat racism'. Certain anti-immigrant activists are also known to have established particularly good rapport with criminal youth gangs who have committed acts of violence against immigrants and asylum-seekers.

3. When marginalised youth gangs, disdained and feared in the community for their criminal behaviour, directed their violence and aggression towards immigrants and asylum-seekers, they often discovered that this brought them support and popularity among wider groups of young people in the community – and even from some adults. Thus, when these criminal bands joined a popular political cause, they did in some cases become 'local heroes' among parts of the population. Violent actions against refugees are normally preceded by heated debates in the local community about, for example, a new refugee centre. The perpetrators feel that they have many behind them. Violence may be seen as an extreme form of an already existing public opinion against refugees.

It is a new and disturbing development that it is possible to muster public support for acts of terrorist violence in Scandinavia. Although only a small section of the population would support or accept such violence, it may constitute a sufficiently large audience for persons who consider carrying out terrorist actions. Until the growth of anti-immigrant sentiments in the late 1980s, racists and right-wing extremists were politically isolated. At this time more-established populist parties put the issue of immigration on the political agenda. For the first time scapegoat arguments were used by relatively respectable political parties. This gave legitimacy to more extreme groups who used the same arguments to direct social discontent, frustration and aggression towards immigrants and asylum-seekers.

MOTIVES FOR VIOLENCE: INSTRUMENTAL, EXPRESSIVE AND GROUP-DYNAMIC ASPECTS

Why, then, do the perpetrators carry out their violent acts? What are the real motivations for attacking 'foreigners' as such? In attempting to answer these questions, we may apply three analytical perspectives – the instrumental, the expressive and the group-dynamic. These perspectives focus on different aspects of the perpetrators' motivations, which tend to be compounded.[9]

The instrumental aspect of violence refers to a means-and-ends rationality: persons and groups use violence to achieve more or less clearly defined objectives. Such violent actors are trying to bring about an effect on the immediate target and on the expanded target groups in order to influence their behaviour in specific ways. One of the common instrumental motives behind the violence is, for instance, to scare or chase away unwanted 'foreigners'.

One example of this was a series of bombings, arson and vandalism against a Pakistani shop-owner in a small Norwegian town. Systematic harassment involving a dozen more or less serious incidents, including several cases of arson and bombings, caused him unsustainable economic loss and anxiety. He finally closed down his shop and left the community as a broken man. 'We won' was promptly painted on the storefront window, along with swastikas, SS and Ku Klux Klan signs. Other immigrants and refugees were also targeted, several of whom moved away because of the harassment.

Thus, instrumental actions are rational in relation to a goal, a means to an end. *Expressive actions*, on the other hand, are rational in relation to a value (to use the term of Max Weber). Such acts are primarily statements and demonstrations on attitudes and identity. They may be acts of defiance, or ways to prove courage and manliness. Expressive acts are meant to 'say' or communicate something – political or non-political. In its extreme form, expressive behaviour completely disregards the reactions and understandings of external audiences. The act is basically self-centred rather than result-oriented. The fundamental point is what the act says about the actor rather than its political effects. Most violent acts, however, are somewhere along the middle of the range. There is an element of communicative purpose, an intention to make an impact on various audiences – within the group as well as outside. Sometimes the communicative intention is straightforward and obvious – like demonstrating one's views on 'foreigners' and immigration politics. Such acts of violence are often accompanied by slogans like 'foreigners out!' Often, however, this is just political icing to cover more private and non-political preoccupations. The violent actor may not even be able (or willing) to express verbally what the act means to himself, and what he wants to convey to others.

This mixture of expressive and instrumental motives becomes more evident if we analyse violent behaviour in a *group perspective*. By focusing on the internal politics of the group rather than on the external political objectives, we may get a more comprehensive understanding of how predominantly expressive acts of violence also acquire instrumental functions. Being a member of a youth gang, or seeking acceptance into such a gang, may provide strong incentives for violent action. Violent behaviour may be analysed as the outcome of the internal group dynamics. The needs of the individuals within the group, or of the group in relation to its social surroundings are often the primary motivating force behind terrorist actions – although these acts tend to be rationalised by political arguments.

Some acts of violence seem to be predominantly instrumental and related to political goals. Other acts may be understood primarily as expressive actions related to a quest for status, and strongly influenced by group processes. But in most cases these various motives are woven together in a complex way. Acts which on the surface may appear to be mainly motivated by racism and opposition to the current immigration policy, may, on closer inspection, turn out to have just as much to do with the perpetrator's wish to present a particular image of himself to his peers and social surroundings. The decision to carry out the act of violence is normally not taken by the individual alone, but emerges from a distinctive social setting where group-dynamic processes play a significant role.

To become a member of a close-knitted youth gang with a violent image is in itself highly attractive to certain types of young males, in particular those with weak identities and social networks (see Heitmeyer, Chapter 2). Many youth gangs cultivate an extremely 'macho' type of group culture, presenting an image of themselves as tough, violent and hostile to outsiders. Blatant racism and provocative use of Nazi symbols may be important components in this image. This may effectively delineate the group from the rest of society. By becoming stigmatised outcasts, in-group solidarity is strengthened. Newcomers feel pressure to live up to these group values in order to win respect and acceptance. This implicit pressure to prove one's manliness and adherence to group values may serve as an incentive to risk-taking and violence.[10]

When some youth gangs discuss immigrants and asylum-seekers it is quite common that hideous plans of violent actions are conceived, particularly when large quantities of alcohol have taken effect. In most cases such propositions should probably be interpreted as part of an implicit competition within the group to display the strongest views and attitudes against 'the foreigners' and – in extension of this – to show off certain group virtues like strength and manliness. Most of the time it is just wild talking. The 'propositions' may not necessarily be taken literally. However, sometimes the participants are trapped by their own proposals. When young men are outdoing each other in introducing imaginative plans on how to scare or 'knock off the blackheads', someone may easily come to say: 'You don't dare that, you coward!' Since there is a competition among the peers for a reputation of bravery and toughness, prestige and social standing within the group is at stake. This is probably of particular importance to those who are on the fringe of the gang, whose group membership is uncertain, and who are striving to achieve full acceptance.[11]

A desire to achieve recognition and group membership by demonstrating bravery, toughness, and other values held high in the group, was clearly a decisive factor when one of the members of a local youth gang took it upon himself to carry out the bombing of an immigrant shop in a Norwegian small town. This was amply illustrated during the trial:[12]

'When I came back into the room after having blasted the window of the Pakistani-owned shop I was welcomed by cheering and cries of victory. The others were satisfied with what I had done, and slapped my back. From that time I felt that I was accepted in the gang.' Thus explained one of the defendants, a 25-year-old Danish citizen, in court. Along with four others he is charged of having blown up the exhibition window of the shop in February 1988.

He did not remember much of what took place before the explosion because he was drunk. He recalled, however, that he and the others had been discussing immigration politics in harsh terms. They had said that immigrants should be shot or refused entry to Norway. The owner of the flat displayed explosives and several guns in his possession. During the discussion they automatically touched on the immigrant shop, and talked about blasting the shop to pieces, the defendant explained.

The others made fun of him, claiming that he did not dare to blow up the Pakistani shop. The defendant felt this as pressure, and wanted to prove to the others that he did indeed dare to blow up the shop. 'I assumed that I volunteered to blast the window of the shop in order to show off. I was a newcomer in the gang and felt that I was still not quite accepted,' the 25-year-old man explained.

Explanations from other cases of anti-immigrant bombings and arson have revealed strikingly similar patterns in the events leading up to the attack: a discussion during which hostile feelings against immigrants or asylum-seekers are expressed, an implicit contest among the participants to outdo each other in reckless proposals, a wish to 'show off', plus a good measure of booze to quell second thoughts.

Internal group dynamics and a competition to express and fulfil central values in the gang culture do seem to play central roles in determining the course of events which lead up to acts of violence. When these group factors are combined with a prevalent hostility against immigrants and asylum-seekers, the violent tendencies take a specific direction.

Violent actions may not just give prestige to individual perpetrators in relation to the rest of the group. When criminal youth gangs turn their violence and harassment towards unpopular groups of 'foreigners', the group as a whole often experiences a dramatic change in social status in the eyes of the community. From being a bunch of nobodies the group members become *somebody*: dangerous racists and neo-Nazis in the eyes of some, local heroes and patriots in the eyes of others.

CONCLUSIONS

The common tendency to equate right-wing violence and racist violence is hardly tenable. Other types of groups than what we would normally call extreme right-wing organisations carry out the majority of the acts of violence against immigrants, refugees and asylum-seekers in Scandinavia. Although neo-Nazi and other right-wing groups are behind some of this violence, these groups also direct much of their violence towards other objects of hate, such as homosexuals, drug addicts, left-wing activists, anti-racists, politicians, and others. However, such right-wing organisations play an important propaganda role in incitement to violence against 'foreigners' and 'racial/national traitors'.

So far, research on racist violence has not been able to establish the necessary and sufficient conditions causing the emergence of racist violence. This may not even be a realistic goal. It is, however, possible to delineate some of the main factors which constitute *circumstances favourable to the emergence of such violence:*

1. On the local and/or national level, a polarised political situation in which immigrants and immigration politics are hotly debated. Government policies towards immigrants and asylum-seekers send out negative signals which depict these groups as 'problems'.
2. On the individual and peer-group level, the presence of hostile attitudes against immigrants and asylum-seekers, often fed by racist propaganda from anti-immigrant organisations which portray immigrants and refugees as a great threat and competitors in the fight for scarce resources.
3. Widespread social frustration due to unemployment, lack of housing, economic recession or other negative social conditions.
4. A familiarity with the use of violence and vandalism.
5. A quest for reputation, respect, status and publicity on behalf of themselves in relation to the peer group, the group in relation to the local community, or sometimes even on behalf of the local community in relation to the rest of the country.
6. Media reports about dramatic acts of violence against foreigners, serving as models for emulation.
7. A drinking party with peers where the consumption of alcohol serves to curb inhibitions and scruples about using violence. This is the social situation where the decision to carry out an action is usually taken.
8. The availability (at short notice) of explosives, petrol, guns or other potential weapons.
9. The presence of suitable hate objects.

The following factors may contribute to make violence endemic:

10. A potential audience in the community which supports or at least condones violence and harassment against 'the foreigners'.
11. Sensationalist media coverage giving publicity (and promising more of the same) to the perpetrators and their potential imitators.
12. Absent, weak, or misdirected reactions to racist violence from the police, politicians and other authorities.
13. A passive public opinion.

NOTES

1. This issue has also been analysed by Merkl (1986).
2. The recorded cases of anti-immigrant violence in Scandinavia have been compiled into a chronology. The chronology, which probably does not include all relevant incidents, is based on a variety of sources: news reports, police reports, court documents, information from immigration authorities, surveys produced by other researchers or anti-racist groups, and interviews with persons involved. The information has been cross-checked as far as possible.
3. The figures encompass bombings, cases of arson (including Molotov attacks), shooting episodes, and similar premeditated, terrorist-type attacks which put the victims in real or potential danger of physical injury. Acts of street violence (including premeditated assault), vandalism or unsubstantiated threats are not included, because these categories of violence are very under-reported. Only acts of violence where the victim is selected *because* he/she is a foreigner (immigrant/refugee/asylum-seeker) or belongs to an ethnic minority are included. Thus, acts of violence from right-wing extremist groups against anti-racist activists or other hate objects, such as homosexuals, are not counted in the statistics. Attacks on property where the intention appeared to be to put inhabitants or owners in a state of fear, *were* counted. Violent acts against immigrants primarily motivated by personal conflicts, or which struck immigrants by pure chance, are excluded from the statistics as far as possible. Known cases where shopowners or others have attempted to disguise their insurance swindle as a racist arson have also been excluded.

   I am grateful to Anna-Lena Lodenius, Stieg Larsson and Gellert Tamas, who have provided me with surveys, chronologies and background on anti-immigrant violence in Sweden. Their findings are published in Lodenius & Larsson (1991), Tamas and Lodenius (1991) and Lodenius and Tamas (1992). Erik Kihl of The Swedish Immigration Agency, Heléne Lööw of the Historical Institution in Gothenburg, and the Swedish Police Authority have also been most helpful. The Swedish Security Police have published chronologies and statistics for 1990–2. In Denmark, Erik Jensen has kindly let me use his extensive archive of press clippings on right-wing organisations and anti-immigrant violence. In Norway, *Anti-Rasistisk Senter* has been most helpful with providing press clippings.
4. The population figures of the Scandinavian countries (1990): Norway (4.2 m), Denmark (5.1 m), Sweden (8.6 m). Immigrants, refugees and asylum-seekers with citizenship from Asian, African and South American countries – which are the groups most exposed to racism and anti-immigrant hostility – constitute 1.5 per cent of the total population in Norway, 1.8 per cent in Denmark, and 2.3 per cent in Sweden. Source: *Yearbook of Nordic Statistics 1992*. During 1992, Sweden received about 85 000 refugees (a sharp increase from the 30 000 the year before). Denmark received 4600 in 1991 and 13 900 in 1992, while Norway received 4500 both years.
5. It should be noted that the increase in Sweden was not as sharp as the chart may indicate. During the late 1980s there were several cases of anti-refugee

riots and assaults which are not included in these statistics of terrorist-type violence. To some extent, 1990 brought a change in the *forms* of violence, but also a real increase. Registration of racist violence has also been improved since 1990 – but mainly as a result of the perception that racist violence was becoming a problem.

6. More precise numbers cannot be given as I was unable to follow the progress of each case. Police statistics and computer records are also generally deficient. The Swedish police has, however, improved its statistics in this field during the early 1990s.

7. *Aktuelt* 17 July 1987.

8. In an important theoretical article on how rebels gradually radicalise through specific stages into terrorism, Ehud Sprinzak (1991) notes that for particularistic (e.g. right-wing or racist) groups, 'violence, and eventually terrorism, only emerge when the group involved feels insecure or perceives an immediate threat'.

9. These three perspectives on terrorism are discussed in more detail in Björgo and Heradstveit (1993), and in Crenshaw (1988).

10. These points are confirmed in interviews with several present and former members of racist youth gangs and neo-Nazi organisations. The argument is also supported by a number of cases presented elsewhere, such as Björgo (1989); Björgo and Heradstveit (1993, ch. 10).

11. Many of the points above are confirmed by a former militant activist in the Norwegian *Nasjonalt Folkeparti*, Ole Kristian Brastad, interviewed in *Det Nye* (No 3–1993) and by this researcher.

12. Compiled from a police report cited in court (Nord-Hedmark herredsrett, 6 June 1989), and a news report from the proceedings in *Hamar Arbeiderblad*, 7 June 1989.

4 The Extreme Right and Racist Violence in the Netherlands

Jaap van Donselaar

In the past few years there has been greatly increased interest in the Netherlands in topics concerning the extreme right and racist violence. To a large extent this has resulted from developments in the surrounding countries, particularly Germany, but events taking place at home have also stimulated interest in the subject. In 1992 there was a sharp increase in the number of criminal offences of a racist nature, and at the same time opinion polls also indicate growing support for the *Centrumdemocraten* (Centre Democrats, CD). In the parliamentary elections of 1989 the CD gained one seat; now, in 1993, the party could most probably succeed in gaining five or six seats.

To date there has been no scientific research into the relationship between the extreme right and racist violence in the Netherlands. Yet this contribution is in no sense intended to fill the gap. Specific empirical research is needed for this. Rather, my intention is to distinguish certain aspects of the connection between the extreme right and racist violence, in the light of information with which, generally speaking, we are already familiar, and to illumine these aspects still further. Although it may sound clichéd to state that this relationship is a particularly complex one, it is nonetheless true. In the Netherlands there has, up to now, been no Weberian 'ideal type' of violent offence of a racist nature attributable to any extreme right organisation. I know of no concrete evidence that could safely be viewed as conforming to this ideal type.[1] The case which has received most publicity is known as the 'church raid' (van Donselaar, 1991, p. 174).

On 29 February 1980, ten or so supporters of the recently established racist *Nationale Centrum Partij*, (National Centre Party, NCP) made their way to the Moses and Aaron Church in Amsterdam. At that time approximately 100 illegal immigrants were camping out in the church, to avoid being deported. At first it was only a matter of shouting, but this gave way to beating some of the immigrants. Two of the three founders of the NCP were arrested and later found guilty of assault and battery. Up to this point this case appears to resemble the ideal type outlined above, but the NCP did not survive the incident a single week. The third founder, Henry Brookman, took the opportunity to disband the NCP, setting up a new party in its stead: the *Centrumpartij* (Centre Party, CP). Its programme remained unchanged from that of its predecessor, but Brookman's two former allies were not involved in the new party.

In this instance there can be little doubt about either the violence in this event, or its racist nature. The problem concerns rather the extent to which the incident can be attributed to an extreme right organisation. In many cases this is rendered still more difficult when, for example, the police fail to arrest the perpetrators of the violence. Such occurrences can then only be labelled as extreme right or racist violence on the grounds of the offence committed, the target selected, and suspicion as to the culprits' identity.

One example is the attempt to set fire to a mosque in Amersfoort at the end of January 1992. Five Molotov cocktails were thrown against the front of the building; a racist slogan and a symbol current in fascist circles were chalked on the wall. The event had every appearance of being a right-wing racist crime. However, so far this case has remained unsolved.

It is often difficult to be certain as to the culprits' identity, their relationship to the extreme right, and the racist character of incidents. In other cases one could ask to what extent one can talk of actual violence. For instance, how does one view the chalking of a racist slogan, or of threats? How do we classify expression of sympathy for indigenous violence against migrants? One often encounters this sympathy in the political propaganda stemming from racist organisations (van Donselaar, 1991, pp. 152, 187), and sometimes this is taken a step further in what can be seen as incitement to violence.

Thus far we have outlined several significant elements in the relationship between the extreme right and racist violence, emphasising the complexity of the subject. This complexity is rooted on the one hand in the problem of definition, and on the other in a lack of factual knowledge, for we are dealing here with a phenomenon that to a large extent escapes our scrutiny.

THE DIFFICULTIES OF ADAPTATION FOR THE EXTREME RIGHT

The Netherlands in the post-war period displayed a broad consensus that there was no longer any place for fascist organisations. Nevertheless, the far Right made its presence known only a few years after the war, and since that time this phenomenon has never disappeared from Dutch society (van Donselaar, 1991, pp. 87–100). The obstructions experienced by these organisations has been of equal duration; every time they appear on the scene, they evoke fierce opposition. Their right to exist is frequently contested, and there are demands for banning them, which is possible according to Dutch law.

Time after time the leaders of the extreme right organisations are faced with the question of how far one can go, of where the exact limits of the permissible lie. When such leaders can be identified with Fascism, they are subsequently discredited and criminalised. In terms outlined by the American sociologist Erving Goffman, they acquire a 'spoilt identity' (Goffman, 1959). This can result in criminal proceedings, and ultimately perhaps in a ban on their organisation. To avoid this danger the leaders are obliged to adapt in one way or another, but adaptive strategies that are too rigorous carry their own risks: the repudiation of ideological principles and the loss of (radical) supporters because the latter see too little difference from the more generally accepted political currents. As a rule, organisations and their leaders distance themselves from the old fascism, at any rate front-stage. Such distancing entails the avoidance or at least the moderation of overt characteristics such as use of Nazi-like jargon, and it certainly entails avoidance of any involvement in violent activism. For survival, the impression one desires to convey is that of respectability and 'democracy' in one's dealings, and in this way the wine is watered down to a greater or lesser extent. More attention is paid to the front-stage and less (and sometimes even very little) to back-stage activities.[2]

The dilemma outlined here is bounded by two extremes: on one hand the open conflict with the law, the ultimate consequence of which is the ban; and on the other, insufficient distinction between the organisation and the more established political currents. Both these extremes can spell the end of the organisation.

The 'adaptation dilemma' we have indicated here presents extreme right organisations, especially their leaders, with problems difficult to resolve since, in everyday reality, the precise boundaries of the permissible are often ill-defined. It is a question of trial and error, and this can easily create internal tensions. Right-wing activists are continually testing such limits, and trying to relocate them to the activists' own advantage. Opponents try to do the opposite, attempting to puncture the façade of moderation erected by an organisation they regard as fascist in nature, for example by demonstrating its involvement in violent actions. In this the aim is to create a 'spoilt identity' for the organisation; to criminalise it in the hope of stimulating judicial intervention. Here, publicity often acts as a catalyst.

A BIRD'S-EYE VIEW OF RACIST ORGANISATIONS

From about 1970 racism came to occupy a prominent place in the manifestation of extreme right beliefs. This development was embodied in the *Nederlandse Volks-Unie* (Dutch People's Union, NVU) founded in 1971. This organisation gradually developed into a single-issue, racist political party. It never succeeded in gaining any seats in elections. The NVU achieved notoriety chiefly for its open and ferocious racism directed at ethnic minorities. The NVU hard line resulted in an unsuccessful attempt to have the party banned.

NVU radicalism was also opposed from the inside, chiefly because of the risk of banning. There was less opposition to the party's central political message: protest against the presence of ethnic minorities in the country. These factors played an important part in the founding of the *Centrumpartij* (Centre Party, CP) in 1980; this embodies a reminder of its short-lived predecessor the National Centre Party, abandoned after the 'church raid'.

The main difference between the CP and NVU concerned strategy rather than the ultimate goal of the removal of ethnic minorities from Dutch society. In other words, there were fewer disagreements between the two parties behind the scenes than there were 'up front'. Right from the very beginning there was controversy within the CP between 'radicals' and 'moderates'. Despite this the party did well; its leader, Hans Janmaat, gained a parliamentary seat in 1982. With this the competition between the CP and NVU was decided in favour of the CP, and slowly but surely the NVU disappeared from the political scene.

In 1983 opinion polls revealed that in future elections the party could well gain several extra seats, but a year later the CP fell prey to internal strife. Janmaat was expelled from the party but kept his parliamentary seat until the 1986 election. At the end of 1984 he established a new party, the Centre Democrats (CD) and in 1989 he made his comeback to parliament. In 1990 the CD did particularly well in the municipal elections of that year, especially in the four big cities. The CP, now called the Centre Party '86 (CP'86) also succeeded in obtaining several seats on municipal councils. The electoral successes of the extreme right continued in the Provincial election of 1991.

Up to this point in our survey, we have dealt with one type of organisation – the political party. However, several other groups need to be discussed, which are not in fact political parties. Most prominent among these are the youth organisations of the NVU and CP, the National Youth Front and the *Jonge Geuzen* respectively. Generally speaking, both youth organisations are somewhat more radical in character than the political parties from which they stemmed.

Next we should mention the *Jongeren Front Nederland* (Dutch Youth Front, JFN) founded about 1982 as a radical offshoot of the National Youth Front; Viking Youth led by former SS-ers; and the *Actiefront Nationaal Socialisten* (National Socialist Action Front, ANS) which came into being shortly after the JFN. There has always been a brisk traffic between the different organisations: an interchange of members, ideas and activities. Many organisations and their members have lent a helping hand to the political parties, especially at election time. The diffuse character of all this is intensified by the fact that invariably there are a few dozen militant youths (especially skinheads) drifting around these organisations, including the political parties, and it is unclear where they belong, or if in fact they do belong anywhere. The murderer of the Antillian Kerwin Duijnmeijer in 1983 fits into the category. In recent times the skinheads appeared to be somewhat better organised, as one can see for instance from the publication of a common magazine, *Keep Contact*.

In 1990 the JFN disbanded. Some of its supporters followed JFN leader, Stewart Mordaunt, into CP'86; Mordaunt represents CP'86 in the Municipal Council of The Hague. The ANS is still in existence but has been more or less paralysed by several confrontations with the law. At present a former ANS sympathiser is sitting on the Municipal Council of Purmerend, representing the CD.

RACIST VIOLENCE

With a few exceptions very little scientific research has been devoted to the subject of racist violence in the Netherlands. Groenendijk has analysed the riots between Italians, Spaniards and Dutch which erupted in Twente in 1961 (Groenendijk, 1990). Jansma and Veenman have studied the riots between Turks and Dutch in Schiedam in 1976 (Jansma and Veenman, 1977, pp. 127–163). De Jong has devoted some attention to the violent exchanges between Turks and Dutch in the Rotterdam suburb '*Afrikaanderbuurt*' in 1971 and 1972. This was in the context of his study of ethnic relations in Rotterdam (De Jong, 1986, p. 143). These are case studies. There is an even greater dearth of publications examining racist violence more over the long term, and those we have were not written with scientific aims.[3] In short, there is little that can be stated with any certainty about the phenomenon of racist violence, on the basis of scientific research. The regular statistics on criminality offer even less certitude since, in these, crimes of racist violence cannot be recognised as such, apart from the more general problem that such statistics only reveal part of the reality, i.e. what is registered.

Those seeking an insight into the extent, nature and background of the manifestation of racist violence are to a large extent directed towards the field of journalism. Using news coverage in daily and weekly papers as my basis, I have attempted to discover several general patterns. Where the extent of the phenomenon is concerned, I have arrived at the following cautious conclusions:

1. Before the 1970s racist violence was a rare and occasional occurrence.
2. In the 1970s the phenomenon became increasingly visible and it increased in frequency.
3. In the first half of the 1980s racist violence was intensified to a great extent, although in the second half of the decade it appeared to diminish again.
4. Recently, and especially in 1992, we have seen a wave of racist violence far larger than any before it.

It is a plausible thesis that the 1970s constituted a turning-point. At all events in that period there was a growing belief that the Netherlands had turned into a country of immigration; that the presence of ethnic minorities would be a permanent one; and that these facts were inevitably accompanied by problems. The risk of racist violence increased with the large-scale nature of 1970s immigration. In the second place one could point to the general rise in crimes of violence becoming perceptible in the 1970s, and continuing since then. This latter factor could also provide an explanation for the third and fourth conclusion, in part because where racist violence reflects general trends in violent crime, one would expect a steady rise. What strikes one about conclusions 3 and 4 are the fluctuations: the sharp increase in racist violence in the first half of the 1980s, its decrease in the second half of the decade, and the sudden steep rise in 1992.

A remarkable aspect of these fluctuations is the way in which they appear, at first sight, to coincide with fluctuations in the electorates of racist political parties. The rise of the CP at the beginning of the 1980s corresponded with an increase in racist violence during the same period. The disintegration of racist organisations in the second half of the 1980s took place at the same time as the decrease in racist violence. The recent new increase coincides with a (predicted) growth in support for racist organisations.

The correspondences are too striking to remain unnoticed, although one could approach them from another direction, i.e. the extent to which the media devote attention to racist violence. In other words, the electoral success of a racist political party increases the news value of the racist phenomenon. Racist occurrences thereby gain further publicity. Conversely, when racist political parties experience a decline, as happened between 1986 and 1989, less attention is paid to racist events.

What kind of 'events' are we dealing with? As already stated, racist violence was only a rare and irregular phenomenon before the 1970s. Groenendijk has summarised a number of incidents occurring since 1945 (Groenendijk, 1990). They usually involve fights between Dutch and non-Dutch youths. In the 1960s there were also several anti-Semitic incidents, mainly damage to property.

In 1970 and 1971 there were repeated fights between Dutch and Moluccan youths (Groenendijk, 1990, pp. 55, 87), while in 1971 again, Turkish and Dutch youths clashed in The Hague and in Rotterdam (Groenendijk, 1990, p. 55). In 1972 the latter city (in the '*Afrikaan-derbuurt*') was the scene of large-scale riots between young Turks and Netherlanders (De Jong, 1986, p. 143). In 1976 a knife fight at Schiedam fair led to scuffles between Turks and Netherlanders which continued for days (Jansma and Veenman, 1977). The year 1977 saw the first fatality: in Amsterdam a Turkish man was deliberately thrown into a canal and drowned. Racist violence increased in a spectacular manner in the 1980s. Holtrop and Den Tex (1984) and Buijs (1988) mention, among other things: intimidation, threats, racist graffiti, destruction of property, arson, fights (several resulting in fatalities), assaults, gun fights, and bombings.

It can be confirmed that not only were incidents like these more frequent; one can also talk of intensification of violence. One incident that attracted a great deal of attention was the murder of 15-year-old Kerwin Duijnmeijer in August 1983. The 16-year-old culprit, Nico B., known as a Nazi skinhead in extreme right political circles, told the police that he had stabbed Kerwin because he was black. Nico B. also claimed that he would do the same again, given the chance (Holtrop and Den Tex, 1984, p. 27). The Amsterdam court which sentenced the culprit several months later caused a furore with its declaration that there was no proof of either racist motive or premeditation. In view of the latter there was thus no question of murder, but rather a case of grievous bodily harm leading to the victim's death, according to the court.[4] In 1989 Nico B. again stabbed someone. The victim, who barely escaped with his life, had noticed that Nico B.'s T-shirt bore the legend 'It's good to be white.'

The years 1983 and 1984 were remarkable for their many cases of arson, or attempted arson. Holtrop and Den Tex have listed the following targets: mosques, a Moroccan coffee-house, a building belonging to a Surinamese organisation, condemned buildings (to frighten away Turks living nearby), and the homes of Moroccan families. In August 1986, exactly ten years after the riots mentioned earlier here, a bomb exploded in a Turkish coffee-house in Schiedam. Three suspects were quickly arrested. All three were members of the Nazi Dutch Youth Front (JFN) and earlier on they had spread racist material round Schiedam and had smashed the windows of a Turkish mosque.[5] The chief suspect told the court that he had taken part in the 1976 riots at the age of 8 years; he had virtually absorbed his hatred of Turks with his mother's milk.[6]

Recently, and especially in 1992, there has been a sharp increase in racist violence and this coincides with a predicted growth of electoral support for the CD. One can distinguish two 'waves' in events taking place in the first four months of 1992. The first wave involved attacks on mosques, and began with the fire-bombing (already noted here) of an Amersfoort mosque at the end of January. According to news coverage in the media, this was shortly followed by attacks of varying kinds on nine other mosques: destruction of property, threats, and arson. As far as I am aware, none of these cases has been solved to date, and it is consequently impossible to confirm with absolute certainty that racist violence was involved in every case. Yet the assumption that such violence is in fact involved, seems to me to be justified since it is unlikely that the choice of target, and the serial nature of the attacks, are due purely to coincidence. It is also far from unlikely that the series may actually have been larger, i.e. that there were more attacks, for example in the form of threats, but that these received no publicity.

In a second discernible wave, the common factor is the place where the attacks were made rather than the choice of target (mosques). Here we are dealing with a series of attacks taking place in The Hague during the first three months of 1992: four bombings, three cases of arson, three (false) bomb alarms, four cases of destruction of property, and several cases of assault. Once again, these concern only offences that have been publicised, and it is probable that the number of incidents is in fact larger.

The cases involving assault – all of them obviously racist in character – were solved more or less immediately, and the culprits (skinheads) were convicted by *snelrecht* (summary jurisdiction).[7] The worst case involved a Haitian man, severely beaten and kicked by a group of five skinheads; one of them was, or had been, active in both the CD and the CP'86.[8]

The bomb attacks on 'immigrant targets' in The Hague in January and February 1992 were also solved. These attacks caused a great deal of disturbance partly because they stimulated the suspicion that they might be the work of (unidentified) right-wing organisations. However, this was not in fact the case. In July the police succeeded in arresting the culprit after he had once again tried to explode a bomb. The 35-year-old man from The Hague had most probably carried out the attacks on his own initiative. There has been nothing to show that he had links with existing racist organisations.

One can find both a consensus and differing opinions among the reactions to recent racist violence. There is consensus particularly in the moral sense: many people reveal repugnance and contempt for it. However, when it comes to interpretation of the phenomenon under discussion, opinions differ to a marked degree. Thus, there is frequent speculation about whether or not we are dealing here with a forerunner of 'German conditions'. Another discussion point concerns the link between the different violent incidents. Can one talk of an organised campaign, or was the 'series' of attacks simply the sum total of otherwise unconnected events? Opinions on the supposed link sometimes differ widely, and differences seem particularly to be prompted by the side of the question – that of the perpetrators or that of the victims – which commentators wish to emphasise. Thus, the government and the minorities' organisations, for example, argue from different viewpoints. In the view of the minorities' organisations there was certainty about the links, if only for the fact that within a short period of time there had been a large number of violent actions all directed against foreigners. In contrast, the Minister for *Binnenlandse Zaken* (Home Affairs) believed that there was no connection between the events: 'Nothing, or at any rate nothing in police investigations indicates a country-wide campaign'.[9] At the end of 1992 there was a glance back at the past:

> For years international attention has been drawn to the fact that, in the Netherlands, there are very few unsavoury incidents. There has been a number of attacks on what have been called Islamic targets here in The Hague. This is certainly very disturbing, but immediately there is the fear that an organisation is behind the affair. Then when the matter is investigated, it appears to be a case of one man acting on his own. There have been incidents, but there is no reason for talking about the growth of right-wing organisations planning this kind of thing.[10]

What the minister appears not to know is that a large number of what she calls 'incidents' have remained unsolved to date: this applies especially to a number of arson cases in The Hague, and to at least seven attacks on mosques, including the one at Amersfoort. There is consequently still much to be investigated. The minister's choice of words seems to have been prompted by the need to calm things down. It is an attitude one frequently encounters among governmental and juridical authorities where racist violence is concerned. Moreover, the low level of organisation behind these incidents is seen by the Dutch government as reassuring, while in Germany it is precisely this aspect that is viewed as a serious problem. As the Public Prosecutor for Hanover puts it:

> I am disturbed by the anonymous character of the group of culprits. I would rather they were organised, then at least one knows how many there are, and where to find them.[11]

THE ROLE OF THE EXTREME RIGHT

Where the incidents occurring in 1992 are concerned, there are only a few cases in which, in my opinion, it is possible to find a direct link between the perpetrators and racist political parties (in this case the CP'86 and the CD). We have already outlined one example: the case of the gross assault on a Haitian man. Another example is more or less identical: in August, the Utrecht police arrested several skinheads who were suspected of having assaulted an immigrant.[12] One of those arrested had stood as candidate for the CD in the parliamentary elections of 1989.[13] A third case concerned near-violence.[14] On 10 October approximately seventy-five extreme right activists allied to the CP'86 gathered in Arnhem; they included the CP'86 leader Mordaunt. They were probably planning to disrupt a multicultural festival. The police arrested eight skinheads with weapons. The festival was still disturbed that very evening by a false bomb alarm. Eight years before this I talked to Mordaunt, then leader of the JFN, about his views on political violence. Mordaunt said:

> We want strong action to keep the members warmed up. You can't hold them if they have nothing to do. I had a Frenchman from the Front National visiting me, and he told us about an Algerian pub in Paris. They smashed it up completely. I like that! But we don't propagate violence because that would put paid to your club. But if my members want to take a Turkish coffee-house apart . . . well, there's nothing I can do about it. It's the members. My hands are clean.

Mordaunt's facial expression gave me the impression that he would actually support an action of this kind. When I asked him this, he answered 'Of course I'd support it!'

During the interview we were discussing a hypothetical question, but two years later a JFN member exploded a bomb in a Turkish coffee-house in Schiedam – we have already mentioned this incident – and hypothesis became reality. Mordaunt declared that he had had nothing to do with the affair and threw the culprit out of the JFN. Subsequently the JFN news-sheet called upon members to correspond with the bomber in prison.[15]

The top echelon of the CD reacted in a variety of different ways to the recent racist violence. Thus the CD member of the Amsterdam municipal council put forward the possibility that the attacks (the case is still unsolved) could well have been the work of the Turks themselves.[16] His colleague from Dordrecht would not exclude the possibility that the attacks were fabricated by the *Binnenlandse Veiligheidsdienst* (Security Service).[17] Or, as in the following:

Sure, if the Dutch citizen can't say 'fuck off' then he'll surely use his fists. Skinheads are really ordinary kids reacting to a culture gone adrift.[18]

Yge Graman 'used his fists' in 1980 in the Moses and Aaron Church. The four-month prison sentence he was awarded for this was no hindrance when the CD placed Graman's name on a list of candidates for the 1991 elections.[19] According to CD leader Janmaat, at this moment Graman belongs among the party's 'top ten'.[20]

Within the CD the member for the Purmerend municipal council, Richard van der Plas, encounters more opposition because of his connections with the ANS. In his home the police discovered incriminating material: a great many stickers bearing the legend 'Free Europe from the Jews'; a gun with ammunition; and a list of immigrant targets for violent attacks.[21] It is clear that van der Plas is in fact opposed within the CD from the fact that, for instance, Janmaat did not place him among his 'top men' for the forthcoming elections. Janmaat, however, defended van der Plas and other CD 'hawks' to the outside world:

Of course we have attracted various people from a somewhat more right-wing or, if your prefer, more extremist sphere. But if they have committed a few youthful sins for which they have not been heavily punished, they can work along with us as long as they respect the party's position.[22]

Things are somewhat different with the CD where skinheads are concerned. The journalist, Robert van de Roer, discussed this with Janmaat and he detected uncertainty and ambivalence in the CD leader:

'Skinheads can distribute leaflets for the CD, just as before', then he (Janmaat) immediately corrected this statement. 'No, that's not the right answer. A large majority of those on the general executive are against that and think it gives the wrong impression. I agree with this view.' Suddenly, this became 'extreme right elements have to be excluded. That breaks the party up'.[23]

The confusion of Janmaat's reaction illustrates the difficulty which right-wing leaders have in handling troublesome, violent political activism. Whatever they may think personally about the use of violence, they cannot permit themselves – at least in a front-stage way – to embrace violent activism. This would place the future of their organisation in jeopardy. An extreme right body openly propagating (racist) violence in the Netherlands runs a great risk of being banned. A political party that openly propagates violence will also very probably discourage a proportion of its (potential) voters.

On the other hand there is an equal risk in keeping a resolute distance from violent activism: alienation of some of the supporters who fulfil useful functions for the organisation. One thinks here of the dissemination of propaganda and the recruitment of (paying!) members. Relations between the 'moderate' leader and his militant followers are often tense. In the leader's eyes, a radical supporter is not only useful: he is also a security risk in the event that he turns out to be an armed hoodlum, thereby bringing the organisation into disrepute. To reduce this risk, a potentially violent supporter is often marginalised, for example, by denying him formal membership of the organisation. This can also be prompted by distrust: someone who proposes violent actions could well be an infiltrator and *agent provocateur*, wanting to smash the organisation.

Conversely the leader can all too often forfeit his credibility in the eyes of radical supporters. They may feel he undervalues them even if he is not actually using them simply as 'pamphlet-carthorses'. The leader's moderate course can easily be seen as 'weak'. Thus a disappointed skinhead – once an enthusiastic CD supporter – let slip the remark that Janmaat 'can't be extreme because then the party would be banned at once'.[24]

Racist parties exert an attraction for people who are more radical or more militant than the image the organisation would like for its own front-stage presentation. The conduct of these people can bring the party as a whole into discredit. Back-stage it is a different matter: there, the 'radicals' are often respected because of what they earn for the party and because of their nerve. They are interpreters for sentiments which many people share but which they do not dare defend in public. Yet the 'radical' position within the party is a vulnerable one. To a great extent it is dependent upon external influences such as media and juridical interest in the doings of individual 'radicals'. Whoever brings discredit upon the party thereby invites pressure on his own position within the organisation.

Personal interconnections are not the only important aspects, since the ideological side of the question also deserves attention. Here we are concerned with such questions as the extent to which racist organisations reveal sympathy for violent actions. Do they try to justify this kind of action, or do they even incite others to commit such actions?

There was indeed incitement of this kind in the riots taking place in 1972 in the '*Afrikaanderbuurt*' in Rotterdam. The NVU spread pamphlets around the area in which Dutch inhabitants of the neighbourhood were encouraged, in covert terms, to continue the violence. In 1976 there was a similar kind of action in the Schiedam riots. Pamphlets distributed by the NVU agitated not only against ethnic minorities but also, and particularly, against 'established' politicians:

> The Mayor and municipal councillors of Schiedam have . . . abandoned, in cowardly fashion, the many hundreds of fellow-citizens who have been unable to control their bottled-up feelings of disgust and despair.

The NVU action aroused a great deal of indignation and also encouraged the suspicion that the riots had been organised by the NVU. This was untrue, but nevertheless NVU involvement in the Schiedam riots brought the party a step closer to being banned (van Donselaar, 1991, p. 161).

When Groenendijk was investigating the Twente riots (in 1961) he found a letter in which sympathy was expressed for the Dutch perpetrators of the violence. The writer, W. J. Bruyn, talked of 'justified self-defence of one's own interests and life-style' (Groenendijk, 1990, p. 76). Later on, Bruyn was to become a member successively of the NVU, the CP, and the CD. In 1984 he wrote a draft proposal for the CP in which the idea of 'justified self-defence' was once again put forward. In a chapter entitled 'The Right to Self-defence' he pleaded that violence used by the Dutch against foreigners, as in Rotterdam in 1972, should be regarded as a form of justified self-defence (van Donselaar, 1991, p. 187). There is nothing new in this line of thought: in *Mein Kampf* Hitler gave a chapter the title '*Notwehr als Recht*' – 'The Right to Self-defence'.[25] The parallel is not confined to chapter titles; it extends to the reasoning itself in which, to put it succinctly, victims are presented as culprits and *vice versa*. Would Bruyn have consciously based his ideas on Hitler's? In his case I would doubt it, but there is less doubt in the case of ANS leader Homan, who labelled the mosque attacks of 1992 as 'justified self-defence'.[26]

FINAL REMARKS

In the prevailing image of racist violence, a major role is allotted to the far right, but this does not accord with the reality of the matter. Many cases of racist violence have never been solved, and thus one can only speculate about the part played in them by the extreme right. Where there is certainty on the matter, the culprits and the extreme right have been linked in only a small proportion of cases. Any demonstrable link is usually an indirect one; the offence cannot be attributed to a particular organisation, but at most only to a person who in some way or other is part of the organisation. Is this fuzzy image a true reflection of reality, or is it based upon defective and superficial insights? Where the latter is concerned, it seems obvious to me that our knowledge of the relationship between racist violence and the extreme right leaves much to be desired. Yet, one can question whether purposive investigation would produce the clarification desired. We have shown here that the extreme right leaders have a strategy for keeping their organisations out of the line of fire. Demonstrable involvement in violence could, after all, spell the end of legal existence for their organisations. This is not to deny that people with a reputation for violence in the arena of racist politics are tolerated, as long as they do not 'besmirch' the organisation too much.

To what extent can the racist political arena influence a climate in which racist violence can flourish? What effect has the propagation of 'self-defence reasoning', in which violence is in fact legitimated? These are important questions for which at present we do not have the answers.

What, in my opinion, can be confirmed without closer research, is that there is good reason for concern. In the electoral sense, racist political parties have never been stronger than they are at the present time. Since 1982 they have been continuously represented on democratically elected bodies, and their supporters have shown a spectacular growth in numbers within a short period. In the past few years there has been a considerable increase in the numbers of militant right-wing youths. The phenomenon of racist violence has never before occurred as frequently in the Netherlands as it has done recently. The only consolation is a poor one: the Netherlands still shows up favourably in comparison with the countries surrounding it.

NOTES

1. 'Ideal type' is here used in its social science sense, meaning 'pure form', without any good or bad connotations.
2. The concepts 'front-stage' and 'back-stage' are taken from Goffman (1959).
3. See for example A. Holtrop and U. den Tex, 'Bij ons in Holland', *Vrij Nederland*, 30 June 1984; H. Buijs, *Beter een verre buur* (Amsterdam, 1988).
4. *de Volkskrant*, 24-1-84.
5. *de Volkskrant*, 28-11-86.
6. Ibid.
7. *NRC Handelsblad*, 19-2-92; *Trouw*, 20-2-92; *de Volkskrant*, 20-2-92.
8. *Nieuwsblad Migranten*, 2-4-92.
9. *de Volkskrant*, 29-1-92.
10. Interview in *Opzij*, vol. 20 (December 1992), p. 151.
11. *Vrij Nederland*, 12-12-92.
12. *Casablanca*, September/Oktober 1992.
13. Ibid.
14. *Casablanca*, November/December 1992.
15. *NRC Handelsblad*, 28-3-92.
16. *Algemeen Dagblad*, 7-3-92.
17. *NRC Handelsblad*, 4-4-92.
18. Ibid.
19. *Afdruk*, February 1991.
20. *Nieuwe Revu*, 2-9-92.
21. *NRC Handelsblad*, 28-3-92, 4-4-92.
22. *NRC Handelsblad*, 4-4-92.
23. *NRC Handelsblad*, 28-3-92.
24. *Krant op Zondag*, 2-2-92.
25. According to Hugo Gijsels, the Vlaams-Blok slogan 'in self-defence' can be viewed in the same light. H. Gijsels, *Het Vlaams Blok* (Leuven, 1992), p. 213.
26. *Leids Dagblad*, 7-3-92.

5 The Cult of Violence: The Swedish Racist Counterculture

Heléne Lööw

> The issue is not Swedish refugee policy. It is the fact that two million in this country have to be exterminated because they are racially inferior or traitors. It might sound hard, but you have to be realistic. That's the way it is. (Interview with VAM activist)

This chapter explores the new radical and revolutionary racism, which has emerged in Sweden during the 1980s and early 1990s, and aims to describe the various organisations, their ideology and political strategies.[1] First of all, however, it should be noted that the Swedish racist counterculture is relatively small. Although the past two years have witnessed gradual growth in the movement, the estimated number of activists, members and sympathisers remains at no more than 500–600.

RACIST SUBCULTURE – THE WORLD OF WHITE POWER

The so-called 'White Power world' in Sweden deviates little from the pattern of revolutionary racist subcultures which emerged during the 1980s throughout most of Europe and in the USA. This counterculture consists of a complex network of National Socialist, anti-Semitic, and other racist groups and individuals. The 'White Power world' is more than merely an umbrella for different groups: its racist underground is a hidden world, with its own language, life style and mythology, cut off from much of the mainstream in Sweden. The White Power network lacks any semblance of political, moral or financial support from any group in Swedish society; and its espoused values sharply distinguish this world from what is generally accepted.

In order to understand this movement, we need to begin with an analysis of its historical roots and organisational components. Sweden was not involved in the Second World War, so Swedish National

Socialists were never compromised by collaboration with a German occupying power. As a result, none of the National Socialist or anti-Semitic organisations were banned after 1945, as was the case in several other European countries.

In 1956 the *Nordiska Rikspartiet* (Nordic Reich Party, NRP) was founded by Göran Oredsson. This is a classical National Socialist party, plagued by a lack of financial support from older and younger generations of National Socialists, by internal struggles, splits, and the acts of violence carried out by its members and sympathisers. Since its early years, NRP members and sympathisers have been convicted for inciting racial hatred, bombings, assault and battery, and harassment. Despite the NRP's lack of political support, the party has functioned as an important bridge between Sweden's pre-war National Socialists and the revolutionary, internationally oriented, racist socialists of the 1990s. A number of key activists in the contemporary racist underground are former NRP members. Today the NRP's political activity is limited to various publications, but its leadership does favour the new militant-racist underground.

VITT ARISKT MOTSTÅND

A cornerstone of Sweden's contemporary racist subculture has been the proliferation of underground youth magazines. Within the network of readers and publishers, and among the young NRP activists of the 1980s, a new militant-racist underground has emerged. The first magazine was the skinhead paper, *Streetfight*; this disappeared in 1989 but was immediately replaced by *Vit Rebell* (White Rebel), a magazine much more political than its predecessor. *Vit Rebell* was the first to propose the creation of a formal network of racist groups. During the *Vit Rebell* era, factional tensions between the revolutionary, anti-democratic racist and the parliamentarian, nationalistic, and basically ethnocentric groupings, such as *Sverigedemokraterna* (Swedish Democrats), erupted into a full split within the nationalistic movement. In *Vit Rebell* (no 2, 1989) it is proclaimed: 'For over 50 years there has been a steady flood of "right-wing extremist" and "racist democratic" organisations, which have achieved nothing by propagating patriotism, while avoiding the brutal truth about our final goal – the necessary extermination of the enemies of mankind.'

In 1990 *Vit Rebell* was replaced by the magazine *Storm*, which aimed to 'lay the foundation for a joint racist front'. In one of its first circulars the *Vitt Ariskt Motstånd* (White Aryan Resistance VAM) network stated that:

> VAM is not a traditional organisation, but an efficient network that helps regional groups, local cells and individuals to get started in their fight for freedom . . . VAM distributes race-revolutionary propaganda through magazines, posters, stickers, leaflets and literature.

This network grew steadily during 1990, with its core consisting of a small group of young men in their early to mid-20s. Despite their young age, they all had a long history of political activity in various National Socialist and racist groups, some with as many as 10 years' experience. The network of the early days operated without a name; one activist explained that it was 'maybe not meant to have a name, only different fronts.' One of these fronts for racist propaganda consists of the magazine *Storm*; another front has been the 'White Power' rock groups such as *Division S*, *Vit Aggression* and *Dirlewanger*.

In 1991 the network made a name for itself through a series of bank robberies, burglaries and attempted burglaries of military depots. VAM made the headlines together with the so-called 'Laser Man' who killed one immigrant and injured ten. On 30 December, a bomb exploded at the main railway station in Stockholm, injuring a bomb squad officer. A man subsequently phoned the police to demand the immediate release of a leading VAM activist, then serving a 6-year sentence for bank robbery. Whether this bombing was actually the work of the network or another group is not known, but the subsequent media attention fed VAM's image as a heavily armed, secretive terrorist organisation.

If 1991 was known for its right-wing political violence and crime, 1992 became significant for its series of convictions for these crimes. Between July and September, six VAM activists were convicted for planning armed robbery. One member of the racist underground in the Gothenburg area also received convictions for robbing a local post office. In November, a member of the Stockholm branch of the VAM network was convicted for his role in a separate bank robbery. Finally, in December a leading 'VAM soldier' was convicted, together with three skinheads, for attempted bank robbery.

VAM's production and distribution of political propaganda also increased in 1992. As of the autumn of 1992 the network had seven contact addresses in the country, and had also established local branches in Finland, Norway and Denmark. VAM leaflets, posters and stickers have also turned up elsewhere in Sweden, but the existence of actual VAM cells in these cities cannot be verified. In most cases the propaganda material is likely to be handed out by local youth with racist or anti-immigrant attitudes. They may not necessarily belong to the network, but the source of the propaganda is relatively easy to trace – the magazine *Storm*; the contact addresses; a mail order service through which *Storm* distributes racist and National Socialist litera- ture, tapes, videos, T-shirts, flags, etc.; the rock groups; and the VAM telephone 'hot-line' – all are part of VAM's public activity. Media attention accelerated the formation of the network, making the symbols, uniforms, addresses and message of the racist underground known to a larger public. This has meant that criminal youth gangs with previous racist ideas could find a political form for their ideas and motivation for some of their criminality. These groups, however, often operate outside the original network and are sometimes unknown to the members of the network. Such 'racist freelancers' are a problem for the original network because the activists cannot control them. Several key activists have complained about how difficult it is to get rid of 'certain lunatics' who operate in the name of the organisations or networks, without being acknowledged as members. One key activist ironically stated that the media attention was to some extent 'like advertising for psychopaths – and unfortunately the response was overwhelming'.

There is also another side to the network. A small, extremely militant group operates in relation to the underground paper *Werwolf*, which is a primitive handbook for political terrorism. This paper gives advice (not very advanced) about bomb construction, murder techniques, street fighting, bank robbery, etc. *Werwolf* provides the militant activist with highly matter-of-fact advice on methods of terror, discussing topics ranging from 'how to phone in a bomb threat' and 'how to harass political enemies', to the more basic 'how to locate the names and addresses of political enemies'. In *Siege*, a similar paper issued by another militant faction of the network, the activist can find a comprehensive guide discussing the best ways to harass homosexuals. During 1993 a third similar underground paper – *Ragnarök* – has turned up. The evidence notwithstanding, most members of VAM deny any knowledge of the existence of these publications.

The VAM-network is not open to everyone. *Anhängarbulletinen*, a newsletter for the network's sympathisers, published the following statement concerning organisational membership: 'To be a member should be a privilege and an honour given to few . . . It can only be earned in the struggle.' The VAM network is built on local cells led by a local leader/organiser, therefore rejecting an organisational hierarchy. The network loosely maintains the following membership ranks: sympathisers/assistants who are, to a certain extent, active in the cause; members/activists, who have demonstrated a dedication to the organisation's ideals and who distinguish themselves through 'good recommendations' either from similar organisations or documentation of participation in racist activities (news clippings, convictions, etc); and local organisers/leaders. VAM lacks a single figurehead, but prefers to organise itself in conjunction with several key activists who have been involved in the racist underground since the early 1980s. This informal ranking of members is what could be described as 'the open component of the network'. Activists have to obey certain rules, such as: no use of drugs; physical training; no media appearances without clearance; silence and moderate use of alcohol; no use of alcohol during network activities. The last rule seems to have had some effects on the racist underground. Drunken activists at rallies and street propaganda activities – a common scene during the 1980s – have more or less disappeared during 1992. The underground is, bluntly speaking, sobering up.

The other, more militant and revolutionary component of VAM consists of small independent groups. The requirement for discipline and dedication within these militant cells is far higher than the standards set for the ordinary street activist. This helps to ensure that the network remains both flexible and difficult to infiltrate, so that it can function well in the event of the entire network being forced underground. The VAM network is organised according to the model created by the US organisation, White Aryan Resistance (WAR), with which VAM maintains relatively close contact. One activist has confirmed that the primary reason for these close contacts between the VAM network and groups in the USA is the fact that most of VAM's Swedish membership is proficient in the English language, but less so in, for example, German.

KREATIVISTENS KYRKA AND *RIKSFRONTEN*

Kreativistens Kyrka, a Swedish offshoot of the US organisation Church of the Creator (COTC), was founded in 1988 by Tommy Rydén, a long-time activist in various racist and nationalist organisations. Part of the COTC has, from the beginning, maintained links with the VAM network. However, during the summer of 1991 a rift emerged between the National Socialist factions of VAM and *Kreativistens Kyrka* because of ideological differences and personal conflicts. During 1992 it seems that part of the COTC and the National Socialists involved in the VAM network began putting their differences behind them in favour of mutual cooperation for the cause. Then, during the late autumn of 1992, a faction headed by Tommy Rydén broke all relations with the US mother-church and established an independent organisation called Ben Klassen Academy – named after the US founder of the COTC. The split is the result of personal and organisational conflicts. In 1993, Rydén returned to the mother-church, since the fraction he belonged to won the battle for control over the organisation. He was also appointed leader of the Swedish COTC.

COTC-Sweden is organised according to the same principles as VAM – not built around one individual but structured in independent units. However, the Swedish branch is controlled by its mother-church in the USA. VAM, on the other hand, seems to be a completely independent network, but the activities of the two organisations overlap significantly. In addition to the COTC, the network has also maintained contacts with an organisation called *Riksfronten/Föreningen Sveriges Framtid* (National Front/Association for Sweden's Future). This group acts upon the basis of the ideological teachings of the fascist leader, Per Engdahl, who since the early 1930s has been the leader of *Nysvenska Rörelsen* (The New Swedish Organisation). However, during 1992 a split emerged between *Riksfronten* and VAM. In May 1993, it seemed as if the differences between the organisations had been put aside in favour of a joint front. VAM has disappeared as a political group and gone underground. Activities have been divided equally between the organisations: the *Riksfronten* has taken over the political, VAM the militant underground and *Kreativistens Kyrka* the religious activities. Activists are free to chose which part of the network they want to belong to.

A CLOSED WORLD – DISCOURSE AND MYTHOLOGY OF THE 'WHITE POWER WORLD'

All the aforementioned organisations together form a radical-racist counterculture with its own language and mythology. Its rhetoric is a mixture of National Socialist terminology of the 1930s and the contemporary code used by Ku Klux Klan and White Supremacist groups in the USA. This becomes apparent when you compare the language used in the organisational press and by the informants with National Socialist texts from the 1930s and literature from US white power groups. Keywords from this genre include a preoccupation with 'The Zionist Occupational Government' (ZOG). Activists in the racist underground believe that the world is controlled by an 'international Jewish world conspiracy'. ZOG includes the media, police, administrators, intellectuals, etc. It is ZOG, not individual migrants, which is the primary 'enemy' to the racist counterculture. ZOG represents the 'corrupt society' which 'poisons the white race through immigration of racially inferior elements, homosexuality and moral disorder', in order to 'destroy the white race'. The 'members of ZOG' are referred to as 'Jew lackeys' or 'race traitors', and are the targets of the most violent hatred.

Another keyword is 'White Warriors'. This refers to KKK activists, members of Hitler's SS as well as those activists involved in the work of the VAM network, and to 'instinctive whites', that is, individuals who emotionally feel that they belong to the 'White resistance' and who feel disgust and discomfort while confronted with non-whites. 'Loyalty' also functions as a guiding principle for members of the network. Loyalty towards the group, its ideas, and its cause is extremely important, and underpins all actions undertaken within the network. The 'Aryan code of honour' – published in *Anhängarbulletinen* – contains the following statements, which show the essence of the network's 'code of loyalty and honour':

I am of Aryan blood. I serve the army that defends my Aryan race. I am prepared to sacrifice my life in the battle for my race. I am of Aryan blood. I will never surrender my soul to my enemies. I will never betray my Aryan people. I am of Aryan blood. If I am captured I will always obey my Aryan duty. I will, if possible, rescue other Aryan prisoners. I will not ask my enemies for mercy.

Loyalty is not only meant to bind the members of a particular network or activist cell, but includes an obligation to all 'White Warriors'. Names and addresses of jailed activists from a variety of nations frequently appear in 'White Power' magazines around the world to arouse sentiments of loyalty and support for all brothers-in-arms. The international racist underground's loyalty also extends to the Swedish 'white prisoners of war' and their families. For example, a member of the Swedish branch of the COTC received significant financial and moral support from fellow US 'Creators' while her husband was serving a prison sentence for inciting racial hatred. The strong emphasis on international solidarity has helped to generate a loose international network that acts as an 'Amnesty International for white prisoners of war'. This way foreign members can be aware of, and sometimes assist, imprisoned members of brother organisations around the world.

Like the international community of radical racists, members of the racist underground in Sweden maintain close contact with one another. It is quite common for activists to share a flat, which perpetuates the tendency of activists to refer to their fellow-members as their 'family' or 'brothers and sisters'. To quote *Storm*: 'VAM is a big family of racial brothers and sisters, who are faithful to each other 110 per cent. If any one betrays the family, that person is thereafter considered an enemy.'

When an activist goes abroad he or she will probably stay with 'brothers and sisters' in other countries. International contacts are extensive, but this does not imply the existence of a 'huge international Nazi conspiracy', as media reports would lead the public to believe. It is more likely that the racist underground is analogous to the militant left-wing underground of the 1960s and 1970s. Activists and sympathisers naturally forge alliances and ties of friendship with similar groups and individuals in other countries (see Jensen's contribution in Chapter 6).

In addition to the code of loyalty and honour, courage is also a central theme of the racist underground. A person lacking courage is considered unworthy of membership in the network. As one of the members of the White Power rock group *Dirlewanger* states: 'If we notice that someone is an idiot who talks a lot of rubbish and does not dare to stand up for what he says, well then he is simply no longer welcome among us. We just tell him to go to hell.' An activist has corroborated the reality of this statement, in his quip regarding the fate of a cowardly member: 'Well, we beat him up first, that happens pretty often.' The appeal to the 'virtue' of Aryan courage is perhaps best illustrated by a skinhead's statement made in court during the trial of a policeman who had shot and killed another skinhead in Malmö on a Nationalist celebration on 30 November 1991. He claimed that he was not at all frightened of getting shot while chasing the policeman, and added: 'It is an honour to die in battle.'

Of vital importance to the activists of the racist underground is the cult of heroes and martyrs. Their heroes are almost exclusively men, since the organisation is dominated by men. The cult of the heroes and martyrs perpetuates the mythology of a 'brotherhood in arms', in which extreme manliness retains its centrality to group identification.

The mythology of the network is also perpetuated through the ritual celebration of Hitler's birthday on 20 April, and the 'Day of the Martyrs' on 8 December, the date of Robert J. Mathews's death. He was the leader of the US organisation called *The Order* and was killed during an FBI raid of the group's headquarters. The Order has to some extent served as a model for VAM, and 8 December has subsequently become an international memorial day for the 'White Power world'. They commemorate not only the death of Mathews, but 'all white warriors who have fallen in battle'. The day also honours imprisoned 'brothers and sisters around the world'. The hero-worship of imprisoned activists can be illustrated by the following statement by the members of the skinhead rock group *Dirlewanger*, in honour of a former member of the Gothenburg branch of the NRP, who in 1985 murdered a homosexual man: 'We want to direct a special thanks and remembrance to *X*, for liberating our world from a Zionist, homosexual bastard, and who instead of his well-earned medal was imprisoned by the bloody system.' This hero-worship and cult of martyrs strengthen members in their ideological beliefs, and confirm the idea of the ongoing racial war – a war which demands sacrifices, but also gives activists a chance of martyrdom. The Swedish racist counterculture also celebrates the death day of King Charles XII on 30 November. The National Socialists' celebration of the Warrior King, who has become a symbol for the far right and nationalist activists in Sweden, goes back to the 1930s. Today's riots between National Socialists and anti-racists are seen as simply a renewal of the first riots that occurred during the mid-1930s.

TOWARDS A POLITICAL STRATEGY

The formation of the contemporary ideology and strategy of this revitalised radical-racist enclave is a combination of ideas from the NRP of the late 1970s and early 1980s, and the skinhead press described earlier. The recent catalyst for action has also come on the heels of a police crackdown on extremist activities. The arrest of a number of activists from the Gothenburg branch of the NRP at the beginning of 1986 marked the start of the Gothenburg 'Nazi trials' which did not end until 1987. Members and former members of the NRP were tried for bombings, assault and battery, harassment, extortion, arson, vandalism, and one case of murder.

Through the police investigations it is possible to generate a profile of the activities of the group and its members. Of the 121 members only seventeen were women. The group had gradually succeeded in creating its own 'world', in sharp contrast to reality as perceived by others. This was a world saturated with 'enemies' – Communists, homosexuals, Jews, immigrants and anti-racists – whom they felt compelled to defend themselves against, get even with, or harass. Defendants in the trials returned to this notion of self-defence time after time during police interrogation. A number of the members had repeatedly armed themselves with chains and knives, leaving the impression that armed confrontation was regarded as normal group activity. Members of the Gothenburg branch also spent a considerable time in meetings drinking alcohol and planning attacks on political enemies. To quote one of the leading members of the group, 'never a meeting without beer'. One drop-out described the meetings as 'beer drinking, drivel and splits'. Asked by the police interrogator if any discussions concerning violence or any direct summons took place during these meetings, party functionary *X* replied: 'nothing else but violence and assault and battery'. Two specific incidents helped to shape this obsession with political enemies. The first occurred on 3 December 1983, when the NRP had called a meeting in Gothenburg. The meeting ended in chaos when hundreds of anti-racists gathered to stop the meeting. After the confrontation the NRP's paper, *Nordisk Kamp*, published the following statement:

> Members and sympathisers! Make it your duty to survey the faces that appear in the media photographs of the riff-raff, on 3 December. Seek their names, addresses, and activities against NRP on this date. We will publish their names and addresses in the NRP media when we know them . . . This will give nationalists a chance to tell these individuals how they feel about their behaviour. Göran A Oredsson [the NRP leader].

This call marked the beginning of an intensive campaign of harassment and extortion against those persons who had participated in the Gothenburg demonstration. The party used the same tactic to identify 'enemies' after a second incident occurred in Växjö two years later. Here the NRP had called a demonstration which never materialised because of the counter-demonstration of thousands of anti-racists who ran the NRP members out of town. A similar incident occurred in late August of the same year in Helsingborg, when ten demonstrating NRP members were forced to seek refuge at the local police station after being chased through town by angry anti-racists. In addition to its internal advertising, the NRP posted the pictures of the individuals involved in the counter-demonstrations as a means of identifying them. As late as 1987, NRP papers published the names and addresses of persons who had taken part in the Växjö incident two years earlier. To avenge their embarrassing setback in Växjö, members of the NRP set fire to the party office of *Vänsterpartiet Kommunisterna* (Communist-Left Party, VPK) in Gothenburg. One of the accused stated his belief that the VPK was behind the rioting in Växjö, and his organisation wanted to get even.

Revenge had clearly become the central focus of the group's activities. Stories of harassment and assaults of NRP members and sympathisers by anti-racists – many of which were true – further reinforced the mythology of revenge for the racist underground. To party members, these anti-NRP incidents demanded revenge and were interpreted as concrete examples of persecution. The notion of a threatening social conspiracy managed by 'lying media, Jews, degenerate liberals, Communists, homosexuals, corrupt politicians, and foreigners' haunted the NRP members. Under this particular interpretation of reality, violence and terror became justifiable. The use of weapons and acts of violence became a natural and necessary extension of the political struggle in a world full of powerful secret enemies. Gradually the group developed terrorist strategy, but their violent acts were not what according to the Swedish anti-terrorist laws would be considered terrorist acts (that is, attacks directed against public institutions or leading politicians). Instead, the NRP sought out those groups and individuals (Jews, Communists, homosexuals and foreigners) that the NRP cell had defined as the secret enemies involved in governing society.

The majority of NRP activists were born in the 1960s. Their members included both students and blue-collar workers. Three main types of members can be found in the group: the lonely contact-seeking, the ideologist and the fanatic. This is illustrated by the case studies below, whose real names have been changed.

'*Jörgen*' was born in 1967. In autumn 1983 he applied for membership in the NRP and soon became one of the most active members of the group. In March 1987 he was arrested. He was charged, with among other things, illegal threats, a crime to which he confessed. He also confessed to the harassment and battery of a drunk elderly man. 'Jörgen' told the police investigators that membership in NRP meant that he was accepted in the skinhead groups. To be accepted was extremely important to him, since he had been harassed as a child and always felt like an outsider. In the NRP he felt accepted for the first time in his life. To impress his new friends he had made it a habit to brag about how often he harassed 'the enemies', with the consequence that he was initially suspected of far more crimes than he had in fact committed.

'*Christer*' was born in 1963. In the early 1980s 'Christer' became interested in the NRP, because he sympathised with the NRP's views on environmental protection and abolition of the right to free abortion. Apart from being a member of the NRP, 'Christer' became involved in the anti-immigration organisation BSS (Keep Sweden Swedish). However, he found the BSS boring, apart from the Norwegian National Socialist, Erik Blücher, who 'opened his eyes to the Zionist problem'. In 1983 'Christer' became increasingly involved in NRP activities. In December 1985 he was arrested for setting fire to the *Vänsterpartiet Kommunisterna's* office in Gothenburg, to which he confessed. 'Christer' continued his political activities after the trials and became one of the founders of *Storm* magazine, and a member of the original group of VAM activists.

'*Roger*' was born in 1967. In 1983 he joined the NRP, and like 'Christer' he was at the same time a member of BSS. At first his membership in the NRP was passive, but in 1984 he became increasingly involved in party activities. In February 1985 'Roger' was convicted of assault and battery. Together with a group of other NRP members he had decided to 'go out and beat up fags'. Armed with truncheons, they went to a homosexual club in the centre of Gothenburg and started to assault people. Afterwards the group went to the red-light district and vandalised a pornographic shop and beat up the cashier. The gang also harassed and assaulted a man they 'thought looked like a drug addict'. The NRP group ended the evening breaking into the office of the Church of Scientology, vandalising the office and beating up a member of the church. In November the same year 'Roger' was arrested for a number of similar crimes. It is obvious that he harbours a strong hatred [of] Communists and homosexuals. Asked why he had threatened a leading Gothenburg Communist, he laconically answered: 'He was a communist'. 'Roger' received a three-months prison sentence. After serving his time he resumed his political activities, which resulted in further criminal acts. In October 1990 'Roger' was sentenced to three and a half years' imprisonment for complicity in assault and battery. 'Roger' and a companion in the racist underground had in August 1990 killed a homosexual man in Gothenburg. 'Roger' is a fanatic who has stated that homosexuals, Jews, Communists, blacks, etc. 'do not deserve to live'. 'Roger's' political activities have continued during his years in prison, and he holds a strong mythological position within the racist underground – where he is counted as one of the respected hard-core veterans.

After the trials the NRP gradually lost its support among the younger activists. Many felt abandoned by the leadership during the trials; others, who disliked the violence, left the party for ethnocentric, democratic and non-violent groups such as *Sverigepartiet*. Still others became the new generation of mythological heroes during their time in prison. Some local branches of the NRP survived, but activity was remarkably low. The years between the Gothenburg trials and the creation of the VAM network can best be described as 'the years of soul-searching' for members of the racist underground.

Since then, the racist counterculture has gradually developed a political agenda which functions on three different levels. The first level involves the official, public propaganda activities described above. Distribution of various types of propaganda material has increased substantially over the past two years.

The second level consists of public demonstrations, such as the VAM demonstrations in Gothenburg on 1 May and 6 November, described as 'the strategy of silence and presence'. Activists, dressed in black uniforms and masks, stand silently with Swedish flags and VAM banners for hours. Demonstrators do not talk to the media or make speeches, but prefer a simple, disciplined demonstration of presence. They project the image of military discipline, a dedicated movement which does not respond to anti-racist provocation. This approach has won them a measure of success. Their demonstration in Gothenburg on 6 November 1992 was the largest demonstration of extreme racists since the Second World War.

The third level of VAM activity centres on the militant cells of individuals responsible for various bank robberies in the past to amass a 'war chest' in support of VAM's cause and to give financial support to activists who often lack employment. The notion of a threatening social conspiracy managed by 'lying media, Jews, homosexuals,' has deepened during the past year, and hard-core activists have step by step broken their remaining contacts with the surrounding society – in favour of a life more or less as outlaws.

THE DREAM OF THE HOLY RACIAL WAR

> As a free Aryan I hereby swear over the green graves of our ancestors, the unborn children in the wombs of our women and the throne of the almighty Gods an unbreakable oath. To unite in the holy union of brothers who are a part of this circle and to proclaim that I hereafter have no fear of death, neither of the enemy. That it is my holy duty to do what is necessary to save our people from the Jews and to achieve a total victory for the Aryan race . . . We hereby proclaim that we are in a full-scale war and that we will not put down our arms until the enemy is destroyed to the last man . . . (Aryan Oath of Liberation – used by the VAM network.)

VAM's renovated ideology is consumed with the notion of the vital white struggle for identity, and survival against other racial groups. The VAM network continuously reminds its members to prepare themselves, physically and mentally, for the inevitable and imminent 'holy racial war'. These activists see themselves as 'White Warriors' in an International Aryan Resistance movement where racism has abandoned its nationalist roots in favour of a pan-Aryan movement. This means that the radical racist groups are anti-immigration only to a certain degree. They can accept, and sometimes even welcome, immigrants – as long as the immigrants are white. This call for international solidarity is evident in the comments of a US activist printed in *Storm*:

> 'To all of you Swedes out there who have the courage to make a stand, I respect and admire you. Nationalism can be a good thing in most wars, but this is not an ordinary war . . . This is a war between the races! Let us break the national boundaries and unite in a pro-white front in order to kill the beast that wants to destroy us.' Tommy Rydén reinforces this US perspective with his claim, 'The holy fight for the survival . . . of our people is universal, the murder of a child in South Africa is an attack on us, the imprisonment of an activist in France is an aggression against us. For us there is only one race and one fight.'

VAM does not openly encourage acts of violence, but states that every activist must be prepared to use violence 'if the situation calls for it' – which suggests that violence is seen as justifiable if the network comes under attack or is banned. On the other hand, the network does not condemn violent or criminal acts committed by individual members of the underground: rather it claims to 'understand' the acts and points out that the activists are free to choose their own way of fighting the race war. The 'struggle for the white race' is individual as well as collective, and all members or activist cells are free to choose their own means of battle. Among activists in the racist underground, important ideological reading on this theme are the books, *The Turner Diaries'* and *Hunter*, by Andrew Macdonald (pen-name for William Pierce). *The Turner Diaries* deals with the notion of the 'global racial war' while *Hunter* is a description of how 'you start your own racial war'. Activists are sometimes referred to as 'hunters' or 'racial wolves' – and the 'Wolf Hook' is the official symbol of the VAM network.

A direct call for violence does, however, occur in *Werwolf*, a paper which is for activists only and not for public consumption. The first issue of *Werwolf* ran the following statement: 'The traitors should never feel secure. There will always be a threat against them. Traitors will be found dead, refugee camps will burn . . . be hard and ruthless in our fight for freedom.' To quote another issue of *Werwolf*: 'If the tax-collector tries to steal your property, blow up his house. If the public prosecutor tries to lock you up, beat up his wife. If the policeman is after you, blow his head off.'

The racial war is, however, more than an armed war. It has been catapulted into a demographic struggle – a 'birth-rate war' – leading the network to condemn abortion for whites. To win the 'birth-rate war' the network has focused on recruiting women to the cause. Women have become central to the future of radical racism. As summed up succinctly by a female member of the COTC: 'After all it is the woman who makes the decision, when she chooses her mate. This is nothing that the men can control. If she chooses a nigger, it is not good, of course, but it is her choice.'

The dream of the global racial war has three dimensions: the propaganda war, the armed war and the 'birth-rate war'. The actual fighting itself is of vital importance to the activists. To quote a leading VAM activist: 'The struggle is the struggle . . . you could say that it is a sort of end in itself.' Dedicated, hard-core activists live according to the notion of 'struggle as a way of life': the daily struggle to survive as outlaws; the struggle against 'racial enemies' – Jews, blacks, coloured, homosexuals; and the struggle against society or ZOG.

VIOLENCE

Is racist violence in Sweden carried out as a part of the political agenda of the racist underground? That is a question very difficult to answer. Few statistics and surveys exist concerning racist-criminal acts to assess whether there exists a politically-oriented pattern to this kind of activity. Between January 1989 and December 1991 there were over a hundred attacks on refugee camps in Sweden, but investigations published by the Swedish security police indicate that the attacks were not part of a directed campaign from any racist organisation. The perpetrators, when found, usually proved to be neighbourhood youth acting under the influence of alcohol. Motives generally involved a search for adventure mixed with a disapproval of Swedish refugee policy. Even if the attacks on refugee camps were not a part of any organised campaign, the police claim that media exposure of racist groups during the autumn of 1991 most likely functioned as a trigger for acts of violence. It should, however, be added that in several cases the attacks on refugee camps represent the final step in a long history of hostility towards refugees in the local community. This includes local politicians who oppose the establishment of a refugee camp, local protest groups, shopowners who refuse to let the refugees enter their shops, etc. The local youths who ultimately attack the refugee camp are in a way the most extreme expression of an existing mentality in the local community.

The activities of the racist underground in the Karlstad/Säffle area can serve as an example. The term 'racist underground' is here to be understood in a broader sense of the word, to include hard-core racist activists as well as surrounding groups of youths who to a certain degree sympathise with the racist ideology. This description is, with one exception, limited to court cases. This area in Western Sweden has a long history of organised National Socialist and racist activities. In some towns there is an unbroken chain of racist organisations reaching from the early 1920s to the present day. In the late 1980s and early 1990s, violent activities from the underground increased.

In October 1987 two members of the Karlstad underground attacked and assaulted a young Swede, who the previous year had caused their anger by pulling down a poster from the anti-immigrant organisation Keep Sweden Swedish.

In August 1988 a mob of around seventy youths attacked the local refugee camp with rocks and Molotov cocktails. During the riot a prominent member of the local racist scene attacked the camp, armed with an axe.

In December 1990, two drunk young men in Säffle initially threatened two migrants with knives and later the same evening tried to set the local refugee camp on fire. In court they stated that they felt there were too many foreigners in the town and that their aim had been to 'scare them away'.

In November 1991 the Jewish cemetery in Karlstad was vandalised. The same year a mob in Säffle – among them some of the more prominent of the local VAM activists – attacked five refugees from Syria and Lebanon. The mob initially shouted racist insults and attacked the refugees with tear-gas. After a while, the mostly verbal attacks escalated into physical abuse, when the crowd attacked the refugees with wooden sticks. One of the refugees managed to get to his car and made an attempt to escape. In the process he injured one skinhead and lost control over the car, which was later smashed to pieces by the mob – most of whom were drunk. The refugee was later convicted of dangerous driving by the District Court of Arvika, a verdict later overruled by a higher court.

During the night of 11 April 1992 four drunk skinheads harassed and injured one migrant and one native, smashed the windows of a cafe belonging to the Church of Sweden and a shop for immigrants. Two of the skinheads later returned and set fire to the place. Later that night they also set fire to several entrance halls in a housing complex where many immigrant families were living.

Apart from the above-mentioned crimes, members of the racist underground and its surrounding circles have been convicted of a number of other crimes without any racist implications. The Gothenburg activists and the core of the Karlstad/Säffle activists, however, do not fit this pattern. The majority of their criminal offences can be defined as 'ideologically motivated' in a broader sense of the word. It should also be pointed out, as noted earlier, that a good deal of the violence and the threats and harassments have been directed not against immigrants but against Jews, homosexuals, drug addicts, anti-racists, etc. – groups who comprise important 'hate targets' for the racist underground.

Apart from the trials of members and sympathisers of the NRP in Gothenburg, Växjö and Landskrona between 1985 and 1987, there has been very little evidence to link racist violence directly to any organised political group, even though individual activists of the militant racist underground have on several occasions been convicted of such crimes.

NOTE

1. This chapter is based on interviews with activists in *Vitt Ariskt Motstånd*, *Kreativistens Kyrka*, *Riksfronten* and *Nordiska Rikspartiet*. Magazines and circulars issued by groups mentioned above: *Vit Rebell*, *Storm*, *Werewolf*, *Siege*, *Tidskrift för Ökat våld mot homosexuella*, *Ragnarök*, *VAM Anhängarbulletinen*, *NS Kampfruf*, *Racial Loyalty*, *The New Order*, *NRP Bulletinen*, *Rikslarm*. The following verdicts are also used as sources: Dom DB 98 B 63/91 Svegs Tingsrätt, Dom DB 639 B 391/ 91 Södra Roslagstingsrätt, Dom DB 682 B 464/92 Uppsala Tingsrätt; Dom DB 175 B 217/92 Ludvika Tingsrätt, Dom DB 464 B 459/92 Alingsås Tingsrätt, Dom DB 584 Jönköpings Tingsrätt (1990), Dom DB 3027 Göta Hovrätt (3 avd, rotel 9, 1991), Dom 1992-10-02, DB 181 B 95/92 Malmö Tingsrätt, Dom DB 759 B 778/87 Kalmar Tingsrätt, Dom DB 326 B 416/86 Göta Hovrätt, Dom DB 276 B 133/86 Växjö Tingsrätt, Dom DB 219 B 50/92 Växjö Tingsrätt, Dom DB 309 B 286/91 Ludvika Tingsrätt, Dom DB 779 B 3422/90 Göteborgs Tingsrätt, Dom DB 234 B 200/91, Dom DB 416 B 299/91 Arvika Tingsrätt, Dom DB 131 B 878/91 Hovrätten för västra Sverige, Dom DB 72 B 35/92, Hovrätten för västra Sverige, Dom DB 6 B 2887/87 Svea Hovrätt, Dom DB 252 B 141/88 Uppsala Tingsrätt, Dom DB 34 B 1/92 Arvika Tingsrätt.

6 International Nazi Cooperation: A Terrorist-Oriented Network

Erik Jensen

Major international Nazi organisations under the leadership of Führers for hierarchic, national organisations do not exist. They never have. The 'black' internationals of the 1930s and the Second World War were nothing but the Fascist state in question, organising among emigrants, local sympathisers and traitors.

On the other hand, since the Second World War many attempts have been made to create an international Nazi organisation. Examples here include:

- The European Social Movement (The Malmö movement)
- The New European Order, NEO
- *Jeune Europe* (Young Europe)
- World Union of National Socialists, WUNS
- Euro Ring, etc.

None of these have been significant on a global or European scale. They have kept some traditions alive, implemented ideas, and cooperated to a certain extent, limited by national interests and ideological intrigues.

Some of the more successful – like the post-war escape-routes for fleeing Fascists – have proved to be no more than covert operations of the Great Powers in the beginning of the Cold War. Likewise, it has been documented that much 'black' terrorism was little more than offshoots of the Cold War or the conflict in the Middle East. Especially in Italy, but also in Spain, Belgium and Latin America, various intelligence services have been directly involved. In Italy it is still impossible to determine exactly who the actors really were during the 'strategy of tension' in the 1960s and 1970s. Leading members of both the 'black' terror organisations and the *Brigate Rosso* (Red Brigades) have been put behind bars, with a feeling of having been manipulated – and having served a cause they were unable to see even while they were in action.

These remarks also apply to much of the international terror cooperation between various organisations in the Mediterranean and across the Atlantic to Latin America. Further north in Europe, there has been less 'black' terrorism, although of a more genuine character. Here, too, the various secret services have tried to intervene, but at a lower level – more often as *agents provocateurs* to contain would-be terror groups.

Especially since the 1970s there has been increasing international cooperation between related Nazi groups – also on the terror-oriented level. During the wave of terror in Europe around 1980, the public gained some insight into the way that wanted Nazi terrorists could go into hiding and disappear, and simply travel from one country to the other. A certain exchange of arms, explosives and know-how took place. The first reports came of joint military exercises in the Ardennes, in Spain, in Germany and in Austria. International cooperation existed, but no international organisation. Contacts were made at frequent meetings – in Madrid, in Diksmuide (Belgium) and elsewhere. Various networks developed, centred on key persons. During the 1980s new forms of right-extremist violence emerged. In Western Europe the victims were to be found among the growing number of refugees and immigrants. After the collapse of the Communist regimes, ethnic antagonism was converted to nationalistic violence – and even civil war – throughout Eastern Europe.

This growing violence has ties to the new right-radical youth cultures. The perpetrators are quite young, the majority being under 20 – predominantly males. Few are organised in a traditional manner, in political parties or the like. They belong to a new and violence-prone culture.

A youth culture, in the making since the 1970s, has from the end of the 1980s accelerated – in numbers of participants and sympathisers and in number of acts of violence. We may venture to say this reached a temporary culmination in the reunited Germany in 1992.

Ernst Uhrlau, head of *Verfassungsschutz* (the security service) in Hamburg, characterises the development as follows:

We are now experiencing how the inner values of major parts of society are being rejected. There is a 1968-movement from the Right, although of another nature and without roots in the universities . . .

The themes of the 1990s will be right-extremism, hostility towards foreigners, nationalism and a return to nature and inner values.[1]

Verfassungsschutz has statistics for this development. Here are the number of violent criminal offences (murder, bomb explosions, arson, malicious damage, bodily harm):

1989	103	including 1 murder (in the old Federal Republic)
1990	128	including 2 murders (in the old Federal Republic)
1991	1483	including 3 murders
1992	2285	including 17 murders (other sources claim 26 murders).

On 23 January 1993 (in an interview with *Deutsche Presse Agentur*), Ernst Uhrlau cautioned against rash optimism in spite of large-scale anti-racist solidarity displays in the past few weeks. The number of organised right-wing extremists had grown from 60 000 to 65 000 in recent months, and at least 6400 belong to the hard-core militant, terror-oriented Nazi scene – mainly skinheads.[2]

The skinhead culture and the violence at the football fields are by and large 'old' phenomena. They date back to the end of the 1960s – and were in a way the response of English working-class youth to the increasing unemployment and extensive slum-clearances which destroyed the traditional social network. At the same time the skinheads were in opposition to the 'Make Love – Not War' Hippie movement.

Initially skinhead culture was basically apolitical. Contacts with the 'Hooligans' were also established during these years. From the late 1970s came a growing politicisation.

It was the now almost non-existent National Front in Great Britain which in its heyday of the late 1970s recognised the potential, and initiated a massive, racial politicisation of the skinhead milieu. Indeed, this was probably one of the few endeavours in which National Front succeeded. With the decline of National Front, parts of the Nazi skinhead movement detached themselves. Today they constitute a relatively large and extremely violence-prone international movement, where smaller groups and bands tour from country to country, spreading their message.

> I stand and watch my country
> going down the drain.
> We are all at fault now, we are
> all to blame,

We're letting them take over,
we just let them come,
Once we had an Empire, and
now we've got a slum.

(from 'White Power', by *Screwdriver*)

Nazi skinheads are not 'organised' in the conventional sense. There are many smaller groups bound to certain localities – but linked together by a highly specific subculture, even across national borders. They are characterised by tonsured heads, boots (Doctor Martens), special brands of sportswear (Lonsdale) and scraps of military uniforms (black or green Bombers' jacket, green or camouflage-printed army trousers). They are often tattooed (with WP for White Power or FTW for Fuck the World). Some have their tattoos inside the mouth, as the ultimate sign of belonging to the same brotherhood. They have developed a special 'Oi' music, as a central element of their subculture. It acts 'racially radicalising and militarising white youth'; 'Oi is warrior music. It's geared towards youth, and it gets Nazis shrieking and storming through the streets in exploding passion . . .'.[3]

Such skinheads exist throughout Europe – also in Eastern Europe. Their concept of who the enemy is – refugees, immigrants, homosexuals, left-wingers and punkers – make them ripe for Nazi agitation. They can be mobilised, although generally they can not be organised in a traditional manner. They form a major part of the foot-soldiers in racial assaults.

The message of the subculture is spread through magazines (fanzines) and Oi music. Their major recording companies are *Rebelles Européens* in France and *Rock-o-Rama* in Germany.[4] The Oi music and the texts are brutalising and inciting to violence and racial hatred:

Er ist ein Skinhead und Faschist,
Er hat 'ne Glatze und ist Rassist.
Moral und Hertz besitzt er nicht;
Hass und Gewalt zeichnen sein Gesicht.
Er liebt den Krieg und liebt die Gewalt;
und bist du sein Feind,
dann mach ich dich Kalt. (Chprqo P83 1993)

He's a skinhead and a Fascist,
He's bald-headed and a racist,
Moral and heart, he has not;

Hate and violence mark his face.
He loves war and he loves violence;
And if you're his enemy,
I'll kill you.

from *Störkraft*'s '*Söldner*' (Mercenaries)

After the set around *Screwdriver* split off from the remainder of the
National Front in Great Britain, they built their own network –
including distribution companies – in the violence-oriented part of the
youth culture. One of the leaders of this subculture is Screwdriver's Ian
Stuart Donaldson, with his 'Blood and Honour' organisation. They
cooperate with other bands and tour in the European countries. In
Sweden they have a faithful audience among the White Aryan troopers
in the 'Storm network'. They have also begun to perform in Germany,
where *Deutsche Alternative* previously arranged the concerts along with
other Nazi organisations, and put them in touch with German bands
such as *Störkraft* and *Kraftschlag*.

'German Alternative' has good connections to the British National
Party, who work together with 'Blood and Honour'. Concerts often
generate orgies of violence, where the excited youths ravage the
surrounding neighbourhood after the concerts – as after the 'German
Alternative'-concert with *Screwdriver* and *Störkraft* in Cottbus in the
autumn of 1991. The police arrested fifty-six violence-intoxicated
youths – including members of *Screwdriver* and their bodyguards.

Ian Stuart Donaldson was not among those arrested in Cottbus.
However, his band is no longer allowed to perform in Germany, and he
has been forced to use *Störkraft* as a back-up group at his later
concerts.

Through concerts and video-shows where the old Nazi smear-films
are screened, politicisation and radicalisation of the very young take
place. These activities are often organised by the 'old-fashioned'
organisations, but very few of the youngsters actually join up. What
they do is create skinhead-gangs and so-called autonomous National
Socialist groups. These are relatively independent, local Nazi groups
who imitate aspects of the autonomous counter-culture: clothing,
battle-forms and squatter lifestyles. When Gottfried Küssel, Christian
Worch and others established their beachhead in the crumbling GDR
in the spring of 1990, it was in a squatters' house in Lichtenberg, East
Berlin. The barricaded house in Weitlingstrasse was declared a
Nationalistic *Hafenstrasse* (a reference to a left-wing squatters' house
in Hamburg), and came to be seen as 'a thorn in the flesh of the Left'.

Society's rejection turns these youths into isolated groups that get swept along by the elevated exodus-mood of the radical Right. And there exist both an international, violence-fixated subculture and a thoroughly organised Nazi network who try to exploit the potential.

On the other hand, the escalating racial violence in Europe *cannot* be said to be caused by the terrorist-oriented cadres and their international networks. Such violence has its roots in a much larger range of social processes and psychological/ideological motivations. The distribution of hate-propaganda and the organised element does, however, play a part, amplifying these processes. They indicate a target, and point at specific enemies. Much of the violence is apparently 'spontaneous' rather than thoroughly organised. It would seem that the cadres participate in inciting to violence; occasionally they may try to 'structurise the struggle', when a major incident is underway. In this phase of 'inspiration' and plotting of targets, the complex that we are going to deal with plays a certain part among 'Boneheads', White Power, football-hooligans and so-called autonomous National Socialists. To quote a report from *Landesamt für Verfassungsschutz in Baden-Württemberg* from 1992:

Important in the increasing aggression of the neo-Nazis are the links to foreign activist groups, especially the National Socialist German Workers' Party/Exile- & Edification Organisation (NSDAP/AO). Propaganda-leader Gary Lauck provides the German neo-Nazi scene with propaganda material from Lincoln, Nebraska, in the USA – especially with swastika stickers and small posters that are used in many actions. *NS-Kampfruf* ('NS-Battle Cry') – NSDAP/AO's mouthpiece – constantly urges the use of violence against the state and its institutions.

In 1989 NSDAP/AO published an 'Action Programme for Aryan skinheads' in their English paper, *The New Order*. It was dedicated to David Lane, a cult figure to White Power-oriented youth in the USA and Europe (he had been sentenced to life imprisonment in the USA for participation in the terroristic 'The Order', which was broken up by the FBI in 1984). This manifesto – ten pages of *The New Order* – is in itself by no means sensational. But its publication signalled a major change in the strategy and recruiting of Nazi cadres. They were now abandoning former National Socialist prejudices and trying to gain influence among the growing right-radical culture by rapprochement.

Even before publication of the manifesto, various German groups had initiated work in these circles, with *Nationalistische Front*

(Nationalistic Front) in the vanguard. (Their leader, Andreas Pohl, was both a text-writer and a musician in a skin-band in the 1980s.) Other neo-Nazis followed suit – closing the circle with the canonisation of Nazi-skins as 'The SA-men of the new age'.

Let us now look more closely into the complex surrounding NSDAP/AO and the 'New Front' (*Neue Front*) – currently the most rapidly expanding part of the terrorist-oriented international Nazi movement, as well as the most successful in gaining access to the growing radical right youth culture. This is no mass organisation, however. Total numbers do not exceed a few thousand in the whole complex.

The acronym NSDAP/AO stands for *Nationalsozialistische Deutsche Arbeiterpartei / Auslandsorganisation und Aufbauorganisation*. It is a descendant of a long-since banned (1973) terrorist group in West Germany, the National Socialist Combat Groups (NSKG). An 18-year-old German-American, Gary Lauck, who participated from the very beginning in 1971, founded an *Auslandsorganisation* in the USA. When the mother organisation was banned in Germany, he continued the work in the USA, reorganising it the same year into NSDAP/AO.

Lauck and his friends felt that the time was ripe to build an underground Nazi movement in West Germany. But because of the ban against the National Socialists, 'headquarters' would have to be situated abroad, in the USA. The group started printing and smuggling their periodical *Battle Cry* (*Kampfruf*) into Germany the same year.

At the same time began the protracted work of building secret 'cells' in Germany. Originally, NSDAP/AO had a specific goal: the legalisation and rebuilding of Hitler's old party, the National Socialist German Workers' Party, NSDAP. The ban was to be undermined by massive – though illegal – swastika propaganda in Germany. Because of this ultimate goal, on which most Nazis could agree, NSDAP/AO grew over the years and gradually changed its character. Today it is an international network aimed at 'promoting a world-wide National Socialist-led White Revolution for the restoration of White Power in all White nations'.[5]

Lauck is not the Führer, but acts as front figure, often traveling to Europe to negotiate with various groups. The political leadership lies with a not-completely-known Führer corps (see later) of several nationalities.

In building the international network they have followed the Leninist concept: political organisation around the publication and distribution of ideological periodicals. Today NSDAP/AO publishes newsletters, bulletins and other propaganda material in at least ten languages.

In 1990 Lauck took the plunge into Scandinavia, where he and his partner, Michael Kühnen, so far had had little foothold. The Nazi Malmö faction of *Sveriges Nationella Förbund* (Sweden's National League) became their beach-head. This quickly led to the building of 'The Nordic National Socialist Bloc', with connections to the terrorist-oriented '*Storm* network' in Sweden and its Norwegian counterparts. Members of VAM – *Vitt Ariskt Motstånd* (White Aryan Resistance) often travel to Germany, just as their German brothers visit Sweden. On at least one occasion Germans have participated in a combat-training camp in Sweden (in Värmland, July 1991).

NSDAP/AO's latest triumph is in Denmark. Riis-Knudsen, leader of the Danish Nazi Party, DNSB, was expelled from the party in August 1992 for 'racial infamy'.[6] He had been one of the pillars of World Union of National Socialists (WUNS) for 20 years and from 1987 its 'World Commander'. WUNS had thus been a main competitor to NSDAP/AO; now the remaining members of Danmarks *Nationalso-cialistiske Bevægelse* (DNSB) have joined their old arch-enemy NSDAP/AO. With 1993 came the first issue of the Lauck-produced Danish *Fædrelandet* (The Fatherland).

A NEW FRONT

The other part of the complex is what today is called *Gesinnungsge-meinschaft der Neuen Front* (Fellowship of Disposition of the New Front) – or *Neue Front* (New Front) for short. This movement has its roots in the activities of Michael Kühnen and a tight circle of his closest comrades (Christian Worch, Heinz Reisz, *et al.*) since the 1970s – in close cooperation with Gary Lauck in the USA.

In the spring of 1984, when Kühnen was in hiding abroad from the German police, he began the building of a European network in earnest. Together with a comrade he proclaimed the rebuilding of the banned *Aktionsfront Nationaler Sozialisten* (National Socialist Action Front, ANS). This time ANS was to become 'the European SA'.[7] The new '*Auslands-ANS*' was not to be an exile organisation. On the one hand it was to organize European National Socialists, including *Europäische Bewegung* (The European Movement, EB), and on the other hand to build a secret support organisation among expatriate Germans. Little is known about this *Deutschlandssektion*, however.

A milestone was the creation of 'The Adolf Hitler Committee' – KAH – in Madrid in 1984, to prepare the 1989 celebration of the 100th anniversary of the birth of Adolf Hitler. The Committee was also meant to act as an international assembly, and as a cover for the continuing work in Germany – for comrades in the ANS-NA, which had been banned in 1983.

Kühnen was unable to create a European assembly – partly because the time was not yet ripe, and partly because he was captured and imprisoned until 1988. While he was incarcerated, the so-called homosexual controversy broke out, splitting the Nazi militants for years to come, both at home in Germany, and in the commenced work for a European organisation.[8] The anti-Kühnen wing assumed power in the EB, and in the spring of 1987 appointed Riis-Knudsen from WUNS as General Secretary. Half a year later – in September – Riis-Knudsen abolished EB and subordinated the remains in WUNS. When Kühnen was released he rebuilt EB, collected the remnants, and integrated them into NSDAP/AO.

Even though his European organisation was a failure, Kühnen made contacts that have lasted till today, and are the foundations in the growing European network. These contacts include:

- The Spanish *Circulo Espanol de Amigos de Europa* (CEDADE) and emigrants in Madrid (SS-General Leon Degrelle and 'Capitän' Walter Matthaei, formerly of the SS).
- Various factions of the banned Flemish-Belgian *Vlaamse Militanten Orde* (VMO), including Bert Eriksson's *Odal* group)
- The French *Faisceaux Nationalistes Européens* (FNE), and some of its factions (after the ban in 1985).

Moreover, he built the more permanent

- *ANS – Gau Niederlande*[9] (with a Flemish offshoot) and a
- *ANS – Gau Ostmark* (Austria), resulting in VAPO.

The periodical of *Die Bewegung* (The Movement), *Die Neue Front* (The New Front) lent its name to the new form, under which the German cadres kept together during the ban. They organised 'independent' study-circles:

'The New Front' is no organisation, but a fellowship of attitude without organisational structures, for the recruiting of supporters from various German-alternative leagues for our ideas.[10]

What it really meant in plain English: a secret cadre-organisation, which from 1984 infiltrated existing organisations and parties (for example, *Freiheitliche Arbeiterpartei*, FAP), and built new ones (for example, *Nationale Liste* and *Deutsche Alternative* (German Alternative)).

The plan was delayed and in part destroyed – one of the reasons being the protracted homosexual controversy, the ripples from which are still noticeable. On the other hand, the prolonged training in many-sided organisation and drilling in conspiratory activity have become useful in the current, so-called 'National Socialist World Offensive'.[11]

During 1992 and especially after the arson murders in Mölln on 23 November, the German authorities initiated a long series of impoundments and arrests. As of January 1993 a number of organisations were forbidden:

- *Nationalistische Front*, NF (Nationalistic Front)
- *Deutscher Kameradschaftsbund* (German League of Comrades, DKB)
- *Deutsche Alternative* (German Alternative, DA)
- *Nationale Offensive* (National Offensive, NO)

Furthermore, Minister of the Interior, Seiters, is trying to revoke the constitutional rights of Thomas Dienel, *Deutsche Nationale Partei* (German National Party) and Heinz Reisz, *Deutsches Hessen* (German Hessen). These organisations and persons have common ties with NSDAP/AO and *Neue Front/Die Bewegung* (New Front). They belong – directly or indirectly – to the network whose leaders hold secret meetings to set out the main directions for the future work. They are the leaders with influence on the 6400 violence-prone Nazis whom the *Verfassungsschutz* mentioned in a press release of 14 December 1992.

Little is known of these summit meetings. But the TV-documentary *Wahrheit macht Frei* (*The Truth Liberates*), part 2, shows some footage from such a meeting in Kollund, Denmark, in July 1990. That the television team was admitted and allowed to film part of the secret meeting and some of the participants, was due to Kühnen's aggressive and in Nazi circles, highly controversial, strategy of publicity.

Little is known of the agenda of this meeting, or of its participants, apart from the following:

At one end of the table	Christian Worch, National List, Hamburg
At the other end	Michael Kühnen and Gary Lauck

Along the sides   Ursula Worch, National List
Berthold Dinter, editor of *Were Dich* and
organiser of the annual Hess-marches (to-
gether with Christian Worch and others)
Thomas Hainke, Bielefeld,
Bereichsleiter West in New Front
Günther Reinthaler, VAPO, Austria
Gottfried Küssel, VAPO, Austria
Toni Douma, ANS – *Gau Niederlande.*

The main assignment for the Germans and Austrians present was to build a Nazi movement in the waning GDR, and strengthen the existing network – at home and abroad. A major project was the propagation of the now-banned *Deutsche Alternative* (German Alternative) to the new Eastern territories, with headquarters in Cottbus, Brandenburg. Some months before the ban, Brandenburg's Minister of Internal Affairs, Ziel – referring to 'German Alternative' and NF – stated: 'The organised leadership of the violence in Cottbus and Eisenhüttenstadt is evident.'[12] Christian Worch and Gottfried Küssel had, together with the late Kühnen (who had allegedly died of AIDS in April 1991), been the chief organisers of the creation of 'German Alternative'. And they had – through Thomas Hainke and others – close connections with the now divided and banned 'Nationalistic Front'. Christian Worch – or at least his car – was observed in Rostock during the unrest there. On the third day his black Mercedes could be seen discreetly parked on the other side of the railway line – a few hundred yards from the Asylum Centre. The cellular car phone was used to direct some of the assault groups. Worch had also inspected a group of members of 'German Alternative' who trained in armed combat at a training camp outside Berlin. Just prior to the ban he participated in forming a North German 'League' with among others 'German Alternative' in Bremen and *Deutscher Kameradschaftsbund* (German League of Comrades) in Wilhelmshafen. Both organisations were banned shortly after. A ban on Worch's own National List can be expected as well.

But these are all front organisations. As the Nazis say: 'One cannot ban people' – that is, the secret organising of cadres which is the basis of it all, and which has deep international roots.

In reviewing the participants in the Kollund meeting we now come to Gottfried Küssel. He has since 1977 been a member of NSDAP/AO and is one of 'New Front's' leaders in '*Gau Ostmark*' (Austria). Although not the brains behind the front organisation *Volkstreue*

Ausserparlamentarische Opposition (VAPO), he is its best-known activist. After being deported from Germany, he became extremely active in Vienna and was the initiator of NSDAP/AO's offensive in Hungary and in Croatia.

In the beginning of January 1992 Küssel and the German Klaus-Peter Kopanski were arrested by the Austrian police (Kopanski had been a military instructor at Küssel's *Wehrsportsübungen*). The following days a number of house ransackings and arrests took place within Küssel's Austrian network. Among the arrested was Günther Reinthaler – another participant in the Kollund meeting – and Hermann Ussner, leader of *Wehrsportsgruppe Trenck*. In his house the police found a weapons arsenal. At the same time Hans J. Schimanek and other friends from 'Lower Austrian League of Comrades' were arrested. They had run Küssel's 'Military Field Practice Group' at Langlois. Schimanek has been a mercenary – in Croatia among other places – so his qualifications should be in order. The existence of the camp had been known since 1990. On 21 October 1991, Britain's *The Independent* could inform its readers about close cooperation between the 'British National Party' and *Die Bewegung* (The Movement), which among other things had resulted in British participation in the military training in Langlois.

After the arrests the public gained further knowledge of VAPO's international contacts. Both Kopanski and Reinthaler (under the alias of 'Hrouda') had close contacts with fellow-travellers in Latin America. But of the most interest were their contacts with Hungary. On behalf of the NSDAP/AO, close cooperation with the Hungarian 'National Socialist Action Group' in Györ had been initiated. (This group was also in contact with Christian Worch in Hamburg.)

On 18–19 January 1992 the Hungarian police arrested and ransacked the house of the leader, Istvan Györkos, and six other members. A large arsenal of Soviet-produced weapons, bought on the black market, was confiscated. The party was banned, as it was scheming to overthrow the new democratic order and establish a Nazi state. Istvan Györkos was the editor of NSDAP/AO's Hungarian newsletter *Uj Rend* (New Order).

Croatia was another operating ground for cadres in Germany and Austria. Since 1991, many right-extremist and Nazi groups have appealed for support for the Croatian side in the civil war in former Yugoslavia, especially for HSP (The Croatian Justice Party) and its militia, HOS (The Croatian Liberation Community). These organisations are viewed as being the south-eastern ramparts of the white race;

and the chances of creating a National-Socialist regime are considered very high despite HSP's meagre appeal to the voters. With its many thousand militiamen, HOS is fighting in both Croatia and Bosnia.

This support for HSP and HOS is by no means coincidental. Both organisations can be traced back to the *Ustasja* movement which in a terrorist manner controlled 'independent' Croatia as a puppet of Hitler's Germany. After the Second World War came considerable *Ustasja* emigration to Argentina, the USA, Canada, Australia and some European countries such as Spain and Germany. The various *Ustasja* groups maintained close links with other fascist emigrant organisations and local right-extremists and Nazis. Among them were a number of terrorist groups who attacked Yugoslavian embassies and consulates and their personnel. These groups enlisted younger Croatian immigrant workers, some of which are now fighting in HOS – and have at the same time maintained their contacts in their adopted countries.

This long-term cooperation is now being rewarded by international support to HSP/HOS. Money and equipment is collected – and since 1991 there has been open recruiting to HOS's small international brigades. NSDAP/AO and 'New Front' are also involved in these projects.

The arrests in Austria in January 1992 hindered the sending of an armed (in 'self-defence', naturally) 'Technical Medical Platoon'. It consisted of fifty Austrians and Germans – but in reality only few of them reached their unit ('Brigade Condor') in Osijek. Plans for Croatia had also been among the topics of cooperation between Küssel and Györkos.

After the moderation of such Austrian activities in Croatia, the initiative has apparently passed over to the German part of the complex. Christian Worch's periodical, *Index* (dated January 1992 but published after Küssel's arrest) states: 'Even though the political warriors at home have enough urgent tasks to perform, we view the support of the valiantly fighting and suffering Croatian People as an important issue.'

Another participant in the Kollund meeting, Thomas Hainke, fought at the front in Bosnia. In early April 1992 he led a convoy of thirty-three scrapped military vehicles from the abolished DDR army – a present for HOS from their German friends.

NSDAP/AO's various periodicals have continued their propaganda for the war effort. French volunteer Michel Faci ('Le loup'), for instance, was interviewed. He spoke ecstatically about 'National

Socialists fighting in Croatia' and about his own contribution: 'I
believe it was the first National Socialist tank attack since April
1945!'[13] *Der Spiegel* (no 39, 1992) paints a less flattering picture of
Faci and his propaganda-contribution, however. Faci is well-known in
the NSDAP/AO and the Kühnen complex. An old acquaintance of Le
Pen, in 1980 he was in the leadership of the then banned *Fédération
d'Action Nationale Européenne* (League of National European Action,
FANE). Faci participated in establishing the successor organisation,
Faisceaux Nationalistes Européens (National European Fasces, FNE)
which collaborated intimately with Kühnen. The first leader of
Auslands-ANS and the first general secretary of 'The European
Movement' (EB), Michel Caignet, came from the leadership of
FNE. It was among the same leadership that Kühnen went into
hiding in 1984, and where he was arrested and deported to the Federal
Republic of Germany.

In the meantime – in 1985 – FNE was banned by the French
authorities. Some of the FNE members have continued their work in
Parti Nationaliste Français Européen (French European National
Party, PNFE), a part of the 'Euro-Ring' which also comprises the
German 'Nationalistic Front'. Others have given up working in France
– according to Faci, because, 'it is subsequently (after the bans)
impossible for us to take part in National Socialist political activism
in France today, we are instead specialised in para-military activities
abroad'.[14] What this specialisation consists of is an open question –
Faci's appearance with Saddam Hussein during the Gulf War can only
be characterised as pure propaganda.

In conclusion, we have followed some of the leaders from the
Kollund meeting and tried to shed some light over activities and
connections among terrorist-oriented Nazi circles and their work to
influence the growing radical and violent youth culture – which is the
real problem. A youth minority, enthusiastic over *Endsieg's Kanaken*
(dark skins)-song, is dangerous for society as a whole.

> *Steckt sie in den Kerker*
> *oder steckt sie in KZ,*
> *von mir aus in die Wüste,*
> *aber schickt sie endlich weg.*
> *Tötet ihre Kinder, schändet ihre Frauen,*
> *vernichtet ihre Rasse,*
> *und so werdet Ihr sie grauen.*
> *Refrain: Türke, Türke . . .*

Put them in jail
Or put them in concentration camps,
Away from me in the desert.
But send them away.
Kill their children, molest their wives,
Destroy their race,
And they will fear you.
Chorus: Turks, Turks . . .[15]

NOTES

1. *Der Spiegel*, 14 September 1992.
2. Among Skinheads today, three tendencies exist: (i) A growing tendency towards racism and national-socialist sympathies. They are called 'Nazi-Skins' and 'Boneheads' by their opponents; (ii) A reaction to this tendency call themselves Red Skins or SHARP (Skin Head Against Racial Prejudice); (iii) The third cathegory try to stay 'apolitical'.
3. *The New Order*, no 82, September–October 1989, p. 4.
4. In early February 1993 the German authorities seized a great many records, cassettes and CDs from the Nazi bonehead music scene, including *Rock-o-Rama*, the distributor of 'Screwdriver' and *Störkraft*.
5. *The New Order*, no 85, March–April 1990, p. 8.
6. In early August 1992 the telephone service of DNSB announced that Riis-Knudsen had been expelled from the movement, as he was cohabitating with a young Palestinian refugee woman.
7. Michael Kühnen, *Unser Weg*, 1986, p. 64.
8. The Frenchman, Michel Caignet, leader of *Auslands-ANS* and Secretary General of the European Movement, elaborated in the summer of 1986 on his homosexual disposition. This led to a violent reaction from a strong wing of FAP around Jürgen Mosler. Kühnen was in jail at the time, but came to the rescue of his comrade, Caignet, as best he could (i.e. with the pamphlet *Nationalsozialismus und Homosexualität*, 1986). Caignet was expelled, Kühnen withdrew for the interim, and a prolonged strife began about what Mosler's wing labelled 'Schweine in Menschengestalt' (Swine in human form).
9. A very small group with no influence in the Netherlands. Its main importance lies in the fact that it acts as a support group for New Front's activities in Germany. '*Die Neue Front – Wiederstand*' is produced and distributed through *ANS-Gau Niederlande*.
10. *Die Neue Front – Wiederstand*, vol. 10, no 78, August 1992.
11. *Sveriges Nationella Förbund* (NSDAP/AO's Swedish-language paper), no 11, Spring 1992.
12. German Text TV, 8 September 1992.
13. *Fædrelandet* (NSDAP/OA's Danish-language periodical), vol. 1, no 1, January 1993.

14. See note 13.
15. Various issues of the following periodicals have proved important: *Antifascistische Infoblatt* (Berlin, BRD), *Antifascistische Nachrichten* (Köln, BRD), *Blick nach Rechts* (Bonn, BRD), *Der Rechte Rand* (Hannover, BRD), *Der Spiegel* (Hamburg, BRD), *Die Neue Front – Wiederstand* (Delfzyl, The Netherlands), *Index* (Hamburg, BRD), *Nachrichten der HNG* (= *Hilfsorganisation für Nationale Politische Gefangener und derem Angehörige* (Witten, BRD), *Ras l'front* (Paris, France), *Reflex* (Paris, France), *Searchlight* (London, UK), *Skinhead Times* (Argyll, Scotland), *The New Order* (Lincoln, Nebraska, USA).

7 Role of the Media in Racist Violence

Tore Björgo[1]

Does the intense mass-media focus on neo-Nazism, racist groups and racist violence serve to calm down these tendencies, or reinforce them? Presented in such a form, the question is far too general to be answered.

It is necessary to identify the *mechanisms* at work when media coverage facilitates racist violence and support for racist or Nazi groups. We also need to identify the mechanisms which operate to discourage the use of violence and reduce support for violent racist groups.

Various mechanisms and influences work in opposite directions. Likewise, various media features on the same subject or event may operate very differently, depending on how the feature is presented. Such features may have different effects on different people and groups at different times. In any event, only a very small minority will be induced by the media to perform acts of violence. All this suggests that it is impossible to supply any general answer to the question of whether the media focus on violent racism reinforces or discourages such action. But it is possible to offer some partial answers on the basis of specific empirical cases, and to identify some mechanisms.

Such an investigation may draw on the results of two research traditions: first, there is an extensive body of psychology-oriented research which has studied whether exposure to violence in the media leads to an increase in violent behaviour (see, e.g., Andison, 1977; Hewitt, 1992). The other tradition, which is the main source of inspiration for this study, is research on the relationship between terrorism and the media.[2] This approach focuses on the social actor who acts strategically in a political context, with media as a resource to be exploited as part of the political strategy of violent organisations or individuals. The media will often have a direct influence upon the actual course of events.

Much of what has been written about the relationship between terrorism and the media is, however, tainted by a somewhat dogmatic claim that terrorists profit from media coverage, and that a symbiotic relationship exists between journalists and terrorists – almost by definition. This is often linked to moralising criticism, that the media cynically allow themselves to be used by terrorists for reasons associated with the media's own interests, namely, to boost sales by creating sensational news.[3]

Too often it is taken for granted that media coverage always serves terrorists and racist groups, encouraging their short-term and long-term objectives. An assessment of both the aggravating and restraining effect of media coverage on terrorism is seldom attempted. Moreover, analyses often draw general conclusions on a thin empirical basis without examining how media coverage operates in specific cases.

This chapter is an attempt to do precisely that: to examine how media coverage has operated in relation to specific cases of terrorist violence directed against immigrants and asylum-seekers. The focus is on the way that events develop, and on the role of the media during specific stages of the events. The analysis is based largely on the way that the perpetrators themselves have described their relationship with the media. Several such evaluations have emerged in the context of the actors' own descriptions of the course of events before, during and after the violence. These have come to light in police and court interrogations, and in interviews given to journalists or to me as a researcher. Some evaluations have also been expressed in the publications of these groups. This material cannot provide a basis for wide-ranging conclusions, partly because the choice of statements has been restricted to a limited number of cases. Also, the statements of some actors may be influenced by having been presented in a context in which it was in their interest to downplay the seriousness and the possible political motives of the act as much as possible, in hopes of receiving a lighter sentence. Taken together, however, these statements nevertheless give grounds for indicating certain patterns which consistently repeat themselves.

On the basis of my own review of extensive material on racist violence and violent racist groups in Scandinavia, and review of the international research into the relationship between the media and terrorism, it is possible to distinguish a number of different mechanisms which operate to reinforce or to inhibit violence and support for violent racist groups. I will describe and substantiate these mechanisms by analysing some specific cases, starting with the reinforcing effects.

THE CONTAGION EFFECT

My own survey of the distribution over time of 168 cases of terrorist actions (bombings, arson and shootings) against immigrants and asylum-seekers in Scandinavia shows that such acts tend to come in distinct waves or clusters (see Figure 3.1, p. 32). A series of acts of violence of the same type has often been directed against the same type of target but at geographically separate locations.[4] Similar patterns seem to emerge from events in Germany and elsewhere. There are in principle four possible explanations of these wave patterns:

1. The clusters of similar violent actions may be a random pattern.
2. The clusters may be caused by particular events or public debates which place asylum-seekers or immigrants in a negative light. This political climate may make acts of violence to some individuals appear as a natural solution or way of reacting.
3. The idea of carrying out certain types of attacks against immigrants or asylum-seekers is spread by mass media coverage of such acts of violence. Individuals or groups read, hear and, especially, see on TV that such acts have taken place elsewhere, and note the great resonance this creates in the media. This gives rise to the idea of doing something similar – a copycat effect in which model acts are passed on, by means of the media.
4. A systematic terror campaign is coordinated by some kind of organised leadership. Alternatively, the same activists may be responsible for all acts.

Explanations 3 and 4 undoubtedly have greater explanatory power. The first two may play a limited role, but they can in no way explain how the same type of action against the same type of target can be carried out at various places at only a few days' interval, whereas nothing happens for long periods. A political climate marked by an atmosphere of aggression towards immigrants and asylum-seekers may, however, be a strong contributory factor. To occur, organised terror campaigns as well as copycat acts are to some degree dependent upon a certain political climate.

Some of the 'waves of terror' in the Scandinavian survey were carried out by a single individual or a group, normally within a limited geographical area. The worst case so far was that of the eleven immigrants in Stockholm who were shot by the so-called 'Laser man' between August 1991 and January 1992.

But in several other cases in which the same type of act was carried out against the same type of target at widely different locations it has not been possible to find any form of organised coordination, or that the same persons were behind these acts. This is the case with a wave of attacks that began in Sweden in May 1990. During May and June, there were twenty-three terrorist-type attacks, mainly in the form of arson or firebomb attacks on asylum centres. In only a few of the solved cases were the police able to link the culprits to political organisations. There are probably more such activists behind those attacks which were not solved. As far as can be judged, the majority of these acts were carried out by local youth gangs and individuals with no evident connection with organised right-wing extremist or anti-immigrant organisations. Many of them have been exposed to racist propaganda from such organisations, and some may be secret members or sympathisers. But there is little to indicate that the attacks themselves were initiated following direct instigation of organised activists. What, then, gave the perpetrators the idea of carrying out the attacks, and why did these occur during a period in which similar attacks were occurring in a number of other locations? In all probability the contagion or copycat effect, spread through the media coverage, is the main factor here.

Statements during police interrogation and interviews with a number of the youths arrested for such attacks confirm that the idea came to them from media reports on similar acts in other localities. A typical course of events in Sweden illustrates how the idea of carrying out such attacks arose, and the reactions it subsequently created. This occurred during a wave of attacks on refugee hostels in May and June 1990. 'Lars' and 'Bengt' (aged 18 and 21) tell their story to journalists Tamas and Lodenius (1991).[5]

It was an 'ordinary' Saturday night. Nothing to do. Just sitting with the boys at Patrick's house watching a video . . . Lars had managed to buy a case of strong beer in a shop in a neighbouring village, where the shop assistant didn't know that he was a minor. The boys became drunker as the night progressed. Soon they started to tell stories about immigrants. They often did. Lars asked what the difference was between a negro and a barrel of shit. The barrel, was the answer. Roar of laughter.

After a while they ran out of beer. The boys went down to the local kiosk . . . They read the newspaper posters with large headlines about new attacks on refugee centres.

'At this point things started to run wild', Lars sighs.

'Shit, it's a long time since [our village] made headlines in the papers', someone said. The boys decided to make that change. After a few minutes they found three empty bottles near the petrol station, and tanked 10 crowns worth of petrol – unleaded. Then Lars, Bengt and Patrick and his girlfriend sneaked up to the refugee centre. They waited until a car from a security company left the place. Lars and Bengt advanced. Patrick stayed behind because his girlfriend pulled him back. A few metres away from the barracks they threw their bombs and ran. They met again at the bus terminal, but nothing much was said. Everybody went home.

The next day the main news story was last night's attack. 'I was shaken as hell', Lars tells. 'When the alcohol left my body I didn't appreciate what I'd done any longer.'

All the same, he could not help boasting to his pals. 'It was me who did it', he told, not without some pride. It is not just anyone who makes the morning radio news. Lars was the big name among his companions. Everybody flocked around him. 'It was cool.' 'It was macho.' 'It was a damned good thing that someone did something', his pals said. Still Lars didn't feel it was right. To his closest friends he admitted that he had a bad conscience. On Tuesday he could not go to work. 'I felt I was going mad. I could not sleep', he tells. When two plain-clothes policemen knocked on his door two days later it almost felt like relief. After a few hours of interrogation he confessed, and 24 hours later he was released.

Neither Lars nor Bengt can explain why they threw the firebombs. 'It just happened', Lars said. 'Something went haywire.' 'You don't think until afterwards', Bengt asserts.

They claim that neither of them really had that much against immigrants. 'It is not the immigrants' fault – it's the immigration policy', Lars maintains. Neither of them have been affiliated to any of the right-wing organisations.

It is noteworthy that, although the idea of carrying out assaults may often spring from media reports, ideas catch on among these people because of their negative attitude towards the prevailing immigration policy or immigrants in general, and because this was a topical subject at the time, both locally and nationally. In many cases, anti-immigrant organisations have been conducting propaganda activities for weeks and months, usually directed against local reception centres for asylum-seekers and against refugee housing.

MEDIA COVERAGE AS MOTIVE AND REWARD

Another aspect of the contagion effect is that potential actionists notice that others who commit assaults on immigrants or asylum-seekers often receive considerable attention and media coverage. The desire to be noticed by the media and by society, and the ensuing status have been central motives for many of the attacks on immigrants and asylum-seekers. In the story of the two young men above, they indeed became 'local heroes' among their friends, not least because of the attention their firebomb attacks aroused in the media. In many cases the deliberate objective is to gain such attention, and the perpetrators are thrilled when the national newspapers and the radio and TV news made news stories on them. A 23-year-old charged with blowing up a Pakistani-owned car outside the immigrant's shop in Brumunddal, a Norwegian small town notorious for a series of racist attacks, was asked by prosecuting counsel:

'Would you have detonated the dynamite if [the car] had been owned by someone other than the two Pakistanis?'

'That's a difficult question. There was a lot of publicity about Brumunddal in those days. If it flared up more I might get into the evening newspaper or the TV news, I reckoned.'[6]

In these and several similar cases, the primary intention is not to gain publicity for a political cause or organisation but to draw attention to oneself and one's actions – in other words, ego-promotion or 'auto-propaganda'. For some who are losers in other social contexts, it may provide a unique sense of importance and power if they can get the national media to cover what they have done. It is said of one young criminal racist who, after an attack, was given 20 seconds on the television news that it gave him an enormous kick which kept him 'high' for several weeks.

Self-publicity can be the main objective of the act of violence. In other cases, the actors discover this status effect subsequently – quite often to their own surprise – when people in the local community praise them because they have 'taught these blacks a lesson'.

For the more organised neo-Nazi racist groups, media attention has been a central motive for carrying out terrorist acts. This has been a recurrent feature in the history of modern terrorism as well, with terrorist action employed as a communication strategy to arouse public opinion and to get an issue on the political agenda. Terrorists exploit the mass media's criteria of 'newsworthy' event. Surprising, abnormal, contentious, dramatic and violent incidents associated with a single individual will always be good material for journalists. If events can be created to meet these criteria, then one is certain to receive full attention from the mass media.

When, in 1985, the *Nasjonalt Folkeparti* (National People's Party, NF) carried out a series of bombings and acts of vandalism in Norway, media coverage was among the main motives – and the best indicator of whether the actions had been successful. One of those participating recounts that, in addition to scaring immigrants, a main objective was to get press coverage – so that resistance to immigration could be demonstrated in a way that would make people realise that at least someone was doing something. After each attack, participants bought all the newspapers the following day. Then they met at the home of the NF leader and discussed 'the results'. The actual content of the report meant little. What was important was the attention itself and the fact that the action was covered. A much-quoted slogan was that 'all PR is good PR'. It did not matter whether the newspaper articles in fact reported the attack in a negative manner.

It is uncontestable that the bombs and the many other unlawful acts drew considerable attention to the National People's Party. But whether these acts and the subsequent trials were particularly good PR for the party is entirely another matter. In fact, this was rather the beginning of the end of the National People's Party, which lost most of its members and was finally dissolved in autumn 1991. Although media attention is easy to achieve through violence, other effects may be harder to anticipate and control.

Other neo-Nazi groups have been more sceptical to media exposure. The Vitt Ariskt Motstånd (White Aryan Resistance, VAM) in Sweden asked their members to boycott the 'ZOG media' (ZOG refers to 'the Zionist Occupation Government'):

> Thousands of race-oriented organisations have . . . failed . . . [because] they have believed that the strength of an organisation can be measured in terms of publicity, and expanded in cooperation with the mass media. How can anyone believe in anything this stupid? The media are definitely not on our side. No, the tiniest little collaboration with the Jewish media is a kind of racial betrayal! We can only spread our own genuine white message through our *own* alternative Aryan news media!

> VAM will do its utmost to make all racially conscious Aryans stop participating in the games of the mass media's scandal journalism.

There is, however, no rule without an exception. In some cases we may profit from using the mass media to spread our honourable message . . . We consider the Jewish media and their lackeys among our main enemies. They spread lies and distortion. They throw dirt on us by their deliberate lies. *Death to the ZOG media!* (*Storm*, nos 5–6, 1991, p. 17).

THE 'ANTICIPATION OF MORE' EFFECT

The intense media-focus on violent racist acts in certain local communities may well have contributed to new acts of violence. But we should not conclude from this that the media ought to avoid reporting violence against immigrants and asylum-seekers. That might give both perpetrators and victims the impression that the public does not care about racist violence. On the other hand, there is reason to look critically at *the way* the media present these events, and at the way that journalists, by their advance coverage, their presence and their behaviour, can have influenced the actual course of events.

One example: Danish tabloid newspapers have been criticised strongly for overdramatising violent clashes between foreign and local youths. Conflicts initially based on reasons other than – or more complex than – race antagonism have been blown up on the front pages as 'Close to Armed Race War'. Such headlines have reinforced fears on both sides; and in some cases the parties have mobilised and armed themselves to meet the threat. After a young Moroccan was stabbed to death in Høje Taastrup, a suburb of Copenhagen, several newspapers reported that racial conflicts had been smouldering in this suburb for a long time, and that revenge could now be expected from immigrant youths. Closer investigation has often shown matters other than ethnic antagonism underlying such incidents as well as several comparable conflicts. In many cases the reason was personal conflicts or random events, but further escalation has taken place along ethnic divisions – well-aided by media reports of 'race war'. Once such oversimplified interpretations are established and accepted, it is almost impossible for outsiders to create understanding and reconciliation between the parties involved.

The tendency of tabloid journalism to simplify and summarise reality can be directly life-endangering in such cases. When *Politiken* was criticised for its constant use of the term 'race war' in headlines and reports on the stabbing, the paper's police reporter simply replied: 'War is such a lovely short word.'[7]

MEDIA REPORTING AS AN ORGANISATION AND RECRUITMENT FACTOR

In several cases, media coverage of racist groups and their assaults has been shown to have a direct effect in the process of organisation-building. The most obvious effect is that reference to the group provides publicity, which may in turn lead those interested to make contact. This is perhaps most obvious when spokesmen of the organisation are interviewed and invited to present their points of view. It often seems as if journalists believe, with the best of intentions, that the extreme opinions of confirmed racists will reveal their nasty faces and have a deterrent effect upon readers. Although this may be the effect on most readers, there is also a small section who may find such extreme and taboo-breaking views exciting and attractive. This is the small group the extremist groups are seeking to reach.

Just as important as the advertising effect itself is the effect that negative media coverage may have as an organisation-building factor within the group. Harassment from the media and other external pressure can act to strengthen within-group loyalty. The group becomes increasingly enclosed, secluded from external influence and correction, and develops a self-confirming image of the world – one in which enemies and conspiracies are central, and where doubt is replaced by conformity. Critical media coverage is interpreted as yet further proof that journalists are obedient tools of 'the Zionist Occupation Government' – or whatever the enemy is to be called.

In several important cases, the media have played the central role of catalyst in a process in which isolated youth gangs have been reshaped into firmer organisations, with a name, ideology and objective. One instance of this took place in the wake of the so-called 'race war' in the Copenhagen suburb mentioned above. A young Moroccan died after being stabbed by a gang of Danish youths which the press called 'the Clan', with clear reference to the Ku Klux Klan.

But 'the Clan' was a group largely created by the media. 'The newspapers call us the Clan. We don't call ourselves anything!', said one of the youths.[8] Local youth workers and the police also maintain that no structured group with such a name existed before the stabbing and the ensuing media attention. The gang was notorious for its criminality and its devotion to beer and 'speed'. They had racist tendencies, and they liked to use Confederate flags and similar symbols. But they were certainly not organised racists.

'It was a bunch of young men – about eight or nine in the inner circle – who used to drink beer together. But following the murder [of the Moroccan youth] there is no doubt that the group has gained an identity – something to live up to', said a youth-worker.[9] This identity was created largely by the media coverage of the youth gang during the days and weeks following the killing. One perceptive commentator described the process as follows:

> With a single stroke, a small group of unnoticed and restless youths in a random suburban municipality was 'promoted' into an effective organisation with a clear and well-defined objective. With a murder as the direct cause, the 'Clan's' members found that they were becoming coveted interview objects, nothing less than media stars the newspapers and TV were lining up to contact. Suddenly, these young people were considered as *something* – equipped with an identity shaped in print – an identity which . . . is perhaps the real reason why the term 'the Clan' arose.
>
> Headlines like 'Race War' and 'Ku Klux Klan Gang Ravages Town' create an obligation – and there is a clear feeling of this among 'the Clan's' members, who since the murder have posed . . . with a new, media-created self-image.[10]

Another consequence of this broad coverage and status in the media is that these gangs are often subsequently contacted by neo-Nazi or anti-immigrant organisations hunting for supporters and new recruits. These organisations presumably consider it advantageous to be in (discreet) contact with hard and violent groups who may be put into action as 'storm troopers' should the need arise.

THE DISSEMINATION OF FEAR

The media may play a dual role in disseminating fear. First, dramatic media reports about 'waves of refugees' who are 'flooding' into the country may create fear and a feeling of threat within the local population. In turn, these feelings may create a political climate in which some people may find it justified to carry out or at least condone acts of violence against the aliens.

Second, sensationalist media coverage of acts of racist violence may amplify the effect of the violence by causing fear and anxiety among other immigrants as well. One powerful characteristic of the media – and television in particular – is to create a feeling of identification and presence. When other immigrants identify with a victim of racist violence, it is with the feeling that it could just as easily have been them. This terrorising experience may in turn affect their behaviour – for instance, making them stay at home as much as possible, or even leading them to consider whether there is any future in this country for themselves and their children. This appears to be one of the effects that many of the racists are trying to achieve through their violence. Success along these lines may thus make violent actions appear an even more attractive political strategy, providing yet further motivation.

So far we have looked at the mechanisms by which media coverage may assist the growth of racist violence and violent racist groups. But media reporting on anti-foreigner violence and terrorism can also have the opposite effect, by calming down violent situations, mobilising counter-forces and making it more difficult for violent racist groups to operate.

MEDIA FOCUS AS A SOCIAL SANCTION

In some cases, strongly condemning media coverage of violent acts against immigrants and asylum-seekers has led the culprits to realise the seriousness of their deeds. As a result, they have shown remorse and publicly distanced themselves from what they have done. Media coverage has in this way worked effectively as one of society's sanctions against breach of the accepted norms of behaviour, thus having a positive educational effect on the culprits and others who might consider committing similar acts.

One example involves two young men who exploded half a kilo of TNT in front of an asylum reception centre at Eidsvoll, Norway. Initially, they were boastful and proud of what they had done. There had been much talk in the town about blowing up the asylum centre, but no one had dared to do so. The intention was therefore to impress friends and 'to scare the asylum-seekers a bit', as they said. Only when they saw and heard the vehement media denunciations the next day did they realise the seriousness of what they had done. They had at most expected a small newspaper report, and they became both scared and ashamed when they realised how the explosion had been presented in the media as a 'terrorist act'.

It is interesting to note that media coverage seems to have had a different effect here from that in some of the other cases we have discussed. There, the media attention had rather the effect of stimulating others to carry out new acts of violence, or to express their racism more openly. By contrast, in the Eidsvoll case it had an educational and violence-reducing effect.

There is no obvious single factor to explain these differences. However, those charged in the Eidsvoll bombing belonged to a youth gang which was *not* particularly criminal, whereas the culprits in those other cases belonged to more distinctively criminal gangs. The degree of previous social marginalisation may thus account for some of the difference. This also means that a strong media reaction to a violent action may have a more positive effect as a social sanction on those who presumably nurture some respect for the police and the law. Members of more criminal and marginal youth gangs may feel that they have little to lose and more to gain in terms of prestige by being presented in the media as 'dangerous terrorists'. More empirical research would be needed to test this hypothesis.

If we turn to the more organised neo-Nazi and racist groups, heavy media focus may also be a strain in itself. This can be seen, for example, from an editorial in the Norwegian skinhead magazine *Boot Boys* (no 10, October 1991) which appeared a few months after a violent clash when the Boot Boys group came to public notice for its active role in attacking anti-racist demonstrators:

> Heil, comrades! Finally *Boot Boys* no 10 is here. Many people have been looking out for us and thinking we were completely extinct, but the fact is that we who produce this publication have been somewhat fed up because we are still witch-hunted by the mass media and ZOG (the Zionist Occupation Government). This explains the 'neglect' in publishing the paper. Moreover, we who are behind the paper feel that we have little or no support from the so-called plastic-nationalistic groups.

Although a media-focus on these groups may be felt as irksome, apparently, most of them still see some PR value in being mentioned and interviewed in the press and on the radio – at least as long as it concerns only who they are and what they stand for. But it is quite a different matter when investigative journalists direct the spotlight on matters which the group want to keep hidden.

DISCLOSURE OF VIOLENT RACIST GROUPS

Organisations and groups who plan to carry out acts of violence and terrorism will usually have quite a few matters they want to keep secret. This applies to details about the number and the identities of their members, action plans, weapons, criminal acts committed by group members, internal matters relating to their own organisation, and links with other organisations. It has in many cases been highly destructive to such conspiratorial groups to have their secrets exposed. This may happen either as a result of detailed investigative journalism (or research) in which apparently minor pieces of information are put together to make a revealing picture, or by the agency of infiltrators, defectors or informers who reveal the group's secrets to the media. In several cases, such exposure has resulted in violent groups being dissolved or neutralised and action plans dropped, while weapons and other incriminating material have to be got rid of or hidden away in a hurry. Exposure in the media has also led to police monitoring of the factions and persons concerned.

THE COUNTER-MOBILISATION EFFECT

Racist harassment of and violence against individuals and groups may continue for long periods if the victims appear to be weak, helpless and isolated, and if 'the silent majority' remains silent and passive. The media may have an important role to play here, by making the victims visible in such a way as to challenge people into showing solidarity and giving concrete support – and standing up against the violent groups. The media can also be the driving force in relation to the police and other authorities, who frequently do not take violence and threats seriously enough. The long-term terrorising of a Pakistani shopowner in Brumunddal is an example of this. Even after this immigrant's shop had been subjected to repeated vandalism, arson and bombings for more than a year, the local head of the county police declared that he saw no connection between the acts of vandalism, and that it was 'hard to accept that it was because of racism'.[11] Once pressure from the local press and politicians was put to bear, the regional Police Authority took over the case, which was then quickly solved. Local newspapers followed the matter closely and helped to form local opinion, which wanted to put a stop to the racist tendencies in the community.

However, an especially biting feature article in one of the largest national newspapers, *Aftenposten*,[12] was what it took to shake up the local population's sleepy attitudes and passivity in regard to racist harassment in the community. People were suddenly forced to take a stand on the violence and hostility towards foreigners. In a full-page announcement in *Aftenposten* two weeks later, the Brumunddalers replied:

A verbal bang on the head. Yet we needed it.

First, we got a shock. And *Aftenposten* was sold out in a jiffy. We read with uneasy eyes. It got worse and worse. Was this really the image of our home town? The place God forgot?

Then we got furious. Who was this . . . Oslo-type who came here unannounced and with a stroke of the pen erased the final remnants of proud Brumunddal's name and reputation?

Then we became more quiet, until we slowly became angry again with ourselves! Why did things have to go so far before we realised how serious it all was; before we realised what we had caused? There *are* racist attitudes. Serious violations have been committed against immigrants. Good God!

In the two weeks that have passed since the curtains were torn apart, 8000 Brumunddalers have scarcely talked about anything else . . . (*Aftenposten*, 4 May, 1991).

The announcement goes on to tell how a group of volunteer citizens took the initiative to rally the population and local organisations to make Brumunddal a better place for everyone to live in, whatever their colour, and to change its flawed reputation. And so the organisation 'Brumunddal along new paths' was created – as a direct result of a barbed and revealing newspaper report. A few months later, the organisation succeeded in mobilising 4000 people who assembled and literally turned their backs on Arne Myrdal, the violence-inciting leader of the organisation 'Norway Against Immigration', who had announced a 'popular meeting'. The ensuing favourable media coverage played an important role in spreading the idea for a non-violent form of counter-demonstration to other towns where Myrdal arrived to hold his 'popular meetings' – the contagion effect in reverse.

THE EDUCATIONAL EFFECT

Hostility towards immigrants and asylum-seekers is often rooted in fear. Such xenophobia is to a large extent aroused by arguments and propaganda based on half-truths, distorted facts and prejudice. Many people stereotype 'foreigners' as a large, undifferentiated mass of garlic-reeking Muslim fanatics. Some sections of the media have played crucial roles in establishing in the public discourse images and metaphors which cause fear: a few thousand asylum-seekers may be described as 'floods' and 'waves' of refugees. Both the media and established politicians pick up and promote slogans invented by anti-immigrant or racist organisations, such as 'bogus refugees' and the image of 'The boat is full' (cover on *Der Spiegel*, 9 September 1991). By influencing the public discourse, the media may also influence the way people think and speak about the issue of asylum-seekers.

None the less, objective and sensitive journalism may also play an important role in eradicating some of the fear, stereotypes and misconceptions. Refugees may for instance to a larger extent be presented as individuals with a specific background rather than as an anomymous mass of people who only enter the headlines in contexts like economic costs, crime or conflict.

However, *some* fear and aggression also springs from real problems and conflicts. It is a fact that there are undesirables and criminals among immigrants, refugees and foreign tourists. Some youth gangs with immigrant backgrounds can be very violent. This creates fear and gives rise to sweeping generalisations.

Among people who are positively disposed towards immigrants and asylum-seekers, it has long been almost taboo to take up such issues for public discussion. The problems are either swept under the carpet and suppressed, explained away, or overlooked. This leaves the field free for anti-immigrants and racists, who use these very real problems to create the impression that *immigrants in general* are violent, criminal and potential rapists as well. In fact, these anti-immigrant activists have managed to win a degree of credibility, since many people feel that they are the only ones to speak openly about what they experience directly.

It is scarcely possible to explain away racism and xenophobia. What *can* be done is to clear up some of the misconceptions and the fear that provide favourable conditions for anti-immigrant attitudes and actions. And it is necessary to take up, objectively and sensitively, the *real* conflicts and problems that arise in the confrontation between immigrants and the established population – which may form a basis for violent escalation.

SOME CONCLUSIONS

It is too simplistic to assert that the media *in general* help to increase racist violence and support for violent racist groups. My findings indicate that media coverage can have effects that work in *both* directions – to aggravate violent tendencies as well as to inhibit them.

A. Violence-aggravating mechanisms

1. Media coverage of acts of violence may spread the idea of carrying out similar acts – the *contagion effect*.
2. Media coverage can confer status and prestige on those who commit such acts. The direct motive for carrying out a spectacular act of violence is often to attract media coverage and attention. This is the *status enhancement effect*.
3. Media coverage of dramatic acts of violence often creates the expectation that there is more to follow – the *anticipation effect*.
4. Coverage of violent extremist groups and their acts can serve to advertise the existence of the group, increase recruitment and play a crucial role in the organisation and consolidation of the group. This could be called the *organisation-building effect*.
5. Media coverage may amplify the effect of violence by causing fear and anxiety among others besides the immediate victim – the *terror dissemination effect*.

B. Violence-inhibiting mechanisms

1. In some cases, condemnatory media coverage may lead the perpetrators to realise the seriousness of their acts, and to regret or publicly distance themselves from what they have done. In such incidents, media coverage may have a *punishment effect*.
2. Well-informed investigative journalism may paralyse and destroy violent organisations by revealing things the group itself wishes to keep hidden – the *disclosure effect*.
3. In some situations, the media may contribute by stirring public opinion into making efforts to counteract trends towards racism and violence. This is the *counter-mobilisation effect*.
4. Factual information and constructive debate in the media may help to avert conflict and to prevent the continued growth of attitudes

hostile to foreigners which may form the basis of violence and terror. This could be called the *educational effect*.

Individual media reports will rarely have a clear either–or effect. A report which directs a critical and revealing spotlight onto violent racist groups can also stimulate the curiosity of individuals attracted to violence, racism and conspiratorial groups. Any message will always operate differently on, and be interpreted differently by, various recipient groups, with effects difficult to predict. This, however, does not absolve journalists from the responsibility of seeking to avoid the obvious pitfalls.

NOTES

1. This study is part of a research project on political violence and terrorism in Scandinavia, financed by the Norwegian Research Council for Applied Social Research (NORAS).
2. Cf. for example A. Schmid and J. de Graaf (1982), Schmid and Jongmann (1989) pp. 108–111, Paletz and Schmid (1992), Heradstveit and Bjørgo (1992).
3. Laqueur (1987) pp. 121–127 represents this tradition.
4. A more extensive analysis of the data will be published later.
5. Quoted with permission.
6. Report of the trial in *Hamar Arbeiderblad*, 7 June 1989.
7. This statement by *Politiken*'s reporter was made in a studio discussion on 'Radio Copenhagen' on 20 May 1987.
8. *Politiken*, 5 May 1987.
9. Dale Smith, interview in *Weekendavisen*, 14–21 May 1987.
10. From an analysis of '*Et mords anatomi*' (Anatomy of a murder) by Jesper Klit in *Weekendavisen*, 14–21 May 1987.
11. *Hamar Arbeiderblad*, 13 May 1988.
12. Vetle Lid Larsen: 'Brumunddal – the place God forgot?', *Aftenposten*, 20 April 1991 (in Norwegian).

8 Racism and Racist Violence: Some Theories and Policy Perspectives

Christopher T. Husbands

A Tamil refugee was beaten to death by a gang responsible for a spate of racist attacks, the Old Bailey [London's central criminal court] *was told yesterday. X, 28, was beaten so severely about the head he died from his injuries four days later, said the prosecuting counsel. 'He was doing nothing more than making his way home, minding his own business,' he said. 'His tragedy was to be in the wrong place at the wrong time'* (*Daily Telegraph*, London, 20 October 1992, p. 9).[1]

All four accused belonged to a group of about thirty to forty youths who, after a stabbing in a discothèque, moved to the Namibians' hostel in order to avenge the incident. Armed with knives and gas guns they broke into the house [in Wittenberge, Brandenburg] and cornered five Namibians. Three Africans were able to escape over the balcony. X and his friend Y fell 15 metres to the ground. It was only thanks to a miracle that they had both survived (*Frankfurter Rundschau*, 24 September 1992, p. 4).

On Friday night the new Jewish cemetery of Eisenstadt in the Austrian region of Burgenland was daubed with such slogans as 'Victory to Haider', 'Foreigners out', '*Sieg Heil*' or 'Jewish pig'. Numerous gravestones were sprayed with swastikas, SS symbols and the Star of David. Those responsible left behind a pamphlet in which they extended their greetings to the leader of the right-wing Freedom Party of Austria, Jörg Haider. The text was signed by a 'Movement of Aryan Resistance', a hitherto unknown grouping (*Süddeutsche Zeitung* (Munich), 2 November 1992, p. 8).

The Amsterdam police are assuming a new attack on an Islamic target after fire broke out yesterday morning in a prayer area in the Turkish community facility in the capital. The fire in the prayer room of a

school on Baden-Powell Weg in Amsterdam caused little damage.
Although no traces of a firebomb or anything similar have been found,
the police are treating it as arson (*Trouw* (Amsterdam), 3 February
1992, p. 3).

Racist violence covers numerous types of incident and process, not
necessarily only actual or implied threats against the person. Such
violence at its most comprehensive includes phenomena that in some
cases have overtones of genocide – such as 'ethnic cleansing' and large-
scale pogroms. It then extends through a mixture of actions with
varying characteristics to incidents such as verbal abuse – either
directed against individuals or as non-specific acts like generalised
racist chanting at football matches, not particularly targeted against
individual black players. All the incidents described in the accounts
reproduced above, taken from events in several European countries,
qualify as racist violence by almost any current definition. Yet, even
though all were of sufficient seriousness to have been reported in
nation-level media, they still have a wide diversity of characteristics.[2]

This chapter analyses and explores some of the features of this
diversity. There are three major sections:

1. A template of dimensions according to which racist violence may
   be classified for analytical purposes.
2. A space-related hierarchy of rejectionism based upon the notion
   that conceptions of what is the appropriate socio-ethnic composition of street, neighbourhood, locality, city and ultimately the
   nation itself assist in understanding the nature and severity of racist
   violence and the characteristics and motives of those perpetrating it.
3. An analysis of policy-related responses, both at the national level,
   where points of legislative and prosecutory principle are usually
   decided, and at the local level, where grass-roots decisions about
   how to respond to specific incidents are necessarily made, often by
   hard-pressed officials whose major work does not include dealing
   with racist violence.

DIMENSIONS FOR THE CLASSIFICATION OF RACIST VIOLENCE

Although, as Bowling (1993) argues, racial harassment is often to be
analysed as a process rather than an individual incident, it is still a

valuable methodological exercise to isolate individual parameters for the classification of racist attacks. Indeed, numerous such parameters may be used as elements for explanation in terms of a space-related hierarchy. Incidents that the most comprehensive definition would recognise as attacks are classifiable according to:

1. **The level of serious physical damage/hurt**
   This may be high or relatively low, to be defined according to what weapons (if any) are used by the perpetrator(s). Clearly, firearms, clubs, cudgels, baseball bats, staves, explosives and petrol bombs offer a high level of threat, as may many physical assaults involving punching and kicking. Verbal abuse or even expectoration (whilst often highly stressful to the victim(s)) will usually be less physically threatening, although the recipient(s) may often have legitimate grounds for fearing that such abuse will escalate into something more threatening, depending upon the character or demeanour of the perpetrator(s) and the context of the actions concerned.

2. **Whether the target is personal or non-personal**
   This dimension distinguishes between: (i) attacks on persons; and (ii) those against facilities, institutions or buildings. The latter may be essentially:

   (a) *cultural/symbolic*, which would include attacks on ethnically-associated religious facilities or buildings. Within this sub-category are attacks expressing hostility to the *symbolic past* (e.g. desecrations of cemeteries or memorials), even if they are intended to cause generalised distress to the living. Or they may attack the *symbolic present and future* (e.g., attacks on mosques, synagogues, or black churches, and profanations of sites intended for such usages). One extreme case of an attack on an establishment of the symbolic past would be the arson in September 1992 of the Jewish memorial at Sachsenhausen concentration camp. The disinterment and mutilation of the burial victim at Carpentras in May 1990 have resonances to past and present.

   (b) *economic*, which would include attacks such as vandalism and fire-bombing on ethnic-owned economic institutions like shops, restaurants, and other particularly visible examples where the motive was racial.

3. **The number of perpetrators**
   This may be high or low, either absolutely or in reference to the number of victims.

4. **The number of victims**

   Similarly, this may be high or low, either absolutely or in reference to the number of perpetrators.

5. **Whom the perpetrator(s) wish(es) to frighten/expel**

   Potential targets of racist violence, as analysed on this dimension, are: (i) the actual victim; (ii) other members of his/her ethnic group; or (iii) both. Sometimes the target may be the members of all ethnic groups in a particular society, but often the well-attested presence of an ethnic hierarchy of social distance means that one or more such groups are particularly despised and attacked (Hagendoorn and Hraba, 1989).

6. **The nature of interaction between the residential base of the victim(s) and that of the perpetrator(s)**

   A residential base may be present or not in the case of each.

   (i) It would be present for both victim(s) and perpetrator(s) if, say, a black person were the victim of harassment in his/her own home from white neighbours after having moved to the locality of the latter.

   (ii) It would be present for the victim(s) but not for the perpetrator(s) when the latter had mounted punitive, pogrom-style raids into the neighbourhood of the former.

   (iii) It would be present for the perpetrator(s) but not for the victim(s) if the latter had innocently wandered into the neighbourhood of the former, or had little or no alternative but to pass through. The 1919 Chicago race riot offers examples of both these possibilities. 'Italian residents on the West Side, aroused by tales about a black man having murdered a neighbor girl, set upon a black youth who happened to ride by on his bicycle' (Tuttle, 1970, p. 49). Other deaths were inflicted on blacks obliged to take streetcars through white neighbourhoods on their way to or from work, or to walk through during a strike by streetcar drivers. Streetcar transfer points could be especially sensitive (Chicago Commission on Race Relations, 1922, pp. 7, 11). Some whites were also killed in complementary circumstances.

   (iv) It would be absent for both victim(s) and perpetrator(s) if both were away from their residential base: for example, a racist attack in a city-centre discothèque or an attack from a car on a pedestrian. Such institutions as schools offer a fertile breeding-ground for the perpetration of racist attacks, as substantial research has shown (e.g. Commission for Racial Equality 1988). Racial harassment within the workplace is similarly within this category.

7. **Whether the perpetrator(s) has/have sympathy or support from adjacent non-participants, or whether such non-participants are indifferent or hostile to the perpetrators**
   Clearly, even sympathy or support from non-participants may vary in character and depth. As reported about the attacks on asylum-seekers'/foreigners' hostels in Hoyerswerda and Rostock, for example, it may involve bystanders cheering and encouraging the perpetrators as they throw petrol bombs or attack the police. Or, it may be adults or parents unwilling to condemn the actions of their juniors and perhaps using them as agents for what they themselves would like to do.[3] In a particularly extreme case in Essen referred to by Heitmeyer (1992a, p. 137), it apparently involved a group of residents recruiting local skinheads, effectively as mercenaries, in order to attack a neighbourhood hostel for asylum-seekers.

Thus, the first of the italicized examples at the beginning of this chapter is classifiable from available information as follows:

1. The level of serious physical hurt was high; in fact, a death resulted.
2. The target was personal.
3. and 4. The number of perpetrators was low ('a gang'), as was that of victims (one).
5. The perpetrators may well have wished to frighten others, as well as to kill the victim, given that there had been previous similar attacks.
6. Although the victim was on his way home, neither he nor (apparently) the perpetrators had an immediate residential base, the attack having occurred on the street.
7. Information about the attitudes of adjacent non-participants is missing, but it may be doubted in this case whether many would have gone as far as encouraging or condoning such an attack.

The other italicised case is also classifiable:

1. The level of serious physical damage was low, even though arson was involved.
2. The target was non-personal and principally related to the symbolic present.
3. The number of perpetrators was doubtless low.
4. The number of victims was probably relatively high.

5. Most users of this community facility will have been inconvenienced and stressed by the event and it was doubtlessly intended to frighten both them and all other members of their ethnic group.
6. Neither perpetrators nor victims had an immediate residential base.
7. The secretive nature of the event suggests that adjacent non-participants (even non-Turks) would not have been sympathetic.

Having offered these general dimensions for classification by no means exhausts relevant descriptive aspects. There are other particular features of many types of racist attack. A large number take place late in the evening or during the night, especially at weekends or on those festive occasions with nationalist symbolisms, such as Bastille Day in France (14 July) or Unity Day in Germany (3 October). The late-night occurrence may impede detection or prevent identification but often the perpetrators have become inflamed by alcohol after extensive consumption earlier in the day; in some cases the alcohol consumption has been to furnish the necessary bravado for a planned racist attack but alternatively it has been the inhibition-removing factor that has led the perpetrators to take advantage of a situation that arose. Importantly too, racist attacks that are otherwise similar in character (at least at their outset) may differ in the extent to which the victim or victims fight back or seek to resist, or again, in the way that the police deal with them if they become involved.

There are also further types of incident that undoubtedly qualify as racist violence under a more generalised definition. For example, there are some older and more middle-class racists who do not attack black people on the streets or in their homes, even if they might have done so had they been younger and not middle-class; most of them may not even incite others to commit such acts. However, they may not be above making malicious and anonymous reports to child-protection agencies or environmental health offices about purported child abuse or infractions of health regulations, either by individual black households or perhaps by ethnic-owned restaurants. From a perspective that restricts the concept of racist violence to incidents where physical damage to persons and/or property occurs or is threatened, these latter incidents might be seen as 'pseudo-' or 'surrogate' racist violence. However, such an exclusion from central consideration decriminalises perpetrators and thus reinforces the limiting perspective that racist violence necessarily involves actual or threatened physical violence.

From a similar perspective, hoax telephone bomb warnings are made to innumerable institutions when there exists a generalised threat of bombs; it would not be surprising if establishments owned by members of ethnic minorities received more than their due proportion of such calls. Such activities may be done as much for their nuisance value as for any serious expectation that the victims will move or be moved away. Finally, there are numerous reported cases of white victims being attacked by other whites for associating with black people, something perhaps to be regarded as 'vicarious' racist violence.

Enlarging the definitional approach to racist attacks to include other phenomena is valuable and important, since it opposes the image of perpetrators of racist attacks as predominantly young (often in their teens or early twenties), white, male and from the more alienated sections of the manually employed or the unemployed. Of course, it is self-evident that those committing *certain types* of racist attack *are* especially likely to be young. Thus, Wolfgang Pfaff, head of the *Verfassungsschutzamt* (constitution-protection office) for the region of Brandenburg, remarked that it is increasingly 15-, 14- and 13-year-olds who are present when asylum-seekers' hostels are attacked (*Die Tageszeitung*, 28 September 1992, p. 3). However, this is to de-emphasise support, albeit passive support, among older groups. In any case, the 'youth' predominance is far from universal. Whereas the median age of those committing extreme-right infractions of the law in the Federal Republic during the period 1981–5 was about 21 years (Husbands, 1991a, p. 103), one particular precipitating event – the synagogue-daubing incident in Cologne in December 1959 – brought out copycat activities from a number of older activists (Dudek, 1985, pp. 87–8). As a later section of this chapter argues, whether racist attacks are to be treated as a general social problem or one that specifically concerns youth is reflected in different perspectives by national and local authorities about how they should be handled.

A SPACE-RELATED HIERARCHY OF REJECTIONISM

A major distinction sometimes drawn by sociologists in theorising about racism is between competition-based theories and culture-based theories; the former may apply during the early period of immigrant arrival, whilst the latter may be appropriate in a later 'settlement' period. There is a further distinction – applicable to theories in both major categories but perhaps especially relevant in the case of the latter – between experientially- and non-experientially-based explanations.

These issues bear upon the perceptions held by indigenous whites about reasons for the presence in their country of particular target groups. In many cases the question of sociological relevance is the degree to which is recognised the economic function, as providers of labour power, of those foreigner groups who came as immigrant labour. Is this perception more real for recently arrived groups than for more established ones? To what extent are various economic motives ascribed to groups, such as asylum-seekers in numerous countries, Moluccans in the Netherlands or *harkis*[4] in France, whose motives for settlement were genuinely non-economic? Finally, to what extent are non-economic motives attributed to particular target groups (e.g. 'to take our women')? One would expect the attribution of 'incorrect' reasons to correlate with the expression of certain types of racism or xenophobia, including a propensity among younger age-groups to commit racist attacks.

Competition-based Theories

Under this rubric one may list the specific arenas in which competition occurs. Some of these are production-based:

1. employment opportunities themselves are the most obvious;
2. more specific are promotion possibilities within a sphere of employment;
3. income is a further dimension (e.g. perceptions that ethnic-group members are 'wage-cutting' or, slightly differently, are competing on equal terms for a share of a finite amount of total income);
4. standard of living (e.g. the feeling that members of a minority ethnic group are diminishing a previous wage differential) is a final arena of relevance, particularly as this includes a subjective 'relative deprivation' perspective.

Other competitive arenas are consumption-based, particularly but not exclusively in the sphere of collective consumption:

1. perceptions of access to social housing, particularly to good-quality social housing, are of likely relevance for some individuals;
2. access to private housing and perceptions about effects of ethnic-group members' presence on rent and price levels are the analogue for non-social housing;

3. access to welfare benefits and perceptions of the legitimacy of ethnic-group members' claims to such benefits;
4. access to public-education provision, usually for children (e.g. the belief that the progress of indigenous children is being 'held back' by, say, the language difficulties of ethnic-group children or that the latter achieve a disproportionate share of educational resources).

Concerning *the experiential/non-experiential dimension*, most competition-based theories are formulated in terms of individuals' actual or perceived experience; i.e. persons who see themselves involved in the competitive situation are those most likely to exhibit hostile reactions towards those with whom they are supposedly in competition. However, such competition may be experienced vicariously by acquaintances or as something that occurs to others, even if individuals themselves have not personally experienced it.

Culture-based Theories

These concern the essentially non-materialist dimensions of potential hostility towards particular ethnic groups. There are numerous possible dimensions that may be relevant for our perspective:

1. hostility based upon language differences;
2. hostility based upon different culinary practices;
3. hostility based upon different religious practices;
4. hostility based upon different marital/sexual practices;
5. hostility based upon fears of supposed cultural dilution or threat: to this latter there is a further, socio-spatial, dimension:[5]
   (i) the street;
   (ii) the locality or neighbourhood (e.g. concerns about ethnic-group members' proprietorship of local shops);
   (iii) the town/city;
   (iv) the nation (e.g. purported loss of national identity);
   (v) in the case of the most militant elements of the extreme right, the 'white race' as a whole.

Of course, racists with primarily locality/neighbourhood concerns might regard it simply as a 'bonus' if those whom they target are also expelled from their city or even country; however, there is evidence of the strongly local, even parochial, concerns of many neighbourhood racists (e.g. Husbands, 1983, pp. 143–4). Being slightly facetious, 'Why don't you go back to Brixton?' may be heard as frequently as 'Why don't you go back to Africa?'

The *experiential/non-experiential dimension* is an especially relevant distinction with respect to culture-based theories. Even more so than with competition-based theories, it is important to distinguish between:

(i) personal experience or perception of personal relevance; and
(ii) perception of those factors happening either specifically to a large and otherwise undefined group of other people of a racist individual's own 'indigenous' group or else generally to all members of that group (i.e. to the individual himself or herself but only incidentally by virtue of his/her membership of the larger indigenous population).

Of course, some factors are much more likely than others to elicit hostility on an experiential rather than a non-experiential basis. Thus, concern about, say, change in local culture at the street or neighbourhood level consequent upon the arrival of ethnic-group members is more likely to be experiential than not.

This formulation provides us with a set of concepts for distinguishing between racist attacks of different types using in part a socio-spatial perspective, which therefore offers a complementary approach to the social-psychological one associated with writers such as Heitmeyer (e.g. 1988, 1992b).

NATIONAL AND LOCAL RESPONSES

Broad policy questions to combat racist attacks are necessarily the province of national governments, especially where high levels of funding are required. Thus, the German government's attempt to evolve a 'youth policy' for the eastern regions that addresses the disorientation of sections of east-German youth (Husbands, 1991b) is to be seen as a longer-term attempt to address 'basic causes', although the actual implementation of such a policy has necessarily been at the local level. Even where practice focuses on individual localities with notorious racist-attack records, the complexities of policy may require intervention and direction from above. The British Home Office's much-vaunted 'multi-agency approach' (itself a commonplace in several other European countries) has been implemented through central initiative in order to transcend obvious initial problems of inter-agency coordination and cooperation at the local level (Saulsbury and Bowling, 1991; and Chapter 16). Even so, there are still some conceptual distinctions to be drawn between national and local responses.

At the National Level

How the national state should respond to particular types of racist attack has led to a lively debate in a number of countries. In the United Kingdom, for example, there has long been a discussion about whether there should be a specific offence to cover racial attacks. Many, though not all, who are active campaigners in this area favour a legislative recognition of the particular racial element of racist attacks, even if the offence concerned could be proceeded with using existing legislation. The British legal and judicial system has, in general, been opposed to making explicit mention of the racial element. Some of this opposition has been based upon definitional anxieties, as well as evidential concerns that, for example, a perpetrator might well be convicted when charged with, say, conventional assault but could be acquitted by a jury when charged with a racially motivated assault because of the difficulty in proving such a motive. The conventional view of the police and the Crown Prosecution Service is that existing legislation (e.g. the Public Order Act 1986 and legislation covering offences against the person) is adequate and that any racial considerations should be introduced after conviction at the point of sentencing.

In the Federal Republic the recent upsurge of attacks on foreigners and asylum-seekers has led to the establishment or reinforcement of special police units (such as the *Spezialeinsatzkommando* in Saxony, which moved against right-wing extremists in fifteen towns in September 1992) and monitoring authorities (*Verfassungsschutz*, the regional constitution-protection offices). Also in September 1992 the Federal Minister of the Interior, Rudolf Seiters, wrote to all regional Interior Ministers to say that the mechanisms of constitution-protection should be used to monitor the extreme-right scene and the police presence at riots is to be reinforced. A couple or so days later Seiters published a so-called Ten-Point Plan against right-wing extremists that involved the tightening-up of powers of sentencing and detention, as well as demanding more powers to use bugging techniques to monitor domestic conversations. Those accused of *Landfriedensbruch* (breaching public order) should be held in detention rather than released immediately to return to the fray. The police should have more powers of crowd dispersal, a proposal directed in particular against passive but sympathetic onlookers (*Süddeutsche Zeitung*, 22 September 1992, p. 1). However, those elements of this programme that involved actual legal changes, as opposed to better application of existing laws, were not at first universally accepted. The *Freie Demokratische Partei* (FDP) Federal Justice Minister, Sabine Leutheusser-Schnarrenberger, rejected the idea that new laws were needed, although later events caused her to change this position (e.g. *Süddeutsche Zeitung*, 27 November 1992, p. 1). The *Christlich-Demokratische Union* (CDU) Federal Minister for Women and Youth, Angela Merkel, perhaps because of her ministerial brief or because of her East-German background, has argued for the appropriate application of existing laws but has tended to focus on attacks against foreigners as a youth problem with a solution to be found in those terms. In East Germany especially new perspectives must be offered to young people, she has claimed (*Süddeutsche Zeitung*, 15 October 1992, p. 7). Others also argued, at least initially, that firmer laws are not the answer. Herbert Schnoor, *Sozialdemokratische Partei Deutschlands* (SPD) Interior Minister for North Rhine-Westphalia, opposed new laws, especially any that would particularly criminalise sympathetic onlookers. The former SPD leader, Hans-Jochen Vogel, has similarly opposed new laws, arguing for the need to maintain contact with 'disoriented young people' (*Frankfurter Rundschau*, 24 September 1992, p. 4). Furthermore, of course, to the extent that racist attacks may be attributed to the organised neo-Nazi extreme right, such groups may be banned, as the Federal German government did with four organisations in November and December 1992. However, such a step is usually undertaken only as a last resort, in view of the disposition of the individuals affected to 'pop up' in another guise.

At the Local Level

Consideration of the local level in actions against racist attacks is important because it is frequently local officials or local police forces who have to decide how to treat a specific incident or series of incidents, unless the matter is very serious or raises issues of general principle that need to be decided at a higher level. The basic function of local-government officials who become involved in handling racist attacks is usually a service delivery that is supposedly far removed from this former activity, such as providing local-authority housing or social services.

There are in principle three different approaches adopted on the local level as practical methods of dealing with racist attacks; most initiatives fit into one or another category. The first is removing or resettling the victim; the second is defending the victim (or potential victim); the third is confronting and, if feasible, prosecuting the perpetrator. These approaches are not necessarily mutually exclusive.

Removing or resettling the victim is a favoured option in the case of racist attacks in social housing. In the United Kingdom at one time many local authorities responsible for the distribution of social housing were reluctant to rehouse because they alleged that black residents invented, or at least exaggerated, accounts of racial harassment in order to be rehoused in more favoured accommodation. This official attitude is now perhaps less current; instead, housing departments are rather more likely to accede to an urgent request by a racially harassed black family to be rehoused. This is despite the argument in favour of confronting the perpetrators: that, when those harassing are themselves tenants, the existing law can be effectively used to evict (Forbes, 1988). The decisions by the authorities to resettle harassed foreigners and asylum-seekers in Hoyerswerda in September 1991 and Quedlinburg in September 1992 were widely criticised in liberal circles as capitulations by the constituted state to the power of the mob. Of course, when as in Rostock-Lichtenhagen accommodation in which attacked foreigners were living has been burned out, there is little alternative to resettlement.

Resettlement is usually a relatively easy option only with individual victims; there are practical limits to the large-scale removals of victims, who may be equally victimised in a new location. As mentioned above, more British local authorities are now willing to confront perpetrators by going to the courts for eviction orders against racially harassing tenants of social housing (though private tenants and home-owners have only the conventional police system from which to seek redress if harassed by racist neighbours).

However, perpetrators are often not readily identifiable for prosecution (or, if they are, others will take their place) and resettlement is not a serious option: in such situations, especially where the victims are concentrated in hostels, the response of local authorities may be defence. Thus, authorities in Brandenburg and elsewhere in Germany have adopted this course. Numerous further examples might be given: a few years ago, after a series of attacks on so-called Sonacotra hostels in the south of France accommodating immigrant workers, the only serious policy option available to the authorities was improved security (*Le Monde*, 21 December 1988, p. 14).

CONCLUSION

Despite its theoretical and policy-oriented concerns about racist attacks, social science has to face an unpalatable truth. Whether on a national or local level, whether oriented to 'basic causes' or specific manifestations and incidents, racist attacks have a pessimistic persistence that is likely to transcend efforts to combat them using any social-science-informed policies. Xenophobic incidents that are the complements of today's racist attacks have been a well-known feature of urban life since the Middle Ages. In the contemporary Federal Republic of Germany, xenophobic attacks have become more violent and more numerous, despite national concern and despite anti-racist gestures by leading politicians, as at the Berlin rally in November 1992 and the demonstrations after the slaughter of a Turkish family in Mölln later that month. Individuals who are sufficiently organised and dedicated to engage in the sort of behaviour behind the incidents described at the outset of this chapter are unlikely to be affected by appeals for tolerance or even by greater investment in youth policy. Of course, the state may successfully move against particular individuals by conviction and long prison sentences but this is a difficult option to pursue as incidents increase in number, escalate in violence and incorporate thousands rather than tens or even hundreds of perpetrators. Moreover, once a wave of racist violence has evolved a self-momentum, even the removal of major perpetrators may merely encourage others to take their place. Even Hercules needed the assistance of Iolaus to kill the Hydra of Lerna. Can the contemporary liberal state do any better without a major sacrifice of constitutionality and incursions into personal privacy in order to gather evidence against organised perpetrators?

NOTES

1. Of these four opening examples, the first and last, both marked with italicised text, are used explicitly in the analytic discussion later in the chapter.
2. In an earlier publication (Husbands, 1989), there is an extensive statement of the level of knowledge about racial attacks in the United Kingdom, plus

references to existing published literature, till about 1988. In general, I have omitted most of the incidental referencing that might have been given. Increasingly in Germany, for example, there is an accumulation of literature on various aspects of this subject, especially with reference to neo-Nazi violence in both old and new regions.

3. Hoyerswerda and Rostock were only among recent examples where perpetrators have been vocally encouraged by a large number of sympathisers looking on. The 1919 Chicago riot produced other examples (Chicago Commission on Race Relations, 1922, p. 22; Tuttle, 1970, p. 37).

4. *Harkis* were Muslim natives of North Africa who served as military auxiliaries on the side of the French colonial power. Most who served in Algeria during the war of liberation were forced to move with their families to France when Algeria became independent. The word is often used to contemporary French to include the children of the original *harkis*.

5. Hesse *et al.* (1992, esp. pp. 127–57) offer a recent English example of a space-related approach to racial harassment – although a more thorough review of past work would have shown that this perspective is not quite the novelty that they claim and they do offer a caricatured account of the 'official' view of racial attacks.

9 The Pogrom Tradition in Eastern Europe

John D. Klier

In the last years of perestroika in the USSR, rumours periodically swept large Soviet cities like Moscow and Leningrad that a pogrom against the Jews was imminent. These pogroms, usually announced by threatening notes in letter boxes, were often predicted for dates in early May, and were linked to the feast of St George (one of the patron saints of Russia) on the Russian Orthodox Church calendar. Many Jews were terrorised – which seems to have been the ultimate objective of the rumour-mongers. In fact, no pogroms ever erupted, nor were they likely to. From the perspective of a century removed, we are far better equipped to understand the nature and the origins of the three great waves of anti-Jewish pogroms which swept the Russian Empire in 1881–2, 1903–6, and 1919–21. This understanding can help us to appreciate why anti-Jewish pogroms were extremely unlikely events before the actual break-up of the USSR.

From the very start, however, we must guard against considering all pogroms in Russian history as conforming to an identical pattern. They did have one very important factor in common – they all occurred at a time of weakened state power and control. Beyond that, they differed significantly from one another in almost every respect. With the recent opening of archives, and the publication of individual studies of the pogrom phenomenon, we have a far clearer picture of the pogroms' unique social pathology: how they arose, what forms they took, how the authorities responded, and how myths grew up around them (Klier and Lambroza, 1991; Aronson, 1990; Wynn, 1992).

Indeed, since the pogrom phenomenon in Russia has become so encrusted with myths, which still surface regularly in the secondary literature, it is appropriate to begin with a discussion of what pogroms were *not*.

First and foremost, the pogroms were not events planned and organised by the central government. They did not occur simultaneously, nor did they progress in a uniform manner. There was no uniform three-day pattern, which some commentators have ascribed to all pogroms, especially in 1881–2. While it is true that conservative ideologues often equated Jews with the political enemies of the tsarist regime, especially after 1881–2, no agency of the central government ever pursued an active policy of encouraging pogroms as a means of deflecting mass dissatisfaction from the failures of the government to the Jews.[1]

The first mass wave of pogroms occurred in Russia against a background of official confusion and panic in the aftermath of the assassination of Tsar Alexander II by revolutionary terrorists. The government was unable to measure the strength of the terrorist offensive, and initially assumed that the pogroms were the product of revolutionary instigation. Most of the territory of the Jewish Pale of Settlement – those areas where most Jews were obliged to reside – had been governed under a state of emergency even before the Tsar's death, so the pogroms were logically seen as the work of the 'anarchists', especially when a revolutionary proclamation appeared in the midst of the Kiev pogrom of 26–28 April 1881 O.S. Local authorities who failed to quell pogroms expeditiously were sharply criticised by the central government, and the archives are replete with telegraphed demands from St Petersburg that decisive action be taken as quickly as possible.[2] No less a personage that A. Kh. Reutern, chairman of the Council of Ministers, warned his colleagues in 1882 that the *pogromshchiki* – as the rioters were called – might begin with the Jews, but they would end with 'the most horrible socialism'. Published archival material depicts a government terrified of pogroms, and determined to quell them.[3] The measures taken were not always as ruthless as pogrom victims demanded, but even here there was logic at work: the government feared that sharp repression would antagonise the masses, and turn them even more against the government. Even so, the authorities ultimately resorted to the crudest form of crowd control – troops were ordered to fire salvos of rifle fire into the midst of rioting crowds.

A central 'proof' of official complicity in scapegoating the Jews for the Tsar's murder was held to be the sustained press campaign conducted against the Jews after 1 March 1881. I have demonstrated elsewhere that there was no such campaign. Although a few pogrom crowds attempted to justify their actions to the authorities – while the latter were engaged in pacification – by invoking the name of Gessia Gel'fman, the lone Jew among the Tsar's assassins, this was a consequence more of rumour than of the written word (Klier, 1983).

The pogroms of 1903–06 actually divide into three separate, if somewhat overlapping episodes, as Shlomo Lambroza has recently demonstrated: the pogroms of Kishinev and Gomel; the recruitment pogroms throughout the kingdom of Poland and the Pale in 1904–5, and the mass pogroms which accompanied the Revolution of 1905, and the political reaction.

The Kishinev pogrom gained notoriety for its symbolic importance as the opening episode of a recurrent series of anti-Jewish attacks. It was a major stimulant for the redefinition of Jewish national identity in the twentieth century. The pogrom sprang from ethnic and economic tensions between Russian, Moldavians and Jews, exacerbated by a relentless anti-Jewish campaign in the local press. Forty-seven persons were brutally murdered in the pogrom, which was made worse by the indecision and ineptitude of the provincial authorities. However, contemporary research has acquitted the Minister of Internal Affairs, V. A. Pleve, of the oft-repeated charge of instigating or colluding in the outbreak of the pogrom (Judge, 1983 and 1992; Lambroza, 1984).

The recruitment pogroms of 1903–4 were urban riots conducted by young village recruits awaiting induction into the army. While at this particular moment they may have represented a protest against the unpopular Russo-Japanese War, they were not unique by any means. Young rural recruits, moved to an urban centre under loose supervision, traditionally enjoyed a last, violent spree before embarking on the rigours of military life. Jews, often concentrated in district towns, were an obvious target. To this might be added the recruits' resentment at the Jews' reputation as a group which successfully evaded military service.

The pogroms of 1905–6 – most notably those which occurred in urban centres like Odessa, Kiev and Ekaterinoslav – were especially dramatic because they erupted in the midst of massive political upheaval and marked a quantitative jump in the lethalness and destructiveness of the pogroms. Scores had died in the pogroms of 1881–2, forty-seven at Kishinev, but as many as 500 in Odessa in October 1905. This was also the juncture at which political complicity appeared strongest. Governors-general, governors, gendarme chiefs, and military commanders dithered while mobs rampaged through the streets.

The question of responsibility may be answered with reference to one close observer: Tsar Nicholas II. A letter which he wrote to his mother shows him well-content that the Jews were being punished for their revolutionary misdeeds, even while he expressed wonderment at this rare demonstration of support for the government (as he chose to interpret the pogroms).[4] Like him, Nicholas's satraps in the field may have rejoiced in their hearts that a Jewish revolution was being drowned in blood; they took a casual approach to the suppression of violence. Local police agents and the 'Black Hundreds' supporters of the regime were active in organising counter-revolutionary and monarchist demonstrations, and these often degenerated into pogroms. While their conduct – and the support given it by the local administration – was often reckless in the extreme, it does not prove the existence of a central 'hidden hand' (Weinberg, 1991).

Polemics continue to rage around the question of responsibility for the pogroms which accompanied the Russian Civil War of 1919–21. Special attention has been given to Ukrainian public figures like Simon Petliura, branded a *pogromshchik* by many Jews, and considered a martyr to anti-Communism by many Ukrainians. Whoever bears ultimate responsibility for these events, the worst attacks on Jews to occur in Europe prior to the Holocaust, their distinctive features must be emphasised. They were seldom perpetrated by the local population, but by external military forces, often badly disciplined irregulars. Whatever toleration they actually showed to troops in the field, all governments in the Ukraine claimed to reject pogrom-mongering, and condemned those who carried them out, usually blaming the other side.[5] Peter Kenez has argued that in lieu of a positive program beyond the restoration of the Tsar and a return to the pre-revolutionary social order, the ideologues of the White Armies used anti-semitism as a mobilising technique. This reflected not so much the 'scapegoating' of the defenceless by a government intent on deflecting criticism away from itself, as a sincere belief that the 'Jew-Bolsheviks', with Lev Trotsky at their head, really were destroying 'Holy Russia'. Whatever the motivation, the results were lethal (Kenez, 1977).

More problematical is the extent to which the pogroms should be considered as containing elements of social revolution, despite the fact that they represented a genuine mass movement. Certainly this was the interpretation favoured by the tsarist authorities for the pogroms of 1881–2, once they failed to find hard evidence of revolutionary involvement. The lead in this regard was provided by the Minister of Internal Affairs, N. P. Ignat'ev. Already unsympathetic to the Jews before taking office after the Tsar's assassination, he became convinced that the pogroms were a response to 'Jewish exploitation'. He worked – against the advice of his ministerial colleagues – to implement legislation to remove Jews physically from the countryside, where they presumably found more scope for their activities. Yet, despite several decades of restrictive legislation, a visibly impoverished Jewish community remained the target in the new century.

So many factors were at work in the period 1903–6 that it is difficult to focus on one alone. The Kishinev and Gomel pogroms grew in part out of ethnic tensions, which may have served as a flash-point for inarticulate social protest. The pogroms of 1905 revealed a strong political element, as will be shown below. The Civil War pogroms grew out of anarchy and chaos, and were more political than social.

Ignat'ev's efforts in 1881–2 to ban Jews from the countryside illustrate another common myth, that the pogroms were primarily a rural phenomenon. Superficially, statistics appear to bear this out. To take Kiev province as an example, there were pogroms in only three cities (Kiev, Vasil'chikov, and Berdichev), but in more than seventy villages, hamlets and *shtetlakh*, the small rural Jewish settlements. In the course of the pogrom in the city of Kiev, 379 persons were arrested (itself a demonstration that the authorities were not inactive), of whom 202 were in the social category of peasants.[6]

A closer examination reveals a different picture. The pogroms of 1881–2 always began in cities, and then spread out along lines of communication, especially the railways, to the peasant villages. Peasants frequently came to the village to participate in looting which accompanied pogroms. Despite the large number of rural incidents, there were very few fatalities, although rural Jews were given much less physical protection than their urban counterparts. An analysis of the 202 peasants arrested in Kiev reveals that the vast majority of them were engaged in some sort of urban trade – they were actually peasants on *otkhod*, a system whereby they were released by their villages to seek work in the city. The urban nature of the pogroms was recognised by Ignat'ev's critics in the Council of Ministers, who gutted his draft law. They reasoned that driving large numbers of Jews into the towns would only increase the tensions and the danger of renewed violence there.[7]

In 1903–6, of course, the pogroms were overwhelmingly urban, as has been noted above. In 1919–21, the decisive criterion was not between urban and rural, but whether a settlement, town or village changed hands in the course of the war, thus bringing troops under loose discipline into the streets. *Pogromshchik*-soldiers were as liable to murder Jews in Kiev as in some remote *shtetl*.

While many factors can be invoked to explain individual pogrom waves in the Russian Empire, all pogroms shared a common framework: they occurred within a context of the weakening or collapse of central authority, the snapping of societal controls, and the disappearance of the customary restraints of law and order. No efforts have as yet been made to connect the Russian pogroms to a climate of carnival or *bacchanalia*, a phenomenon identified in Western Europe by a number of social historians, but this might prove a useful avenue of research (Ladurie, 1979). Certainly the anarchic settings of pogroms encouraged protest by segments of the population who were accustomed to express their frustrations in displays of violence.

Violence was a commonplace in Russian daily life. Corporal punishment, seldom accompanied by legal safeguards, was routinely administered in public to the 'lower orders'. Both public and private arguments quickly and easily degenerated into fisticuffs and brawls. Immigrant workers in the cities preserved their links to their villages by gathering for mass brawls, village against village. Alcohol abuse was a frequent source of public disorder. Church holidays, especially Easter, were celebrated with rampant drunkenness and consequent violence. The pogroms often drew all these ingredients together: the first pogrom of 1881, for example, grew out of a brawl between patrons in a Jewish tavern in Elizavetgrad.

Indeed, the decisive security consideration in the Russian Empire was the *prevention* of violence. Despite its reputation as the quintessential police state, Russia, urban and rural, was woefully underpoliced (Lieven, 1989; Weissman, 1985). Once violence – a pogrom or anything else – actually broke out, it was very difficult to control. The disastrous attempts at crowd control by the army in the unsettled period after the peasant emancipation of 1861 resulted in massacre in the village of Bezdna. Army commanders were very reluctant to deploy the army against civilians, because of its effect upon morale (Field, 1976; Fuller, 1985).

Crowd control in urban areas was even more difficult without wholesale casualties. Contemporary descriptions of pogroms invariably faulted the authorities for inactivity in the face of mobs of looters, who carried out their raids under the very eyes of troops called in to patrol the streets. When groups were attacked, they scattered, only to reform elsewhere and carry on. The authorities had the unappetising choices of restricting themselves to the defence of prosperous areas of the city (and thus seeming to condone looting elsewhere), of clearing the streets by cossack charges, of arresting masses of people (who could not be effectively imprisoned or tried), or, in the extreme, firing into crowds. The use of deadly force was always a last resort, since it demoralised the troops and turned the crowds against the authorities. In the end, however, such an expedient was employed. In the pogrom wave of 1905, when Jewish political groups organised self-defence brigades, critics of the government complained that the army failed to differentiate between *pogromshchiki* and Jewish defenders. To complicate matters further, Jewish self-defence not infrequently had an antigovernmental, political character (Lambroza, 1981).

Understandably, the first manifestations of violence were directed against those who were perceived as the most weak, unprotected, and vulnerable, one space removed on the spectrum of disenfranchisement and misery. The pogroms were an attack upon the highly marginalised by the less marginalised, according to crude categories of popular social differentiation. Jewish communal spokesmen argued in 1881 that the Jews were a target because they were widely perceived as outside the protection of the law, a group which could be assaulted without fear of punishment or retribution. This assumption was given greater credence by the delay and hesitation which accompanied the suppression of the pogroms, whatever might have been the underlying motive for such delays.

There was indeed much to emphasise the ambiguous legal status of Jews in the Empire. Kiev, a major political, economic, religious and cultural centre in the Ukraine, and a scene of major pogroms in each of the three periods, may stand as a good example. Although located in the midst of the Pale of Settlement, where most Jews in the Empire were required by law to live, most of the city was off-limits to Jewish settlement. On a regular basis the police conducted round-ups of illegally-settled Jews, and dispatched them, under armed guard, from the city. The capriciousness with which the law treated the Jews, argued their representatives in 1881, placed them outside the law. The peasants and workers had a badly developed understanding of law (although a strong sense of justice). If the authorities could deal so brusquely with the Jews, why not the rest of the population?[8]

A further demonstration of this theme of violence against the marginalised is illustrated by another event in 1881, which has been totally overlooked by commentators because it took place on the fringes of the Empire and was totally overshadowed in scale and duration by the pogroms. Contemporaneous with the anti-Jewish pogroms in the Ukraine, there were anti-Muslim riots carried out by Christians in Baku, an imperial (i.e. Russian) city located in Azerbaijan. Times of confusion and relaxed constraints were dangerous for any minority in the Russian Empire.

The theme of the breakdown of community and control as a mechanism for the release of violence is thus the major factor linking all of the pogroms, as the following summaries will show.

1881–2

The Russian government was briefly paralysed by the assassination of the Tsar on 1 March 1881. Following the Tsar's death, a mined street was discovered in the capital, and the strength of the terrorist movement was widely exaggerated. The security of the new Tsar, Alexander III, was thought to be at risk, and he became a virtual prisoner of the security forces in his suburban palace at Gatchina. In the period before the assassination, the government had embarked upon a new reformist political course, 'The Dictatorship of the Heart', designed to enlist the support of moderate opinion in the struggle against revolutionary terrorism. Within the Cabinet of Ministers there was a debilitating debate over the future political course of the regime. The period immediately before the pogroms was filled with fantastic rumours in the countryside, some of them identifying the assassins with the nobility or the Tsar's ministers, said to be angry with the ruler 'for giving land to the peasants'.

When the pogroms finally erupted, they were traditionally carried out by the 'Barefoot Brigade', a motley assortment of homeless vagrants, immigrant workers, and casual labourers. Their motive was clear: a bit of excitement, plundered vodka, and looted shop goods. Russian Judeophobes were eager to characterise the pogroms as a popular response to 'Jewish exploitation', and they created a myth that the crowds left the person of the Jews alone, and did not loot but only destroyed account books and credit tickets, 'the fruits of exploitation'. 'This is our blood', the crowds were alleged to have shouted. In fact, the pogroms displayed all the features of unbridled mob violence: beatings, rapes, wanton destruction, and copious looting. Significantly, the fatalities of every pogrom included those who had drunk themselves to death on looted alcohol.

1903–6

The pogroms in Kishinev and Gomel occurred against the background of rising popular discontent, while the recruitment pogroms accompanied an unpopular war. Most significant were the urban pogroms in centres like Kiev and Odessa in the aftermath of the grant of a constitution by Tsar Nicholas II in October 1905, in response to the rising tide of revolutionary violence and industrial unrest. Jews, both those who hoped to receive full civil rights from the 'October

Manifesto' and those involved in the socialist activity of the Jewish Bund, were prominent in the crowds which welcomed the Tsar's concessions with street demonstrations, red flags and rejoicing.

Counter-demonstrations – the first efforts of the defenders of the old order, the so-called Black Hundreds – easily degenerated into violence and then into pogroms. The frustration of the counter-revolutionaries was compounded by the participation of the politically-marginalised Jews in the revolutionary crowds, a clear expression of a world turned upside down. The raw-material for pogroms remained the same: the 'Barefoot Brigade', casual labourers, and 'workers lacking in class-consciousness', in the words of frustrated revolutionary activists. So prone were workers – any workers – to move from protest to pogroms, once restraints were removed, that, as Charters Wynn has shown, revolutionary agitators grew wary in late 1905 of staging political demonstrations (Wynn, 1992).

1919–1921

The Civil War pogroms were a product of war and anarchy. In a conflict where White Terror alternated with Red Terror, where the taking and shooting of hostages was routine, and where violence against the civilian population was commonplace, it is not surprising that the Jews should serve as an easy target for all sides. Events since the outbreak of the Great War had all served to isolate and indict the Jews. Early in the war, they were accused by tsarist military commanders of spying and collusion with the Germans. The lack of confidence in the Jews led to their wholesale transport to the rear, military defeat thus serving as the catalyst for the destruction of the Pale of Settlement. Since anti-semitism served as a major ideological mobilising device for the White Armies, it is small wonder that badly disciplined troops routinely turned on Jews in zones of occupation. The pogrom-mongering of the Red Armies is less-well-documented, although anti-bourgeois rhetoric was easily directed against the stereotypical Jewish tradesman. The irregular armies of the various national movements had no reason to assume the benevolence or cooperation of the Jews. Even the invading Poles were hostile to the 'Zyd-Kommunist'. In times of the breakdown of law, order, and the social fabric, Jews were a familiar and ready target for frustration and violence.

* * *

This survey of pogrom violence in the Russian Empire demonstrates that while it was a common phenomenon in past periods of change, the period of perestroika was an inappropriate setting for pogroms. Until the August Coup of 1991, the security forces of the USSR were still intact, and closely monitoring all political movements. While perhaps engaged in the occasional provocation, there is no evidence that the KGB – despite its well-known anti-Jewish bias – ever contemplated organising a pogrom, or permitting others to do so. It would have been a dangerous mobilising device, as our survey has suggested. Had such a pogrom been organised, moreover, it would have resembled the organised Nazi Kristallnacht attacks of 1938, rather than the mass riots of the Russian past.

The disintegration of the Soviet Union, on the other hand, has brought about exactly those conditions which permit and encourage pogroms. Ironically, the Jews no longer feature as the central target for prospective violence, despite the noisy rhetoric of right-wing splinter groups like *Pamiat'* (Memory). Violence in the post-Soviet Union concentrated on the frontiers in the form of civil war and inter-ethnic violence in the Caucasus or Transdnistria. If ethnic murders or pogroms threaten any group today in the Russian heartland, it is surely the diasporas of the Caucasian peoples, accused in cities like Moscow and St Petersburg of being the 'Mafia', responsible for crime and corruption. They, not the Jews, are targeted as the 'exploiters of the Russian people', and it is against them that violence is most to be feared.

NOTES

1. See Hans Rogger, 1986. Even without the archival evidence which has now become available, Rogger offered cogent arguments why the regime did not encourage pogrom violence.
2. Central State Historical Archives of Kiev (TsGIA-K), Fond 274, opis' 1, delo 238, ll, pp. 1–161 (1881).
3. P. A. Zaionchkovskii, *Krizis samoderzhaviia na rubezhe 1870–1880-kh godov* (Moscow, 1964), 417. G. Ia. Krasnyi-Admoni, *Materialy dlia istorii antievreiskikh pogromov v Rossii*, T. 2, *Vosumidesiatye gody* (Moscow, 1923). Cited as *Materialy*.
4. 'Perepiska Nikolaia II i Marii Fedorovny (1905-1906 gg.)', *Krasnyi arkhiv*, XXII (1927) p. 169.
5. See Saul S. Friedman, (1976); Taras Hunczak, 'A Reappraisal of Symon Petliura and Ukrainian-Jewish Relations, 1917–1921', and Zosa Szajkowski, 'A Rebuttal', *Jewish Social Studies*, XXXI (1969) pp. 163–213.

6. *Materialy*, pp. 529–42.
7. Iu. I. Gessen, 'Graf N. P. Ignat'ev i "Vremennye pravila" o Evreiakh 3 Maia 1882 goda', *Pravo*, 30 (27/VV/1908) pp. 1631–7 and 31 (3/VIII/1908) pp. 1678–86.
8. For the complaints of Jewish communities on this score, see *Materialy*, pp. 226–41; 312–21.

10 Racist Violence: An Issue on the Political Agenda?

Rob Witte

In August 1981, eighty National Front sympathisers rampaged about the Brechwood area of Dundee, Scotland, attacking Asians and their property. When the police arrived six Asians who had tried to defend themselves were arrested (including one Asian who had been injured).[1]

On 21 August 1983, 15-year-old Kerwin Duinmeyer was stabbed to death in Amsterdam, in the Netherlands. In his statement to the police, the perpetrator said he had killed Kerwin, because 'he is black and dirty niggers should not look at me in an ugly way'. In spite of this, the judge explicitly denied in the verdict that there were any racist motives.[2]

In March 1990, African street vendors in Florence, Italy, were frequently under racist attack. Pamphlets were distributed stating that 'the hunt for blacks and other minorities had started'. The Italian Head of Police, Parisi, went to Florence and had 240 policemen sent in to seal off the city centre to African street vendors.[3]

In May 1990, the desecration of Jewish graves in Carpentras, in France, attracted international media coverage. As an immediate response to the desecration, and for the first time in French history, the President headed an anti-racist demonstration and the French Parliament interrupted their debates to honour the dead of Carpentras.[4]

In August 1992, a racist siege of asylum-seekers and migrants in Rostock, in Germany, lasted a whole week. Just a few weeks later, a German–Romanian treaty was signed concerning the repatriation of some 40 000 Romanian asylum-seekers. Roma gypsies constituted the vast majority of this group of asylum-seekers in Germany. They were the first and main target of the racist attacks in Rostock.[5]

139

In May 1991, a pogrom was carried out against gypsies in Mancha Real, in Spain. In October 1992, a regional court decided to dismiss the city council of Mancha Real because of their part in this pogrom.[6]

Six examples of different incidents of racist violence in Europe[7], and six examples of different state responses to this violence. In the early 1990s, racist violence is increasingly attracting the attention of the public, the media and politics all over the continent. Countries differ with respect to the many and varied aspects of racist violence, such as the perpetrators, groups of victims, and the intensity and scale of the violence. Differences also exist with respect to the responses by various sections of society. In almost every European country, however, national and local authorities are facing racist violence in one form or another. Authorities are often forced to formulate policy and to take measures.

The situation with respect to both racist violence and the response of the state to such violence appears to differ widely from one country to the next because of various historical, political, social, socio-economic and ideological factors. But it is also partly due to the different moments in time at which racist violence emerges in each country. Nevertheless, the response of the state to racist violence is an important, if not decisive, factor in the future development of such violence. The way in which the state responds to racist violence will to a large extent determine whether this violence will increase, or whether it will disappear from the pattern of day-to-day life of specific social groups.

International comparative analysis could give greater insight into state responses and into ways of combating this violence (more) effectively. Comparison of state responses in different countries at a specific moment in time raises difficulties because of the very different situations in the individual countries. In 1981, for instance, racist violence was a political topic in Britain, while in France it was hardly significant, and in the Netherlands it received no attention at all. For the purpose of an international comparative analysis, one country can serve as a frame of reference for studying the situation in other countries. But, in carrying out such analyses, differences in discourse are often overlooked. These differences are important because different ways of perceiving and defining a situation result in differences in policy and practice. In addition to this, the analysis often has an abstract theoretical basis, as a result of which the specific historical circumstances of individual countries are often neglected (Bovenkerk, Miles and Verbunt, 1990a).

Therefore, by means of the so-called 'political agenda approach' (Cobb & Elder, 1983), an idealised process[8] has been described through which a social phenomenon such as racist violence may go before it reaches the political agenda as an issue for state action. From this idealised process a model of types of state responses to such violence can be derived. This model (see Figure 10.1) has been developed in greater detail elsewhere (Witte, 1993). Here, the main features will be outlined and different types of state responses to racist violence will be considered in more detail using examples from all over Europe.

FROM AN INDIVIDUAL PROBLEM TO THE POLITICAL AGENDA

In analysing the ways in which social phenomena reach the political agenda, an idealised process would consist of all the possible phases it may pass through. Four general phases can be distinguished. In relation to racist violence these phases are:

(a) racist violence as an experience or problem of the individual;
(b) racist violence that is experienced directly or indirectly by different groups in society, and that is perceived as a social problem;
(c) racist violence as a social problem that has to be dealt with by the state in accordance with (broader) public opinion (the public agenda);
(d) racist violence as an issue on the political agenda requiring serious attention and action at state level.

This, of course, is an idealised process. A specific social phenomenon may appear in any one of these phases and disappear from it without moving to another phase. A specific phenomenon does not, by definition, have to go through the whole process before it appears on the political agenda. But, this idealised process enables us to structure and compare specific state responses to specific phenomena in a particular phase in several countries. For example, how do, or did, the authorities respond to racist violence in Britain in the 1960s, and in the Netherlands in the 1980s, when it was not yet on the political agenda? The process may also enable us to analyse general and specific

Figure 10.1 Phases of the idealised process of racist violence 'on its way' to the political agenda in relation to different types of state responses

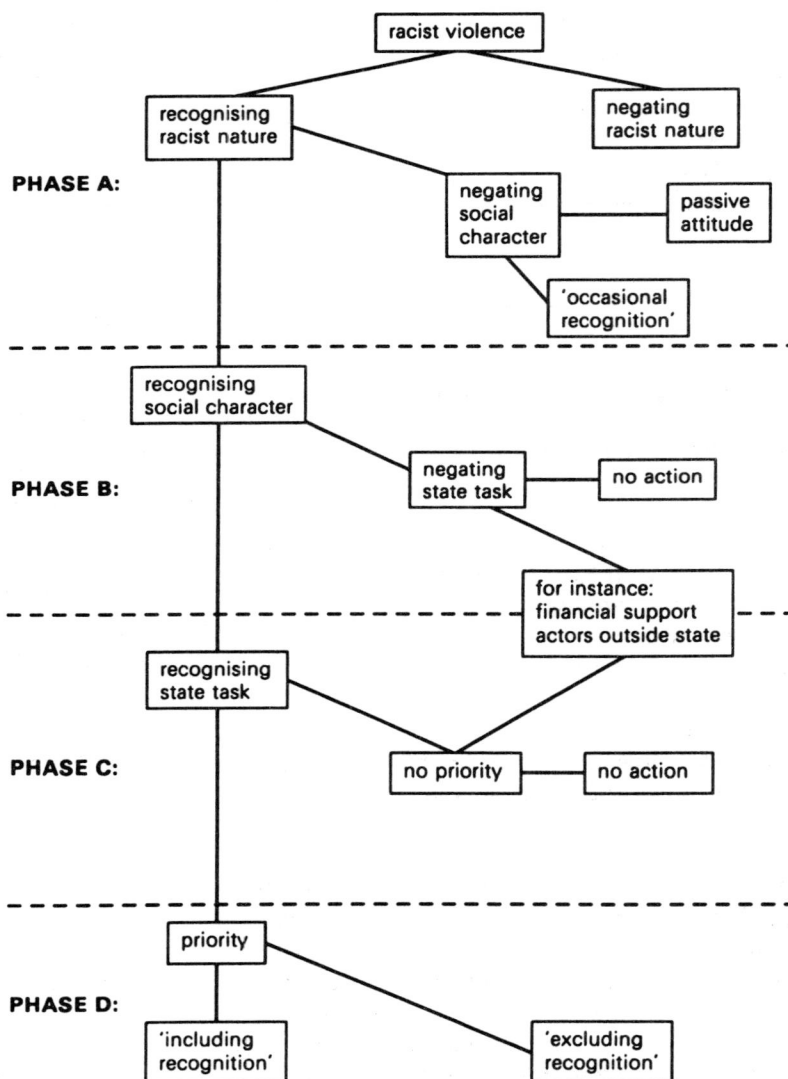

causes for major changes in the status of racist violence in relation to state responses. For example, why did racist violence reach the political agenda in Britain in the early 1980s, and in Germany in the early 1990s? What were the major state responses to the changing status in each of these countries at the time?

It should be noted that the state is not to be perceived as a monolithic unit. State activities are the result of internal struggles and compromises (Bovenkerk, Miles and Verbunt, 1990b, p. 480), and are constantly subject to very different influences from outside the state. This means that different, and even contradictory state responses to racist violence may and will occur simultaneously in any one country.

A distinction needs to be made between the national and the local levels. Although the main focus of attention will be on the national level, the local level needs to be taken into consideration for at least four reasons:

1. social problems usually occur for the first time on the local level;
2. in those phases of the idealised process in which racist violence is not perceived to be a social problem by the public at large, state responses will mainly be visible at a local level (especially response by the police);
3. the difference between the intention of policies and their practical effects induces one to study the national level at which the intentions of policies may be formulated, as well as the local level at which policies are implemented and will (or will not) have specific effects;
4. Initiatives to combat racist violence as well as resistance against such initiatives or policies alike may be prominent on the local level.

Let us now return to the four phases of the idealised process described above and to the different ways in which the states of Europe have responded to racist violence during recent years.

(a) Racist Violence as a Problem of the Individual

In this phase, racist violence is experienced by (groups of) individuals in society, but is not perceived as a social problem by the public at large, nor by the state. People who suffer such violence are more or less thrown back on their own resources, and are unable to draw broader attention to this problem. This may well be because of the marginal position that groups of potential victims occupy within the power relations in society. This, in itself, is one of the main reasons why they become victims of racist violence. Victims are representatives of minority groups in society – minority groups, that is, as regards number, as well as in terms of political and socio-economic power relations.

It is most likely that where a state response occurs in this phase, it will be at the local level. The racist nature of the violence is often not recognised as such at all. Examples are manifold in Europe. Statements by victims and others, or other indications of racist motives, are often trivialised or neglected.

On 14 December 1973 a bomb exploded at the Algerian Consulate in Marseille, in France. Four people were killed and twenty injured. Although an anti-immigrant organisation ('Charles Martel') claimed responsibility for the attack, the police stated that this attack was not racist (Viard, 1984). Official statements by authorities often explicitly overlook the racist nature of the event by referring to the (alleged) attackers as 'drunken pranksters', as people without any knowledge of (racist) ideologies, or as vandals who are merely trying to attract publicity.[9] In more than one instance, such statements refer to the incident as something of which anybody could have become the victim. Sometimes the incident is compared with vandalising bus shelters or other public property, or as 'ordinary' street fights. Being a victim of this kind of violence is depicted as a matter of 'bad luck'.

On 20 August 1992, three Nigerian asylum-seekers were beaten up in Hoorn, in the Netherlands. The perpetrators acted in response to a rumour that a friend had had an argument with someone 'with dark skin'. The asylum-seekers had nothing to do with this. 'Racism? Rubbish!' According to the police spokesman 'the suspects don't have any notion of ideologies or any deeper thoughts. They simply let fly.' He also pointed out that this could have happened to anyone.[10]

Maintaining 'law and order' is one of the main functions of the state with its monopolised right to use violence. Therefore, it is the state that must and will respond to any incident of violence. However, experience of racist violence shows that such action is not assured. This is illustrated by the fact that the police sometimes emphatically refuse to report an incident of racist violence. There have even been several cases in which the victim was arrested after he/she insisted on reporting the incident. In 1981, Satwinder Sondh was attacked in London and had the initials 'NF' (National Front) carved on his stomach with a knife. At first, the police simply denied that there was any racist motive. Later, Sondh was charged with wasting police time. He was convicted but later completely cleared on appeal (Gordon, 1990, p. 20).

Numerous incidents of racist violence have involved the arrest of the victim(s), especially when the latter tried to defend themselves. Elsewhere in this volume (Chapter 12), Paul Gordon gives some examples of this in Britain. The example of Dundee, given at the beginning of this chapter, is another in which people were attacked, tried to defend themselves and were arrested as a result. This Dundee example also illustrates the afore-mentioned need to make a distinction between the national and local levels. While in 1981, racist violence reached the political agenda in Britain at a national level (Home Office, 1981), the Dundee example shows racist violence still in the phase of an individual problem at a local level.

Of course, even when the racist nature of the violence is not recognised by the state authorities, the perpetrators of such violence may be arrested and convicted. The main perpetrator of the violent attack against three Nigerian asylum-seekers in Hoorn, in the Nether-lands (already mentioned) was sentenced to two years imprisonment.[11] Although racist motives were not included in the verdict, his violent past was. The murderer of Kerwin Duinmeyer (second example at the beginning of the chapter) was also convicted. In the verdict, racist motives were explicitly denied, on the basis of a psychological report that pointed out the very unstable personality of the perpetrator.

In this phase, in which racist violence is not perceived as constituting a social problem, incidents may occur which most people and authorities agree are of a racist nature. Yet, the main response in such cases will then point to the 'occasional character' of the incident. In these cases, the fact that racist violence constitutes a social problem is denied, whether implicitly or explicitly.

On 24 January 1992, an arson attack damaged a mosque in Amersfoort, in the Netherlands. Public opinion held it to be a racist attack. The Dutch Minister for Home Affairs and the Minister for Justice stated that they were appalled by the event. Yet both also made statements to qualify the incident, to counteract any 'panic' and to warn against exaggerating the seriousness of the Dutch situation with respect to racist violence (van Donselaar, in Chapter 4 of this volume). Their statements pointed to the 'occasional character' of racist violence by referring to the number of known(!) incidents in relation to the situation abroad, which is perceived and depicted as being more serious. In these instances, while the racist nature of the violence is recognised, it is seen as consisting of isolated incidents and as only an occasional problem. One could thus speak of 'occasional recognition' as the specific type of state response.

Motives for denying that racist violence is a social problem can be diverse. The denial may be based on the need to prevent possible panic or violent counterattacks against (potential) perpetrators. It may also be based on the opinion that racist violence should not be given any – or not too much – attention, motivated by the imagined or real danger of 'over-exposure'. Sometimes, it is motivated by the possible influence of mass media publicity on potential perpetrators ('copy-cat actions'). While the racist nature of the incident may not necessarily be denied here – sometimes, it is even explicitly recognised – no further state action is taken (except, perhaps, by the judiciary).

(b) and (c) A Social Problem on its Way to the Political Agenda

If racist violence is perceived as a social problem by different groups in society, this does not mean that state action to combat this problem follows automatically. Because of the marginal position of most groups who become targets of racist violence, the attention of the public at large and shared public concern and consensus that state action is needed, are essential before such action is to taken (Cobb and Elder, 1983, p. 85). These may be achieved by activities to attract public attention, and by formulating demands. Public awareness and pressure on state authorities in favour of the demands may be increased by organising demonstrations, publishing documents, exerting direct influence on decision-makers, etc.

During the early 1990s, many demonstrations were organised throughout Europe to protest against racism in general, and racist violence in particular, and to demand state action. Some of these appear to have had a major influence on public opinion and on state responses to the issue. Examples of these are the demonstration in Brumunddal, in Norway, in 1991 (see Björgo, Chapter 7 in this volume on the role of the media) and the weekly 'candlelight' demonstrations in many German cities since the end of 1992. Sometimes state representatives respond to demonstrations by joining them, such as President Mitterrand of France in 1990 (fourth example at beginning of this chapter). By leading a demonstration of this kind, he actively supported the idea that racist violence is violence directed against the whole of society, and that it should be placed on the political agenda.

However, this does not mean that racist violence is, by definition, placed on the political agenda after every demonstration. Often demonstrations get hardly any political attention or media coverage at all. If they do, their importance is often trivialised. Sometimes demonstrations do attract a lot of attention, only to be portrayed as a danger in themselves with an effect contrary to that intended. This occurs particularly when the state and, for instance, mainstream media and public disagree with the demands of the organisers. Small disturbances may even be enough to criminalise the demonstrators and to depoliticise and trivialise their demands. Several demonstrations in Britain at the end of the 1970s and in the early 1980s were treated in this way by the political authorities and the media. Partly as a result of 'over-policing' at demonstrations, the demonstrators, instead of the racism and racist violence they were protesting against, were portrayed as the main problem. One example was the demonstration against a meeting of the National Front (who were seen to be linked with many incidents of racist violence) in Southall, London, on 23 April 1979 which led to major disturbances resulting in the death of Blair Peach (CARF/Southall Rights, 1981). Another was the demonstration, following the racist killing of Akhtar Ali Baig by a skinhead gang, on 19 July 1980 in Newham, London which resulted in at least twenty-nine arrests (Newham Monitoring Project/CARF, 1991).

Registering racist incidents, publishing criticism of (the lack of) response to incidents and publishing documents, are other ways of increasing pressure and drawing attention to the problem. Gordon (in Chapter 12 of this volume) points out the importance of the publication of the 1978 report by the Bethnal Green and Stepney Trades Council (*Blood on the Streets*), and of the 1979 report by the Institute of Race Relations (*Police against Black People*). These two reports had a major influence on future developments concerning the perception by the state of racist violence as a social problem in Britain in the 1980s. But the fact that a less well-documented report by the state-related Joint Committee Against Racism (1980) was needed to get the issue on to the political agenda, indicated the state response to the first two reports by non-state organisations. It is obvious that the latter reports were perceived to be 'coloured' and 'politically motivated' and needed to be checked by a 'state inquiry'.

The afore-mentioned are examples of the action that specific groups in society can take to get racist violence on the political agenda. Action may, of course, also be taken by people or institutions within the state. In 1975, for instance, the British MP, Mr Paul Rose, started to keep records of racist incidents. Another example is the hearing on racist violence organised in 1984 by the *Vaste Kamercommissie voor Justitie* (standing committee for justice in the Netherlands).[12] Other examples are proposals for new legislation or new policies by Members of Parliament. An example of a recent initiative taken by a person from within the state at an international level was the speech by the Prime Minister of Norway, Mrs Brundtland, in a session of the parliamentary assembly of the Council of Europe in Strasbourg (4 February 1993). She spoke of the 'ever more frequent reports [which] describe both organised and spontaneous acts of racism and racially motivated harassment in our societies'. She then proposed a European Plan of Action against Racism, Xenophobia and Intolerance, including:

- renewed commitment by governments to use the full potential of their legal systems, administrative procedures, educational systems and information agencies to counter all forms of discrimination;
- increased research into the nature and extent of racial violence; international cooperation in the field of legal instruments and law enforcement procedures;
- integration of multinational tolerance into all relevant fields of inter-governmental cooperation within the framework of the Council of Europe.[13]

Once racist violence is perceived by the public at large and by state authorities to constitute a social problem that needs to be dealt with by the state, the issue has entered the so-called public agenda. Still, this is no guarantee that state action will be taken to combat the violence. State authorities may refer to other important issues which are, implicitly or explicitly, given higher priority. Often this is motivated by the opinion that racist violence is only a matter of 'being watchful'. Sometimes the state increases or starts financial support to non-state organisations, such as organisations of minority groups or anti-racism organisations, to help them carry on their work in combating racism in general. No further measures are taken for the moment.

On many occasions, an issue has reached the public agenda more or less suddenly, as a result of a specific event which is felt to be shocking by a large part of society. With respect to racist violence such events may be assassinations (such as the murders in Mölln, Germany, in November 1992), riots (such as Hoyerswerda in August 1991 and Rostock in August 1992 in Germany), and desecration of graves and places of worship (such as Carpentras, France in 1990; Amersfoort, the

Netherlands in 1992) – events that surely are not the first signs of racist violence, but are nevertheless perceived to be shocking and attract massive media coverage. A notorious type of state response in this respect is the establishment of a 'special inquiry commission'. Often, this is an either intentional or unintentional policy aimed at releasing anger and gaining time to avert 'panic'. Whether any state action will be taken later, and whether racist violence actually will be put on the political agenda, remains uncertain. On more than one occasion, the issue has, after some time, disappeared from the public agenda without ever reaching the political agenda.

(d) Racist Violence on the Political Agenda

If racist violence is perceived to constitute a social problem which has to be dealt with by the state and is given priority, it enters the political agenda. Racist violence in this phase is an issue of active and serious state action. In this phase, two types of state response may be distinguished: 'including recognition' and 'excluding recognition'. In general, the terminology 'including versus excluding' refers to the position of the groups of potential victims in relation to society as indicated by the state response, whether implicitly or explicitly. If these groups are perceived to constitute an inextricable part of society ('inclusion'), racist violence will be perceived as violence against society and it will be treated accordingly. Policies and measures will be directed against (potential) perpetrators of racist violence and against circumstances in which this violence may flourish. If, on the other hand, groups of victims are perceived to form separate, more or less isolated groups, partly outside society ('exclusion'), policies and measures to combat the violence will mainly be directed against the (increasing) presence of such groups.

An example of an 'including recognition' type of state response is changing legislation in a such way that racist motives play an important role in the prosecution procedure and are explicitly seen as aggravating circumstances. In the Norwegian Penal Code, for instance, racist motives form an independent aggravating circumstance (Björgo, 1993). 'Including recognition' does not always have to be translated into new legislation. Sometimes, a more strict enforcement of existing legislation is possible. In many European countries, giving a 'Hitler salute', carrying a swastika, and shouting racist slogans are prohibited. Yet there is hardly a policeman in Europe who will arrest people who behave in this way. Since the second half of 1992, the police in the

Netherlands seem to have been instructed to act according to existing legislation and to arrest people who violate these laws. During a recent football match between Turkey and the Netherlands (24 February 1993 in Utrecht, in the Netherlands) the police were instructed to mingle with the audience as soon as racist slogans were heard and to arrest every individual who shouted these slogans again.

The sixth example at the beginning of this chapter also illustrates the 'including recognition' type of state response to racist violence. The decision to dismiss the entire city council of Mancha Real, in Spain, because it had played a major role in a pogrom against local gypsies is clearly directed against the violence and its perpetrators. A special aspect here is the fact that this is an example of a state response against other state authorities who are the perpetrators.

Other examples of 'including recognition' as a type of state response to racist violence have been seen in Britain since the 1980s, and occurred in Germany at the end of 1992. During the second half of the 1980s, the so-called 'multi-agency approach' was developed in Britain as a method of combating racist violence in society at a local level (see Bowling and Saulsbury in Chapter 16 of this volume). In its intent, this form of cooperation between different local agencies to combat racist violence seems to be an example of the 'including recognition' type of response. In December 1992, after the Mölln murders (three Turkish women killed in an arson attack), the German state imposed a ban on several organisations which propagated racism and racist violence (Atkinson, in Chapter 11 of this volume). This can be seen as another example of 'including recognition', because it was directed against perpetrators and organisations who contributed to an atmosphere in which racist violence flourished.

It should be noted that a state response of this kind in no way guarantees that racist violence will disappear from society. Measures may be directed at just a few of the many causes of such violence, and may be symbolic rather than effective on the practical level. Nevertheless, such policies and measures are clearly directed against the violence, the (potential) perpetrators, and against the circumstances in which racist violence occurs.

'Excluding recognition' is a type of state response in which the violence is perceived to constitute a social problem, but in which measures and policies are directed against the presence of the potential victims. Statements that explain violence as resulting from the increasing number of immigrants, asylum-seekers, ethnic minorities, etc., are manifold in Europe in the 1980s and 1990s. But such arguments have been heard before. In the aftermath of the occurrences of civil disorder in Britain in 1958, which were clearly initiated by increasing racist violence, state action was not directed against racism nor against this violence in British society. State action and statements politicised the debates about restricting migration and prepared the legislation (Commonwealth Immigrants Act, 1962) to implement such restrictions.[14] In 1973, there was a massive outburst of racist violence in France starting in the Provence region and in the area around Marseille and spreading all across the country. At least twelve Algerians were killed (Viard, 1984). This led to many debates about the presence of 'migrants', especially Algerians. During the 1974 elections migration was a central political issue and the new government acted immediately to halt all further immigration (Lloyd and Waters, 1991). No state action was directed against the outburst of this racist violence.

The German–Romanian treaty (fifth example at the beginning of this chapter) – the first significant state response at the national level following events in Rostock in August 1992 – is another 'excluding recognition' type of state response. Being the first response, the presence of these asylum-seekers was, whether intentionally or unintentionally, portrayed as the main cause of the violence – as if there should be a 'natural' limit to the presence of asylum-seekers and as if it were 'human nature' to start to become violent if this limit is exceeded.

At a local level, the Florence case (third example at the beginning of the chapter) is also an example of 'excluding recognition'. The main reason for the extra police was to seal off the city centre of Florence to the African street vendors. This portrayed the victims of racist violence as the main cause of the violence. Parisi, the Head of Italian Police, stated that the violence against the street vendors was nothing more than an individual act of vandalism. The 1200 illegal immigrants were felt to be the ones to blame for the insecurity in Italy. According to Paresi, these 1200 were capable of committing as many crimes as all the 1.2 million Italians in the city and the Province of Florence taken together.[15]

These examples of 'including' or 'excluding' recognition are types of state response that occur when racist violence reaches the political agenda. It should be noted that these two types of state response may occur simultaneously. As already stated, state action is the result of internal struggle and compromise that is constantly being modified by influences from outside. Because of this, and because the state is not a monolithic unity, different and contradictory responses may occur together.

CONCLUSIONS

The idealised process by which a social phenomenon such as racist violence may reach the political agenda consists of four possible phases. These distinguishable phases enable us to analyse and compare state responses to racist violence in each phase in different countries over a period of time. This is an idealised process and does not mean that racist violence must necessarily pass through each of these phases before it reaches the political agenda. Shocking incidents, increasing public awareness, demonstrations, individual state institutions, etc., may each be the cause of the 'sudden' appearance of this topic on the public or the political agenda. Sometimes racist violence is brought to the political agenda before it reaches the level of a broadly experienced problem. Racist violence may appear in any phase and disappear from any phase without moving to the next phase.

By distinguishing the phases mentioned, we are able to analyse the main causes of change in the status of racist violence and in the state response to racist violence and their influence on the violence. For instance, what was it that triggered the appearance of racist violence on the political agenda in the early 1980s in Britain? What were the main state responses before and after this? Who or what influenced these changes? These are some of the questions that need to be asked.

The model also enables us to compare, for instance, the appearance of racist violence on the political agenda in Britain in the 1980s with that in Germany in the 1990s. Were both 'appearances' typified by shocking events, such as Rostock and Mölln in Germany? And did both countries at the time of this appearance realise an increasing 'threat' of self-defence by groups of potential victims? Similarities may be analysed as well as specific differences. The same is possible for the state responses to racist violence in any other phase. What were the main differences and similarities between state responses in different countries in the phase of racist violence as a problem of the individual? How did groups victimised by racist violence, whether directly or indirectly, and perceiving it as a social problem, try to draw attention to this problem and to their demands? How did the state respond to such action and demands? In an international comparative analysis the answers to these and other questions may give greater insight into the ways in which states respond to racist violence, how such responses influence future developments of this violence and ways of combating racist violence in Europe in the 1990s.

NOTES

1. *Searchlight*, no 76, October 1981, as cited in Institute of Race Relations, 1987, p. 69.
2. *Panorama*, 21 September 1983.
3. *De Volkskrant*, 14 March 1990.
4. *De Volkskrant*, 12 May 1990.
5. *Parool*, 25 September 1992.
6. *De Volkskrant*, 24 October 1992.
7. Racist violence is the (threat of) violence against (groups of) individuals or their property because of their real or imagined membership of minority groups in society, based on skin colour, religion, cultural, national or ethnic origin.
8. This is a term often used in social science for an ideal type, without any positive or negative valuation.
9. Björgo's two contributions in this volume demonstrate that the perpetrators' use of alcohol, their criminal records, and their wish to attract attention are typical traits of racist violence. They certainly do not exclude either possibilities that there might also be racist motives involved.
10. *Alkmaarse Courant*, 29 August 1992.
11. *Parool*, 16 December 1992.
12. *NRC Handelsblad*, 30 August 1984.
13. Address by Gro Harlem Brundtland, Prime Minister of Norway at the Fourth Part-Session of the 44th Ordinary Session of the Parliamentary Assembly of the Council of Europe, Strasbourg, 4 February 1993.
14. See: Miles (1984), Pilkington (1988), Fryer (1991) and Hiro (1992).
15. *De Volkskrant*, 15 March 1990.

11 Germany: Nationalism, Nazism and Violence

Graeme Atkinson

The day when reunification of the two Germanies was formally consummated, 3 October 1990, will arguably be seen as a watershed in the history both of Germany and of Europe.

Certainly, few observers could have predicted then the rapidity with which right-wing nationalist extremism would begin to mount a serious challenge to the State, precipitating earnest discussion inside Germany and abroad about the scale of the danger and reopening the question of exile amongst Jewish people and others plunged into fear by these developments.

Yet, this has happened and the situation has taken on increased urgency following the formidable escalation of right-extremist or neo-Nazi political violence and of racism and anti-Semitism.

The precise level of the violence of the past two years is not easy to quantify, a fact which stems from the gathering of statistics by a variety of agencies including the Federal Interior Ministry; the Interior Ministries of the individual state governments; the *Bundeskriminalamt* (BKA), Germany's main police agency and the *Bundesamt für Verfassungsschutz* (BVS), the country's internal security watchdog.

Frequently, the statistics issued by these agencies – or by some of their constituent parts – are at serious variance with each other. For example, on 9 December 1992 the BKA issued statistics showing that up to the end of November 1992, a total of 4587 'xenophobic indictable offences' had been perpetrated as against a total of 2426 the previous year.[1] Two months later, the Federal German Interior Ministry issued its own latest figures – based on BVS estimates – to indicate that in 1992, it had registered 2285 'right-extremist acts of violence', a 54 per cent increase on 1991.[2]

These figures revealed that 1953 of these attacks had had foreigners as their victims, that 686 of the attacks had involved arson or the use of explosives and that seventeen people had been killed and 542 wounded. The corresponding BVS total for 1991 was 1489 attacks of which 1255 were perpetrated against foreigners.

Especially noteworthy was the Interior Ministry/BVS revelation that more than 70 per cent of suspected perpetrators were under the age of 25 years old and only 2 per cent over the age of 30. It was also reported by Johannes Vöcking, Secretary of State for the Interior, and later confirmed in the Interior Ministry's figures that in 1992 there had been seventy-seven desecrations of Jewish cemeteries and other property – more than double the number of the previous year.[3]

In any case, the real toll of attacks is probably higher since not all attacks are reported and then again not all racist attacks are treated as such by the police. A case in point here is the *murder* of three Sri Lankan asylum-seekers in an arson attack in Lampertheim on 31 January 1992. At the time, the investigating authorities ruled out arson but, in November, three German youths under investigation for other alleged offences, confessed to police that they had set fire to the asylum-seekers' home.

Cases similar to Lampertheim account for the differences in the assumed numbers of deaths as a result of racist and neo-Nazi violence. While anti-Fascist researchers estimate the number of racist killings in 1992 to be closer to twenty-six, the BVS figure stands lower.[4]

Either way, the figures are appalling and have tarnished Germany's international image. This latter factor, as much as the internal situation, accounts for the sudden and very belated flurry of action by the Federal State Prosecutor, Alexander von Stahl, and the law enforcement authorities in the wake of the neo-Nazi atrocity in Mölln on 23 November 1992 in which three Turkish people were killed in a fire-bomb attack.

Mölln has been claimed to be the alleged catalyst for a series of raids, arrests and the banning in rapid succession of four neo-Nazi organisations, the *Nationalistische Front, Deutsche Alternative*, the *Deutscher Kameradschaftsbund* and *Nationale Offensive*, whose members have both engaged in and inspired much of the violence in the past two years.

Definitely it was a factor, but this begs the question of why the government did not act before to stamp out racist and neo-Nazi violence, and brings into focus other factors in the political situation.

Of these, the most important is undoubtedly that of rising German nationalism which has been given a massive boost by reunification and which has also given a dubious legitimacy to many arguments of the extreme Right.

When the Berlin Wall opened completely unexpectedly on 9 November 1989, the enormity of the economic, political and social crisis of the German Democratic Republic (GDR) became apparent and was shown to be far deeper than had been imagined.

For Helmut Kohl's ruling Christian Democratic Union (CDU), however, it was a godsend; an opportunity to make a reality of a long-held programmatic advocacy of German reunification but also a chance to outflank a looming electoral threat on the CDU's right.

This threat, represented by the neo-Fascist *Die Republikaner* (REP), was already on the political scene, agitating against the presence of West Germany's 4.5 million foreigners and capitalising on the electorate's weariness with the rule of the CDU and its junior coalition partners, the Free Democrats (FDP) and the Bavarian Christian Social Union (CSU).

Even before the 'turn' in the East, the REP had functioned as a kind of harbinger of nationalist revival. In January 1989, the party had won more than 90 000 votes and eleven city parliament seats in local elections in West Berlin. The initial media and political reaction was a mixture of shock and dismissiveness and it was confidently predicted by numerous observers that this 'protest phenomenon' would disappear like its Fascist predecessor the *Nationaldemokratische Partei Deutschlands* (NPD) had done at the end of the 1960s after another supposed far-right 'breakthrough'. Within two months, the dismissive view was subjected to bitter irony when this same NPD took seven seats in the Frankfurt am Main city parliament and re-established the presence it had lost precisely at the end of the 1960s.

And, just to emphasise that this far-right electoral progress represented no fluke, the REP took more than 2 000 000 votes in the European Parliamentary elections on 18 June and won six seats in Strasbourg. The total vote for the Fascist Right in Germany in that election was even bigger: more than 2 600 000 votes for four parties in all.

Most interesting was the REP's programme – broadcast very skilfully in TV 'spots' – calling for a strong Germany, for reunification within Germany's 1937 frontiers, for national self-determination and spiritual and moral renewal and, above all, for draconian curbs on the number of foreigners – all of which touched deep chords within a segment of the German populace. Significantly, the REP was also able to establish a firm and broad base of support, particularly amongst young working-class men, and also inside sections of the state apparatus like the police and armed forces. According to the official Report of the European Parliament's Committee of Inquiry into Racism and Xenophobia in Europe, published in 1991:

... surveys ... suggest that support for the REP among policemen is especially strong. In Bavaria, for example, more than 50 per cent of policemen declared their support for the REP while in Hessen more than 60 per cent of officers expressed similar loyalties. In addition, the REP now has serious backing in the Federal Republic's armed forces with more than 1000 serving soldiers and officers in party membership.[5]

The two most powerful planks of REP policy were its anti-immigrant, anti-foreigner stance and its demand for a strong, *reunified* Germany, something which, at the time, was not remotely conceivable. Within months, the incipient collapse in the East changed all that. To begin with, the movement against the Stalinist dictatorship was concentrated on the development of a renewed, democratic but still socialist and definitely separate German Democratic Republic.

This was summed up in the slogans roared by tens of thousands on the weekly Monday night demonstrations in cities like Leipzig and Dresden: *Wir sind das Volk* – 'We are the people' – a slogan which emphasised the collective democratic will against the rule of the Stalinist bureaucracy. Immediately, political discussion in Western Germany shifted to the question of whether unification was a real possibility. For the CDU, there was little hesitation from the outset and almost the entire media was set in motion to bring it to fruition.

Thus, there began a propaganda blitz, perhaps the biggest in recent German history, to push events with a haste that was almost indecent in the direction of German unification. Newspapers, magazines, radio and TV were turned over to the themes of 'German nationhood', 'German sovereignty' and 'German unity'. Between the winter of 1989 and the summer of 1990, the national and regional TV broadcasting schedules were frequently rearranged to make way for 'special' programmes, especially studio discussions and East–West '*vox pop*' link-ups on the future of Germany.

The mass-circulation *Bild* consistently ran 3-inch headlines in the black–red–gold of Germany's national colours. People in the GDR were confused and bewildered but above all intoxicated by the new-won freedom. And their vision and expectations of the future began to change under the impact of the blandishments and promises coming their way from the West.

As early as the end of December 1989, new slogans were heard on the streets of East Germany as the Monday night demonstrations continued into the New Year. *Wir sind das Volk* underwent a tiny verbal but enormous political alteration to become *Wir sind ein Volk* ('We are *one* people'), the CDU's own campaign slogan.[6] At the same time, the chants of *Deutschland, Deutschland, Deutschland* became more insistent and the unequivocally racist slogan, *Deutschland den Deutschen! Ausländer Raus!* (Germany for Germans! Foreigners out!) accompanied by neo-Nazis, also made its debut.

Ironically, the REP, the most ardent and consistent advocate of German national unity, saw its support begin to slide while Kohl's CDU took its chance to be the party that united Germany. What had happened was quite simple. The REP, which was becoming a perceptible threat to the CDU's re-election prospects, was outflanked by the latter. The CDU could make its own independent and long-held 'unite the Fatherland' policy a reality while all the REP could do was to make propaganda for it.

Nationalism, though, was not weakened by this process. On the contrary, it was strengthened above all by the media's obsessive coverage of the 'new Germany' and the determination of the CDU to make that 'new Germany' a reality. Running hard to keep up with the *Bild* was the highly-respected *Der Spiegel* which metamorphosed from a 'left'-leaning journal into a nationalist journal.

Spiegel covers during the run-up to reunification displayed clear evidence of this. For example, the cover of the 15 January 1990 edition featured a photograph of Gregor Gysi, leader of the Party of Democratic Socialism, the successor organisation to East Germany's former ruling Socialist Unity Party (SED). SED leader Gysi – the only German party leader of Jewish origin – is labelled *Der Drahtzieher*, the 'wire-puller', 'the manipulator'. If this expression seems familiar, it is – to most educated Germans, at least.[7] In Frankfurt am Main's Jewish Museum one can even see the 'original' of the *Spiegel* cover: a late 1920s poster from Adolf Hitler's NSDAP displaying a caricature 'Jewish capitalist'. The words over the poster? *Der Drahtzieher.*

This anti-Semitic cover was part of the magazine's growing fixation with Germany's nationhood and 'sovereignty'. On 18 May 1990, *Der Spiegel* ran a cover which voiced this obsession. Over the title 'When will Germany be sovereign?', Bush, Thatcher, Mitterrand and Gorbachev – the leaders of the victorious Allied powers – are portrayed sitting astride the horses which surmount Berlin's historic Brandenburg Gate. The message speaks for itself.[8]

A few weeks later, on 2 July 1990, an article on this theme by *Spiegel* publisher Rudolf Augstein himself got front-cover treatment in the shape of a stylised pre-Raphaelite German warrior who adorns the cover, sword in one hand and national flag in the other. Augstein's article, nine pages in all, however, contained one sentence which entirely revised the history of the twentieth century. He wrote: 'Prussia–Germany was no more anti-Semitic than France or Poland, even during the years 1933 to 1945.'[9] Astonishingly, this comment – unthinkable, never mind unsayable, a decade ago – drew not a single protest from any senior politician.

However, the assumption of the nationalist role by the CDU and its coalition partners created more problems than it solved. As bait to win support in the West for reunification, Kohl solemnly promised that there would be no tax increases to pay for reunification. It was not long before this promise was shown to have been written on water. The cost of reunification turned out to be more than anyone could have predicted. The introduction of the Deutsche Mark on 1 July 1990 alone cost 120 billion DM.[10] As evidence mounted of just how decrepit the GDR's economic infrastructure really was, the pressure for sacrifices in the shape of higher taxes in the prosperous West became irresistible – just to maintain a semblance of stability in the East and to prevent a total disintegration of the ex-GDR economy.

As early as the Spring of 1991, increased taxation in the West became a 'live' issue. In TV coverage, strangely, news items about increased taxation and cutbacks in public spending provision in the West were almost invariably preceded or followed by items about the number of asylum-seekers entering Germany or about their cost to the economy. In this way, the questions of asylum and the number of foreigners – now increased to 5.8 million (7.4 per cent of the population) – which had been a campaigning point both of the REP and the CDU *before* the opening of the Berlin Wall became inextricably linked with that of the economy.

In the summer of 1991, against the advice of Germany's President, Richard von Weiszäcker, the CDU opened what it called the 'Asylum Debate' whose keynote was a flood of media claims, repeated day after day that Germany was about to be 'invaded' or 'flooded' by 'millions' of refugees. Again, this did not correspond even to the Federal government's own statistics which showed that, in 1991, 274 000 sought asylum of whom 4 per cent were accepted and that around 400 000 refugees were expected in 1992.[11]

Bild meanwhile concentrated very heavily on painting a picture of a refugee threat and where *Bild* led, *Der Spiegel* again followed.

And not just *Bild*. The Fascists of the REP and *Deutsche Volks Union* (DVU) had already taken over the Hamburg CDU's election slogan 'No to fake asylum-seekers'. Now, *Der Spiegel* was to take over the REP and DVU slogan 'The Boat is full!'[12] On 9 September 1991, it published a cover depicting a boat in Germany's national colours. The boat, surrounded by a sea of struggling humanity, was massively overcrowded. This tasteless pictorial representation of a *fascist* slogan was topped by the headline 'The Onslaught of the Poor'.

At the same time, CDU politicians added their voice to an increasingly racist campaign designed to divert attention from the social and political problems and to prevent the defection of racist votes to the REP and the DVU.

As soon as asylum became an issue, there were immediate strident demands to curb the right to it as enshrined in Article 16 of the German constitution. The CDU determined to get rid of Article 16. To do so, it required a two-thirds majority in the Bundestag, a feat that could only be accomplished by dragging the opposition SPD into the nationalist and racist vortex. Only evidence of massive public pressure would force the SPD's hand.

During the course of the 'Asylum Debate', politicians from both the CDU and the Christian Social Union raised the political temperature to boiling-point. For example, Klaus Landowski, the CDU leader in Berlin said 'We cannot allow foreigners to . . . shout "asylum" and live at the taxpayers' expense.' He was echoed by Otto Zeitler, the Bavarian Deputy Minister for Development and Environment, who told listeners that 'we have to think of the ecological consequences of unlimited immigration'. Another top Bavarian CSU member, Manfred Ritter, went even further, comparing refugees with 'locusts who leave a desert in their wake' and demanding 'a total closure of Europe to all immigration from the developing countries'. And to indicate that these were not merely individual musings, the then leader of the CDU Faction in the *Bundestag* Alfred Dregger, avowed that 'foreigners are guests and not citizens'.[13]

Such statements gave the proponents of systematic race-hate and terror the green light for action – legitimised by no less a party than the CDU.

First to reap the benefit of the Asylum Debate was the fascist DVU which scored 6 per cent of the vote in state elections in Bremen and strengthened its foothold in the state parliament. However, the intervention of the Fascists was not limited to electioneering. They took the campaign into the streets and applied a match to the powder gathered by the CDU with a week-long pogrom in the Saxon town of Hoyerswerda (population 70 000) where hundreds of local residents joined neo-Nazis in terrorising and then forcing out all 230 foreigners living there.

What was in fact a pogrom was conducted for six days under the watchful gaze of police officers who did nothing to intervene while a Nazi-led racist mob put its victims under siege by smashing their windows and beating them with baseball bats and bicycle chains in the streets.

Hoyerswerda – Germany's first 'foreigner-free city' – was a victory for violence in German politics. Astonishingly, neither Kohl nor any of his ministers saw fit or felt able to make an unequivocal condemnation of it. Always, condemnations were qualified by statements about abuse of the asylum laws. For example, the then Federal Interior Minister, Wolfgang Schäuble, commenting on the events in Hoyerswerda, said 'popular worry and fear that our country is being flooded with refugees must be taken seriously'.[14]

This followed a similar statement by Volker Rühe, the then General-Secretary of Kohl's CDU, and now Defence Minister, who proclaimed that Hoyerswerda showed 'that the population is overstrained by massive abuse of the right to asylum'.[15] Kohl did not disavow either of these statements.

Hoyerswerda, however, was the flashpoint for an autumn of horrific violence in which, during October 1991 alone there were, according to BKA chief Hans-Ludwig Zächert, 904 acts of racist violence, including 167 fire-bomb attacks and 683 cases of criminal damage and other violent behaviour.[16]

Opinion polls conducted during the autumn of 1991 suggested some measure of public support for the avalanche of violence. For example, polls conducted shortly after Hoyerswerda and published in *Der Spiegel* indicated that 21 per cent of East Germans and 38 per cent of West Germans had 'sympathy for the aims of the right-radicals'.[17]

In elections, too, the hostility to asylum-seekers found expression. On 5 April 1992 the REP gained 538 000 votes (10.9 per cent) in Baden-Württemberg. On the same day, the DVU took 93 000 (6.3 per cent) votes in Schleswig-Holstein at the opposite end of the country. It should be noted that in neither of these two German states is there mass unemployment, bad housing, poor education, low wages or any of the other features so often used to account for the growth of Fascism. Neither are they part of the former GDR.

Likewise, in Berlin, in May, the REP won 8.1 per cent of the vote in the first all-city elections there since 1933. In all these elections, the main emphasis was given to anti-foreigner campaigns by the Fascist parties. The CDU was the main loser and its attempts to use the Asylum Debate to further its own political goals clearly backfired. Similar consequences may well ensue when it is perceived that planned changes to Article 16 have failed.

The changes, aimed at imposing severe restrictions on the right of asylum, cannot alter the circumstances – civil war in the former Yugoslavia, persecution of Roma people in Romania and catastrophes in the Third World – which are giving rise to dramatic population movements.

Ever since Hoyerswerda, violence against foreigners, Jews, political opponents, homeless people, homosexuals and, increasingly, handicapped people, has escalated into an ugly feature of daily life in Germany. And the right-extremist scene now numbers, according to Ernst Uhrlau, the head of the *Verfassungsschutz* (security service) in the state of Hamburg, over 65 000.[18]

The xenophobic feelings on which the continuing violence is based have a wide resonance within the German population. Nowhere was this shown more frighteningly than in the Baltic city of Rostock at the end of August 1992. There, again, violent action – the storming and fire-bombing of a house for foreigners by Nazi-led hooligans, was applauded by thousands (in Hoyerswerda, it was hundreds) of local residents. The police were passive and senior politicians like Mecklenburg-Vorpommern Interior Minister, Lothar Kupfer, openly expressed sympathy with the Fascist rioters.

Rightly, *Stern* magazine commented in an editorial that 'The constitutional state has capitulated before the terror' and that 'the events in Rostock show above all that Germany's security forces have neither the will nor are in a fit state to protect innocent people against the terror troops of the radical right'.[19] The exact extent of the truth of *Stern*'s assessment was revealed in February 1993 when, following exposure of a police 'deal' with the neo-Nazi rioters in Rostock and the resulting cover-up, Kupfer was dismissed.

However, sympathy with the rioters went far beyond Rostock. A poll carried out by the respected and highly accurate Infas Institute eight days after the Rostock pogrom followed the same pattern as polls taken after Hoyerswerda.

Despite, or possibly because of, the Rostock pogrom, Fascists would have won 19 per cent of the vote in Western Germany and 12 per cent of the vote in Eastern Germany if an election had been held on 30 August 1992. In the West, 24 per cent of young people aged 18–25 would have voted for 'a party to the Right of the CDU/CSU', according to Infas.[20]

A further Infas survey broadcast on ARD TV on 12 September 1992 showed that 26 per cent considered the slogan 'Foreigners out' wholly or largely justified, that 37 per cent agreed that 'Germans should defend themselves in their own country against foreigners' and that 51 per cent supported the slogan 'Germany for the Germans'.[21]

Though support for these slogans receded after the shock of Mölln, failure of the changes to Article 16 and worsening economic circumstances will probably deepen rightist support within the population. This is foreshadowed by Infas's finding in the same study that amongst the jobless 30 per cent would vote extreme-right in Western Germany compared with 19 per cent in the five new eastern states.

Generally, polls, when they provide East–West readings, shatter the myth, widespread in the international media, that the East is the focal point of a right-extremist trend which does not touch the West. This myth does not stand up to scrutiny. Whichever set of indicators one selects – voting patterns, voting intentions, attitude formation, existing prejudices – the rightist tendency is markedly stronger in the West than in the East.

Anti-Semitic prejudices, for instance, are much more pronounced in Western Germany than in the east. A survey published by the Emnid Institute in Spring of 1992 indicated that 16 per cent of the West Germans admitted to being anti-Jewish, as opposed to 4 per cent in the former GDR.

The same is true of the violence. According to the *Bundeskriminalamt* (State Police), 74.9 per cent of racist attacks in the first nine months of 1992 occurred in the former Federal Republic as compared with 25.1 per cent in the former GDR. Although, of course, one must also measure the attacks in their ratio to the size of population and the number of foreigners – which indicates a higher *intensity* of violence in the East – the fact remains that there is far more of it in the West.

Empirical evidence from court cases involving rightist terror also challenges another keenly-held media myth: that the perpetrators of violence are largely unemployed and socially disorientated youth from unstable family backgrounds with no connection to rightist groups or politics.

Quite the contrary. In the overwhelming majority of cases surveyed by this author, the opposite facts emerge. Young, the practitioners of violence certainly are. Unemployed and from 'bad' family backgrounds, they certainly are not. And, in the majority of cases, police evidence discloses possession of racist or fascist literature, flags and other paraphernalia.

The main, and perhaps most frighteningly long-term, impact of the wave of violence has been to show that it 'works'. The anti-foreigner terror in Hoyerswerda and Rostock was emulated in Wismar and Quedlinburg with similar results: Government surrender and evacuation of refugees, leaving so-called 'foreigner-free cities'.

And so the violence swept on. Until Mölln. Then, because the fire-bombers bawled *'Heil Hitler'* in a telephone call made to announce their crime Federal State Prosecutor, Alexander von Stahl, declared this to be a threat to 'restore a Nazi dictatorship in Germany'. After two years of relative inactivity, the State and sections of the population, independently of each other and for different motives, decided something had to be done about Nazi terror.

The Government's dramatic lurch into action with the declaration of bans was, of course, not purely altruistic but intimately connected with the fact that it now had what it wanted from the SPD: an agreement to accept changes to Article 16.

Powerful reactions from such diverse sources as the US State Department, the Russian government, the Israeli and European parliaments and internationally respected human rights organisations like Helsinki Watch, put enormous international pressure on the German government. Combined with popular mass revulsion in Germany, it was this, rather than the belated actions of Kohl and his Interior Minister, Rudolf Seiters, which forced the extreme-Right into temporary retreat at the end of an extremely violent 1992.

Across Germany, there were massive candle-lit demonstrations, torchlight vigils and other actions involving hundreds of thousands of people in Berlin, Munich, Hamburg and scores of other cities, towns and villages in protest at the Mölln atrocity and against 'hatred and violence'.

However, despite these positive – if overdue – actions, the portents for 1993 are not good. This was forcefully brought home in the local elections in the state of Hesse on 7 March when the fascist REP took 8.3 per cent of the vote at state level and, in Frankfurt, together with the NPD and the DVU, won more than 13 per cent of the vote.

The REP's share in Frankfurt was 9.3 per cent, but they won as much as 33 per cent in parts of some working-class districts like Sossenheim and now have ten seats in the city parliament. Elsewhere in Hesse, the REP scored double-figure returns in Giessen (10.4 per cent), Wiesbaden (13.9 per cent), Hanau (14.0 per cent) and Offenbach (15.1 per cent) and registered altogether 245 344 votes.

The so-called *Rechtsrück* (jolt back to the right) now runs very deep and is clearly part of the new German political tapestry. As Hamburg *Verfassungsschutz* President, Ernst Uhrlau, stated in an interview with *Der Spiegel*:

> The themes of the 1990s will be right-wing extremism, xenophobia, nationalism and self-absorption. The violence is increasing constantly . . . More than 20 per cent of the younger generation sympathises with the right-wing parties. Once they have established themselves, they will change society, although with the opposite goals, more significantly than the leftists of 1968 ever hoped.[22]

Not a comforting prospect. Least of all in a Germany, which has so far escaped the worst effects of the world recession but which cannot do so indefinitely. At the turn of 1992, unemployment rose by 325 000 to a national figure of 3.45 million. To be added to these figures are 2.1 million on job-creation schemes and 857 000 on short-time working: 6.4 million in all. Zero growth in the economy is predicted for 1993 and contraction thereafter. Rising unemployment is forecast. With a mass basis for Fascism already at the beginning of formation, the consequences of economic crisis piling on top of political and social crisis could be incalculable.

NOTES

1. *Die Welt*, 10 December 1992.
2. *Neues Deutschland*, 21 December 1992.
3. *Allgemeine Judische Wochenzeitung*, 17 December 1992.
4. *Antifa Info-Blatt* no 21 (19 February 1993).
5. Inquiry into Racism and Xenophobia in Europe, *European Parliament Report* (1991) p. 10.
6. *Searchlight Magazine*, March 1990.
7. *Der Spiegel*, 15 January 1990.
8. *Der Spiegel*, 18 May 1990.
9. *Der Spiegel*, 2 July 1990.
10. *Time*, 25 June 1990.
11. *Statistisches Bundesamt*, quoted in *Stern* no 38, 1992.
12. *Der Spiegel*, 9 September 1991.
13. Originally in *Stern*. Quoted in *Searchlight*, January 1992.
14. *Die tagefzeitung*, 2 October 1991.
15. *Die tagefzeitung*, 24 September 1991.
16. *Frankfurter Rundschau*, 25 November 1991.

17. Originally in *Der Spiegel.* Quoted in *Searchlight,* January 1992.
18. *Deutsche Presse Agentur* (German Press Agency), 23 January 1993.
19. *Stern,* no 37, 1992.
20. *Searchlight,* October 1992.
21. *ARD TV,* 12 September 1992.
22. *Der Spiegel,* 14 September 1992.

12 The Police and Racist Violence in Britain

Paul Gordon

Racist violence[1] was a phenomenon of the life of black[2] people in Britain long before the police – or any other official agency recognised it as such. The riots which occurred in various seaports after the end of the First World War were probably the first in a century-long history of such violence. Black people, usually seamen and their families, were attacked in London, Liverpool, Cardiff and Glasgow. In Liverpool, racist violence was to claim its first fatality when Charles Wooton was chased to the docks where he drowned trying to escape his attackers. The government's response to the attacks was to encourage black seamen to return to their countries of origin by offering them cheap berths on ships. In the 1930s, there were attacks on Arab seamen in Tyneside and after the Second World War there were further attacks on black people in London and elsewhere. Such semi-orchestrated violence culminated in the 1958 Notting Hill riots when hundreds of white people attacked black people on the streets and in their homes over a period of days.

Throughout the 1960s and 1970s too there were numerous reports of attacks on black people, both Afro-Caribbeans and Asians, and their property. During this period, thirty black people lost their lives in what appeared to be racist attacks. There were numerous delegations to parliament and the Prime Minister's residence in Downing Street and repeated calls for concerted action by government and the police. But none was forthcoming.

Accounts of racist violence published in these years invariably criticised the police for their failures to respond effectively. An early report had criticised police failure to protect black people at the same time as accusing the police of themselves attacking and harassing them (Hunte, 1965), while a study by the Runnymede Trust of one town found that the police took racist attacks seriously only when black people started taking action to defend themselves (Jenkins and Randall, 1970). At the other end of the decade, two important reports

167

gave eloquent voice to the situation. Bethnal Green and Stepney Trades Council (1978) reported in *Blood On the Streets* that East London Bengalis had little confidence in the police, considering them to be either uninterested in attacks on them or even biased against them. The following year, the Institute of Race Relations in its evidence to the Royal Commission on Criminal Procedure cited a number of cases of police refusal to take action against alleged offenders even where there were witnesses or other evidence, of failure to provide adequate protection to black people, of refusal to recognise the racist element in incidents, and of hostility to victims of attack. This latter included cases where it was the victims of racist attack who were arrested (Institute of Race Relations, 1979). The literature from this period showed a remarkable degree of consensus about the failings of the police, generally highlighting inactivity in the face of racist violence, a slowness to respond to incidents, a refusal or failure to recognise or accept a racial motivation (or the possibility of one) and hostility to those complaining (Klug, 1982).

It was not until 1981, however, that racist violence was recognised as a problem by the government. That year was an undoubted watershed in British 'race relations' with riots in numerous cities and towns throughout the country, many of them fuelled by long-running tensions between the police and young black people and often sparked off by particular instances of racist policing. This resulted in the creation of a Home Office working party to look at the matter and the publication of its report a few months later. There were, it would seem, a number of reasons for the setting-up of the Home Office inquiry.

First, the situation had become very serious indeed. Six people had died as a result of racist violence in 1980 and the situation appeared to be worsening every day. A fire in New Cross, South London, at the start of 1981 claimed the lives of thirteen young black people. Although this was never officially acknowledged as arson the tragedy was widely viewed among black people as being at the very least an incident having a possible racist motivation.

Second, in the face of police failure to defend them, black people had increasingly turned to self-defence measures. Street patrols were set up in various areas of the country. In the summer of 1978, Bengali workers had staged a one-day strike against racist violence in East London and hundreds had sat down in Brick Lane in protest at the police arrest of anti-racists. And in 1979, the mass demonstration against a fascist meeting in Southall was a statement by the local community that it would not be intimidated by racists. Such actions were presumably seen by those in power as a threat to public order.

Third, the inquiry was set up following a report by the Joint Committee Against Racialism on which all the main political parties were represented (Joint Committee Against Racialism, 1980). Although this said little that was new, the JCAR report was important in that it indicated the extent of concern that existed in all the main political parties as well as church groups. Racist violence, it seemed, was no longer a marginal issue that could be ignored.

The Home Office report, *Racial Attacks*, published in November 1981, asserted, against all the evidence that had been published over the years, that the government's failure to appreciate the seriousness of the problem had been largely due to a lack of reliable information about it. Nevertheless, the report accepted that racially motivated violence was a serious and probably worsening problem and estimated that about 7000 incidents would be reported to the police in England and Wales in a year. As far as the police were concerned, in contrast to virtually every report on the subject previously published, the Home Office report claimed that they had not underestimated the seriousness of the problem and dismissed allegations about the failures of the police. Indeed, the report found 'a considerable degree of overall agreement' between victims and police as to whether or not incidents were racially motivated. This conclusion was not, however, supported by those victims of racist attacks who were interviewed by the authors of the study and they also conflicted with the report's remarks elsewhere that the police tended to 'underestimate the significance of racialist incidents and activities for those attacked or threatened'.

But the Home Office report appeared to have little impact on the police at operational or policy level. One year after the publication of the report, a survey by the Runnymede Trust of those forces which had participated in the Home Office study concluded that such forces had not yet shown that they fully understood the significance and seriousness of the problem. Criticism of police handling of racist incidents was still widespread, it said (Runnymede Trust, 1982). Even more telling, during the trial in 1982 of twelve youths in Bradford, accused of conspiracy after they had made petrol bombs which they claimed were for the purposes of self-defence, police officers involved in the case claimed never to have heard of the Home Office report even though their force was one of those which had taken part in the study.

REDEFINING THE PROBLEM

Although the 1981 Home Office report was widely welcomed as a long-overdue official recognition of the problem of racist attacks, it was less widely noticed that it involved a redefinition of the problem. It was not about racist attacks as such – that is, attacks motivated in some way and to some extent by racism. Rather it was about *interracial* incidents or attacks and was thus equally concerned with attacks on white people either by Afro-Caribbeans or Asians as it was with racist attacks properly speaking. Hence the comparison it drew when it said that Asians and Afro-Caribbeans were between fifty and sixty times more likely than white people to be victims of racial attack. This comparison stated quite clearly that whites could be the victim of racial attack (Home Office, 1981). In this, the Home Office inquiry was following police thinking and practice. Since 1978, the Metropolitan Police had been recording as 'racial incidents' not just incidents where there appeared to be some racist motivation, but those involving 'concerted action by or against members of an ethnic group'. Thus to the police, a 'racial incident' could equally be a racist attack on a black person or a robbery of a white person by a group of black youths. The Home Office, therefore, following the police, refused to recognise the existence of racism and the specificity of racist attacks. It chose instead to follow popular 'common sense' racist ideas which equate attacks on black people with ordinary criminal attacks on white people where the attacker was thought to be black.

The definition now used by police forces, although modified, still permits the classification of attacks on whites as racist in that it requires officers to submit reports on all incidents which are alleged to involve a racial motive or which appear to the reporting officer to include such a motive. Although this definition was presented as recognising the importance of the victim's perception of the offender's motivation, its effect has been to allow for the recording of incidents involving black assailants and white victims as 'racial incidents' in the same way as racist attacks. Leicestershire Police, for instance, recorded seventy such cases in 1990, while the Metropolitan Police recorded 439. But in no meaningful sense can such incidents be regarded as *racist*.

Black people may attack whites for a whole number of reasons – greed, anger, frustration, envy – but racism is not among them, not if by racism we understand hostility towards people because of their skin colour, or ethnic or national origins, in the context of a *system* of unequal power relations. While black and white people may have equal power as individuals, black people as a group in Britain lack the social, economic and political power of the white majority who are not only considerably greater numerically, but have the power also to define and determine the situation of others. So, as far as the police figures go, either a great many white people claim to be the victims of racial attack – although they appear to be doing this only in some areas – or the police are redefining the problem. Either way, the specificity of racist attacks is lost. By a sleight of hand, therefore, racist attacks have become just an aspect of interracial crime to be found, indeed to be expected, in any multiracial society. The racism that informs and underlies such attacks is thereby denied.[3]

A further problem in the police response lies in the way that police forces have conceptualised the issue. The police response is essentially based on the idea that racist violence consists of specific and discrete incidents. Yet, as a growing literature shows, racist harassment is in reality a *process* of repeated attacks. As Bowling describes it, it is a dynamic series of events, a process both in the sense that it involves several 'incidents' and in the sense that it has a social, political and historical context (Bowling, 1990). Such a view is supported by a detailed study of one East London borough which argued that racist harassment consisted of 'connected crimes with discernible social and spatial contours' (Hesse *et al.*, 1992) and by research from within the Home Office itself which found, in relation to one housing estate, a clear pattern of repeat victimisation of a small number of families and a significant degree of spatial concentration of attacks (Sampson and Phillips, 1992). A police response based on an idea of responding to incidents and which refuses to recognise the spatial patterning of attacks is ill-equipped to tackle the problem effectively.

THE CRIMINALISATION OF SELF-DEFENCE

Faced with the inability or unwillingness of the police to attend to the problem of racist violence, black people have, on numerous occasions, been forced to defend themselves against attack. In the 1960s it was reported that the police in one area only began to take the problem seriously when there were reports of Asian families buying guns to protect themselves (Jenkins and Randall, 1970). In the 1970s, numerous defence committees were set up, involving practical defence activities such as street patrols as well as symbolic protests. But while the right to defend oneself is recognised in law, it has been denied in practice by the police. In the 1977 case of the Virk brothers, four Asian brothers who defended themselves against an attack while they were repairing their car in East London were arrested while their attackers went free. They received heavy prison sentences. Although some of the sentences were reduced on appeal, their convictions were not reversed. While the right to self-defence was confirmed by a multiracial jury in the 1982 trial of the 'Bradford twelve' – twelve young Asian men who faced serious criminal charges after they had made petrol bombs to defend the Asian community from an attack they believed to be imminent – this was in the face of police attempts to criminalise those involved. As indicated above, the police in this case revealed considerable ignorance about the nature and extent of racist violence in the area. The following year police arrested a group of eight Asian men in East London who had formed a self-defence group following a series of attacks on Asian school pupils.

In these and other cases, the police acted in such a way as to deny not only that there was a right to defend oneself against attack but that self-defence was a necessity. So, too, have police officers from time to time attacked defence campaigns and police monitoring groups which have tried to assist victims of racist violence and to highlight the general issue. In 1983, when three such groups published a dossier of attacks in East London and criticised police inaction, the Metropolitan Police Commissioner criticised the involvement of what he called 'third-party organisations – often motivated by political activism'. Some years later he said that the sole purpose of such monitoring groups seemed 'to be to call for every possible adverse comment they can make about police activities . . . They project an atmosphere of misrepresentation, tendentiousness and distortion' (*Today*, 11 March 1986). In other words, those who were concerned about racist violence and who were, moreover, prepared to do something about it were, as far as the police were concerned, part of the problem.

PROGRESS OR DIVERSION?

Five years after the 1981 Home Office report, the parliamentary Home Affairs Committee concluded that the police had still not made racist attacks a priority and it recommended that they do so. The report described the incidence of racial attacks as 'the most shameful and dispiriting aspect' of race relations in Britain and spoke of the 'fear and blighted lives' to which they gave rise. It said also that where there was sufficient evidence, the police should also prosecute for the offence of common assault where there was evidence of racial motivation. They should not leave it, as they had been doing, to victims to take out their own private prosecutions. The committee also recommended that the police be given special training in the handling of racist violence. All this suggested that the police, five years after the first Home Office inquiry, were still not taking the action necessary to deal with the problem. But the Home Affairs Committee went on to argue that racist violence could only be effectively tackled through a 'multi-agency approach' – that is, one which coordinated the efforts of all the different agencies having an interest in the matter, including the police, local authorities, community relations councils and ethnic minority organisations (Home Affairs Committee, 1986). In its formal response, the government announced that a working party had been set up to develop such a multi-agency approach and to help to coordinate the work of local agencies (Home Department, 1986).

The Metropolitan Police launched a high-profile campaign against racist violence in January 1987 in the boroughs of Ealing and Newham, both areas with substantial ethnic minority populations and significant recorded levels of racist violence. This campaign involved the distribution of 100 000 copies of a 16-page 'action guide', together with leaflets in ethnic minority languages, advising victims of racist violence on the course of action to take. The guide promised that such attacks would be given a high priority by the police. Two years later, the campaign was extended, at a cost of £400 000, to cover nineteen London boroughs and again an 'action guide' and ethnic minority language leaflets were distributed to residents. Police stations also displayed posters stating that 'Racial violence is a crime'. In the West Midlands, police set up a telephone 'helpline' for victims of racist attacks, which gave advice and allowed callers to leave a message if they did not wish to visit a police station. In West Yorkshire, a helpline was set up, staffed by officers who spoke Asian languages; and police also distributed information cards describing the action to be taken when reporting an incident to the police.

The problem with such efforts is that they are primarily concerned with giving advice, explaining the role of the police and countering criticisms of the police. They are not directed at effective action against those responsible for attacks. Nor do they address the problem of police ineffectiveness (Hesse *et al.*, 1992). The London Borough of Newham criticised the police effort in its area as a failure on the grounds that it was employed as a vehicle for police objectives and not for addressing the needs of local people' (quoted in Hesse *et al.*, 1992).

By 1989, all police forces, it was claimed, had defined procedures for recording and monitoring racial incidents but the Home Affairs Committee, while welcoming the action which had been taken, described the police response to its 1986 report as 'unsatisfactory'. It recommended that police forces develop methods of encouraging people to report racial attacks and establish procedures for the proper scrutiny of all racial incident reports and for their proper investigation. The Committee also emphasised the need for greater recruitment of police officers from ethnic minorities, recommending that all police forces adopt equal opportunities policies (Home Affairs Committee, 1989).

It is extremely difficult to judge the extent to which the policing of racist violence has changed, beyond the better recording of incidents.[4] Public discussion of the subject has undoubtedly made some individual officers more aware of the problem and more sensitive to victims and potential victims. In some areas and some cases, this has been reflected in an improved police responsiveness. At the same time, criticisms of the police continue. In Newham, East London, for instance, the creation of a specialist police racial harassment squad has been criticised by the local Newham Monitoring Project, set up to monitor racist violence and the police response, as absolving other officers from any responsibility for the problem. In other areas, initiatives such as telephone helplines and information cards have been criticised as cosmetic and leading only to the reporting of more incidents and not to improved policing.

Particularly since the 1986 Home Affairs Committee report, the 'multi-agency' approach to racial violence has come to be seen by many, including those in the police service, as *the* answer to the problem. An interdepartmental working group report published in 1989 came out fully in favour of a multi-agency approach, arguing that no one agency could provide a total response to what was sometimes a 'complex social problem'. While individual agencies should take unilateral action, a multi-agency approach which brought together the police, education authorities, housing and social services departments and voluntary and community bodies would be more effective (Interdepartmental Racial Attacks Group, 1989). The multi-agency approach is dealt with in more detail in the Chapter 16 by Bowling and Saulsbury. Here, it should be noted that while concerted action by concerned agencies is surely necessary, the multi-agency approach can also be used by individual agencies to absolve themselves of their own responsibilties, a point made in the Racial Attacks Group report itself. There is as yet too little evidence of how such cooperation works – or does not work in practice, but there are fears that some police enthusiasm for this approach may derive from a wish to shed what has become too much of a problem.

POLICE RACISM

The policing of racial violence has to be considered in the context of police dealings with black people generally and, specifically, in the context of a history of police racism. Thus, in its evidence to the Royal Commission on Criminal Procedure in the late 1970s, the Institute of Race Relations viewed the failure of the police to respond adequately to racial violence as the other side of the coin of police abuse of black people. This history of police racism, which stretches back to the early years of this century, is one in which the police have consistently viewed black people as a social problem and as being inherently criminal. There is not space to rehearse this history here. Readers are referred to the voluminous literature (e.g. Hall *et al.*, 1978; Gordon, 1983; Smith and Gray, 1983; Institute of Race Relations, 1987; Cashmore and McLaughlin, 1991) all of which testifies to widespread and endemic abuse of police power in relation to black people, whether as individuals or communities.

This abuse has taken a number of forms. Individual black people have been subjected to racist abuse, assault, unjustified stop-and-search, and arrest and prosecution for crimes they have not committed. Areas with significant black populations have been subjected to special policing measures involving the targeting of specific locations and the use of heavy-handed tactics, including armed raids on homes and clubs. And, of course, attempts are made all the time to link black people to crime: at various times this, it has been asserted, has been a matter of illegal drinking, gambling, prostitution, illegal immigration, drug-taking and drug-trafficking and street crime ('mugging'). Research has shown the extent to which racism and racial prejudice are embedded in the 'canteen culture' of the police and how the acting out of racism is inadequately dealt with by existing disciplinary or other measures (Smith and Gray, 1983).

One particular case may provide an illustration of police attitudes and behaviour. In October 1992, Trinidad-born Frank Crichlow was awarded £50 000 by the Metropolitan Police in settlement of an action for false imprisonment, assault and malicious prosecution. Mr Crichlow was arrested in 1988 in a police raid on his 'Mangrove' restaurant, in London's Notting Hill area. He claimed that he was kept face-down on the ground for 20 minutes with two police officers sitting on his back. He was charged with possession of heroin and cannabis with intent to supply, and with permitting the supply of heroin, cannabis and other drugs. Mr Crichlow was held in prison for five weeks and when granted bail was not allowed within 500 yards of his restaurant. He was acquitted the following year of all charges, despite evidence against him from thirty-six police officers. He then began his claim for damages against the police.

Mr Crichlow had, his counsel said, 'been wrongfully and unlawfully arrested and detained at a police station, assaulted and injured in the course of the arrest and charged and prosecuted in relation to criminal offences, of which he was innocent, on the basis of evidence fabricated by the arresting officers'. The police were sued for damages and aggravated damages to compensate Mr Crichlow for 'the anxiety, distress and humiliation caused by his degrading treatment, and exemplary damages to reflect the arbitrary and unconstitutional nature of the police conduct'. In making the settlement and in paying his costs, the Metropolitan Police denied the allegations and refused to offer an apology (*Daily Telegraph*, 13 October 1992).

This was far from being an isolated incident, an understandable if unfortunate mistake by the police. Frank Crichlow was no stranger to the police for he has been arrested over fifty times since he first set up a coffee bar in the Notting Hill area in the 1950s when he arrived in Britain from Trinidad. The 'Mangrove', a restaurant-cum-community-centre, quickly became the focus for police–black tensions. It was first raided in 1969 by police looking for drugs but none were found. After a demonstration against police harassment in 1970, nine people (including Frank Crichlow) were arrested and charged with serious public-order offences. But after a ten-week trial in 1972, all were acquitted of riot charges and only two convicted of affray for which they received suspended sentences. The 'Mangrove' was to be 'visited' by police more than forty times between 1972 and 1977 (Gordon, 1983).

Police behaviour towards Frank Crichlow and the 'Mangrove' is emblematic of police attitudes and behaviour towards the black people of the Notting Hill area generally which, in many ways, can be seen as a microcosm of the black experience in Britain. All the alleged abuses of black people by the police can be found here, from the harassment of people on the streets through the misuse of stop-and-search powers to attacks on the social and cultural life of black people as exemplified in police hostility to, and overpolicing of, the annual Notting Hill Carnival, the largest cultural manifestation in Europe.

The experience of Frank Crichlow and the 'Mangrove' and the black community in Notting Hill encapsulates the experience of many black people and of places used by them. It illustrates the sustained attempt by the police to criminalise black people, using all the powers at their disposal, accompanied by unlawful violence. It also illustrates that police racism is not a matter of a few individual officers but rather of police practice and police culture. While the most recent assault on Frank Crichlow may have been carried out by a few officers, it should be noted that the police *as an institution* not only failed to apologise to Crichlow but continued to deny his allegations and have, at the time of writing, taken no action against the officers involved. The police, as an institution, have viewed black people, whether Asian or Afro-Caribbean, as a people apart, undeserving of even the minimal protection granted to others and constituting a major policing problem in their own right by virtue of their presence in this country.

THE LIMITS OF POLICING

Critics of the police (including the author) have pointed to the failures and deficiencies of the police in dealing with racist violence and demanded better police responses. But the problem of racist violence raises the question of what can be expected even from a reformed and enlightened police. There is no question that the police can and should devote more resources to the investigation of racist crimes and should better understand the significance of such crimes – including those which seen in isolation may be thought of as 'minor' – to those affected. Black people are entitled to the same degree of protection and vigilance as others and crimes against them merit the same application of police investigative powers as would other serious offences. The nature of racist violence should also lead to a reappraisal of policing methods and a shift away from a focus on *incidents* to an understanding of violence and harassment as a *process*.

Yet policing can never be the sole answer to the problem of racist violence, any more than it can be the sole answer to most other forms of violence. This is not, it should be emphasised to avoid misunderstanding, to absolve the police of any responsibility. It is to argue that the problem of racist violence is embedded in a racist culture and can only, ultimately, be addressed by addressing that culture. A society that wishes to deal effectively with racist violence must face the uncomfortable and inconvenient fact that such violence, while a serious problem in and of itself, is also a manifestation of something larger: it is an expression of racism, in particular of white exclusionism or territorialism. If it is serious about wanting to do something about it, rather than mere remedial work, then it must address that racism. In Britain, this is the racism that for more than three decades has defined black people as a problem for white society, whose entry must be controlled. Time and again it has expressed its concern, in the clichés of the racist imagination, at possible 'swamping', 'flooding' and 'invasion' by Third World immigrants. Racist violence, on the streets, in the housing estates, at work and in schools and colleges, is the everyday expression – and consequence – of this policy of white exclusionism.

NOTES

1. I use the word 'racial' (rather than racist) when this is the word used by the agencies being discussed and I use 'racist' when speaking for myself.
2. I use the word 'black' to include people of both Asian and Afro-Caribbean origins.
3. The problem is compounded in that many of us have used the term *racial* when we really mean *racist*.
4. In 1988, British police forces recorded 4682 incidents; in 1990, 7095 and in 1991, 7882 (England and Wales only). For details, including figures by individual police force for 1988–90, see Gordon, 1992. No other national figures are available.

13 Double Standard: The Turkish State and Racist Violence

Yücel Yeşilgöz

In present-day societies, racism and racist violence appear on the public agenda with increasing frequency. In the past, Europeans associated these terms with victim groups such as Jews and gypsies. Today, as a result of labour migration in Western Europe, other groups such as Turks and North Africans are added to this list, in addition to refugees. In some countries, the Turkish population is among the groups under racist attack. The environment in Europe is not sufficiently safe to allow Turks and other minorities to live a quiet life without worrying about racist attacks.

What does it mean to be 'a potential target' and 'to live with fear'? What do the people living with these feelings understand about the racism that threatens them? Do they oppose racism as an ideology or are they 'anti-racist' because it threatens them? What does Turkey as a country, whose citizens abroad live with these feelings, understand about racism? Individual members of groups which are the potential victims of racist violence, are often by definition perceived as being anti-racist themselves. Many times racism places groups of people in a hierarchy based on skin colour, religion, and cultural, national or ethnic origin. Racist violence is inflicted on those groups who find themselves in the 'lowest' ranks of this hierarchy. However, this does not necessarily mean that these victims of racist violence cannot themselves advocate racist beliefs and ideologies. This should not be taken as a matter of 'blaming the victim'. Racist violence should always be combated as such, regardless of the person on whom it is inflicted. And it should be fought wherever it occurs, if necessary, within the very groups who are victimised by racist violence.

This chapter deals with the Turkish state, and with the Turkish people who live all over Europe. Two questions are considered: on the one hand, how do the Turkish people respond to, and what is their role in violence directed against minorities within Turkey itself and abroad?

179

And on the other hand, what is their response to violence against Turkish minorities in the countries of Western Europe?

First, a few remarks are needed about the ideological structure of the Turkish state without which Turkish policy and behaviour cannot be properly understood. Second, an explanation is given of the Turkish influence on the everyday life of Turkish people living abroad. Third, examples of the response to the violence against Turkish minorities in Europe that appeared in the Turkish press and were published all over Europe are presented.

KEMALISM: THE IDEOLOGICAL STRUCTURE OF THE TURKISH STATE

> No idea can be upheld against the interests of the Turkish nation, the foundation of the indivisibility of the Turkish existence with its state, its country, its history and moral values, Atatürk's nationalism [Kemalism], principles, revolutions and civilisation.

This statement is from a section of the Constitution of the Turkish republic, which was ratified in 1982. It not only proves that Kemalism still prevails in Turkey, but also means that Turkish law will not accept any idea that is in conflict with the interests of the Turkish nation and Turkish nationalism.

Kemalism, presented in Turkey as an ideology, is named after Mustafa Kemal (1881–1938), founder of the Turkish Republic. In 1923, Kemal declared republican rule over the countries remaining of the Ottoman Empire in 1923. Up to the time of his death, he continued to assume total control of Turkey's destiny. In Turkish history, this period of time is known as the 'one-party period' or the 'one-party dictatorship'. Kemal, later named Atatürk ('father of the Turks') and 'Chief for Eternity', launched a series of reforms concerning a great variety of matters, ranging from clothing to the alphabet. In these reforms, Western norms were adapted to Turkish conditions. At the same time, he began activities to create a state based on 'being Turkish'.

Since the turn of the century, there has been evidence of attempts to create a state structure based on 'being Turkish'. An organisation, first known as the 'Young Turks', and later called the 'Committee of Union and Progress', was actively committed to this issue. The main goal of this Committee was to prevent the division of the Ottoman Empire. This Committee was represented in the main administration of this Empire after the announcement of the Constitutional Government in 1908. This continued until 1918 (see Tunaya, 1984, and Haniôlu, 1985). The national and cultural requirements of non-Turkish elements, which were unknown because of previous oppression, began to surface after the Constitutional government was formed. 'Union and Progress' governed according to a dual policy. It oppressed non-Muslim elements and tried to make all Muslim groups Turkish. Albania, Macedonia and Yemen took their share of this oppression, which was aimed against nationalist movements. In 1915, this period drew to a close with the holocaust of 1.5 million Armenians. Although there was a Kurdish group among the founders of this Committee, they were unable to prevent these policies developing towards Turkish nationalism based ultimately on notions such as 'Turan' – the idea of realising the 'Great Turkish Empire' in the place of the Ottoman Empire.[1] The Kurds were deported to different parts of the country under the Deportation Law of 27 May 1915 (Beşikçi, 1977).

The founders of the Republic (1923) were part of this Committee. Of course, these ideas were developed by the 'Union and Progress'. But during the years that followed, Kemal made a definitive distinction between the unionists and himself. During the 1930s, in particular, he began efforts to create a new Turkish nationalist ideology. From that time onward, there was no 'race' in Turkey other than the Turkish 'race', and no language was allowed but Turkish.

There were 'One Party', 'One Nation', and 'One Leader' in the country. Ideological theories were formulated in the magazine, *Kadro*, first published in 1932, and banned by M. Kemal in 1935. The main goal was the creation of a 'coalescence nation without classes or privileges'.[2]

The famous Turkish sociologist, Ismail Beşikçi, observed that Mussolini's ideas were very influential in determining this ideology, and established that there were significant parallels to be drawn (Beşikçi, 1990).

In the same period, M. Kemal ordered that scientific conferences be held. At one of these conferences, a theory (the 'Son-Language Theory') was accepted following 'scientific' discussions. According to this theory the Turkish language was 'the mother of all languages'. The 'Turkish history thesis' was accepted at another conference. According to this theory 'the superior Turkish race' was the 'mother of all civilisations and races' (Beşikçi, 1977).

The Turkish Janissary Corps (*Türk Ocaklari*) was responsible for the organisation of these conferences. In one of his speeches at a ceremony on 23 April 1930, the President of the Turkish Janissary Corps, Abdullah Suphi Tanriover, made the following statement establishing the parallel between Fascism in Italy and the developments in Turkey:

> A form of nationalism, also known as Fascism, has appeared in Italy after a very difficult struggle. We see some of our own political and social ideas as being similar to aspects of this movement. Fascism concerns economic, political and social harmony based on the ideal of the 'motherland'. Like the Fascist youth, nationalist Turkish youth will also take up arms and will defend the Turkish revolution against anything that threatens it. We see both our past and our future in the enthusiasm of Fascism.[3]

While this ideology was created within Turkey, friends and enemies were also identified according to *Türk'ün Türk'ten başka dostu yoktur* (The only friends of Turks are Turks). Internal enemies were identified as communists, socialists, Muslim fundamentalists, Kurds and other ethnic minorities such as Armenians, Lazes, Greeks and Suryanis.[4] Attacks were launched against these groups. Anybody who opposed these ideas was immediately removed. As a result of the assimilation policy, anybody who did not speak Turkish was punished. *Bir Türk dünyaya bedeldir* (One Turk is worth all the world) and *Ne mutlu Türk'üm diyene* (What a happiness to say that I am Turkish) became the slogans of the day.

After the death of M. Kemal in 1938, his colleague and close friend, Ismet Inonu, succeeded him. During the Party Congress on 26 December 1938 he was given the title of 'National Chief' and was proclaimed the irreplaceable leader of the Party. It was decided that Kemalism would continue to be the country's sole ideology.

Although Turkey had a non-biased policy during the Second World War, the government interned people who were close to the Hitler regime. Many people, most of whom were scientists fleeing the regime in Germany, were accepted as refugees in Turkey. However, according to documents which were discovered recently, some people, including Turkish citizens, were handed over to the Nazis and killed in Nazi concentration camps.[5] Representatives of the Hitler regime had organised their supporters, especially within the army. In December 1942, the German Ministry for Foreign Affairs sent 5 million German Gold Marks to their Ambassador in Ankara, Franz von Papen, for their 'Turkish friends'. In documents found later, Alparslan Türkeş is named as one of the people who had connections with the German Fascists (Soytemiz, 1988). Türkeş, also known as *Başbuğ* ('Führer'), frequently appears in the recent political history of Turkey. After the defeat of Germany, Türkeş and his friends were arrested and tried. Not because they had established relationships with Nazis, but because they had formed a 'Turanist' organisation in 1944. They were found not guilty by the Court in 1947 because 'an organisation, based on an idea which is not considered to be criminal, is not a crime either'.

In 1950 Turkey embarked on a multiparty regime. To this day, this regime is a multiparty regime that is peculiar to Turkey. The groups that had been identified as internal enemies during the 1930s, were not given the right of political organisation. All parties had to follow Atatürk's route. The Democratic Party, which had started as the opposition movement within the Republican People's Party, won the 1950 election with an outright victory. Their policy was 'to follow Atatürk's route' and to maintain close ties with the USA. On 27 May 1960, the government was overthrown by a military coup that was motivated by the assumption that the government no longer followed Atatürk's route. Prime Minister Adnan Menderes was executed. The coup was directed against the reactionary attitude of the government and was Kemalist and progressive. Its spokesman was Colonel Alparslan Türkeş, who had been a sympathiser of Hitler in the 1940s. Later, this man was to lead the extreme Right and his name was mentioned in relation to numerous murders committed by his organisation, known in the West as 'The Grey Wolves'.

The government of the Justice Party, formed to replace the Democratic Party, faced another military coup in 1971. The reason for this coup was again the assumption that the Republic had moved away from Atatürk's route and that the Muslim fundamentalists, leftist and Kurdish movements were gaining power. They had already been identified as 'enemy forces' during the 1930s and were seen to threaten Turkish democracy.

The last military coup occurred on 12 September 1980. The reason for army interference was again the assumed move away from 'Atatürk's route' and the increasing number of terrorist activities. The daily newspaper with the largest circulation, *Hürriyet*, announced that the new policy to be followed was a 'continuation of Atatürk's route'.

All movements and opinions have the right to be organised as a political party in Turkey. Yet, no party can be created which opposes the state's unity with its nation, its country, and secular republican principles, or which depends on classes (Constitution, para. 68). This means that the Constitution, which was ratified in 1981, still supports the notion of 'enemy forces' identified in 1930, such as communists, Muslim fundamentalists and Kurds. Any political party which opposes this law is prohibited. Although some parties, which did not follow official ideology, have existed in Turkish political history from time to time, they were all banned later on. So too, the Muslim fundamentalist National Regularity Party and the Turkish Workers Party which indicated in their programmes that they are nationalist, were banned after the 1971 coup although they had elected representatives in parliament. Again, the motivation was that they did not follow Kemalism. In 1992, the Socialist Party which mentioned the existence of the Kurds in Turkey, was banned by the *Anayasa Mahkemesi* (Constitutional Court) for this reason. Within the context of the right-wing and left-wing ideas that are allowed in Turkey, this automatically means: Kemalist right-wing and Kemalist left-wing parties. They all have to have one point in common – to be a better Kemalist. As a matter of fact, the present-day structure is like this. With one exception, all the parties in Parliament have stated in their programmes that they are 'nationalist'.

After the Republican People's Party, founded by Atatürk, was banned together with the other political parties by the 1980 military coup, the Social Democratic People's Party was created to replace it as a left-wing party which accepted as its tenets the six main principles, identified by M. Kemal in the 1930s. This party is currently led by Erdal Inönü, the son of the 'National Chief', Ismet Inönü. The *Halkin Emek Partisi* (People's Labour Party), which takes its place as a more left-wing party and which is outside the Kemalist context, is known as a pro-Kurdish party. The lawsuit to ban this party still continues at the Constitutional Court. The right-wing parties which continue to exist compete for the status of the 'most nationalist' party.

OFFICIAL UNDERSTANDING OF RACISM IN TURKEY

Turkey is one of the countries which signed the United Nations 'International Convention on the Elimination of All Forms of Racial Discrimination' (1965), but this has not been ratified by Parliament. The 'International Convention on the Suppression and Punishment of the Crime of Apartheid' (1973) has been neither signed nor ratified by the Turkish state. Yet racism is prohibited by Turkish law. But this does not include 'Turkish racism'. Minorities, who oppose this and identify themselves as non-Turkish, are actively being portrayed as racist, and there are various legal measures directed against these 'racists'. In the Constitution of the Turkish republic, the following phrase is mentioned thirty-three times: 'Anybody who opposes the indivisibility of the Turkish Republic with its nation and its country, will be deprived of their basic human rights and freedoms.' In addition to this, and according to the Turkish Criminal Law (para.125), the Anti-Terror Law (para.8) and a number of other laws, anyone who tries to divide the country, who says that there is more than one nation in Turkey, who acts on or organises on the basis of this matter, can be punished by various penalties, including imprisonment and execution.

It is also a crime to say 'Hurray to the Turkish–Kurdish brotherhood.' The Kurdish deputies who added this statement to their pledges at the opening ceremony of Parliament in November 1991 were first beaten and then taken to court for attempting to divide the country.

To have Turkish nationalism accepted by the people, all institutions, especially in the field of education, are held responsible for its propaganda. In elementary schools, all pupils have to rise when their teacher enters the classroom and have to respond to his 'Good Morning' with 'Thank You'. And then they have to recite a long text starting with the phrase 'I am Turkish, I am honourable, I work hard.' This text ends with 'I give my existence as a present to the Turkish existence.' This is not only the case in elementary schools, but also in High Schools. In all universities, academies and colleges Turkish Revolution History is a mandatory course. The objective of the main textbook is to explain Atatürk's revolutions. This book shows that these revolutions were based on nationalism and that they secured Turkey's place in the world (Eroğlu, 1974). Turkey's largest educational institution, Turkey's Teachers Association, campaigned to remove the chauvinistic elements from the educational system. After the 1980 coup, this Association was banned by the military court for 'conducting activities to divide Turkey' and its leaders were given sentences of up to 8 years imprisonment.

The slogans, which were identified in the 1930s are not only valid in schools, but are also widely accepted by the population. It is not difficult to activate the people. In order to 'help' themselves with their socio-economic problems, government officials have, on numerous occasions, manipulated the feelings of the people. In 1955, for example, the Cyprus problem was the most important 'national issue'. At the end of August a conference was arranged in London, with Greece and the United Kingdom – the other parties involved – to determine the status of Cyprus. Turkey planned an activity to demonstrate the sensitivity of this problem within the Turkish community. The newspaper, *Istanbul Express* (6 September 1955), published the news of the bombing of Atatürk's birthplace in Selanik, Greece. Student protests started the same day. It developed into a nationwide response and within two days, shops, cemeteries and churches belonging to Greeks were destroyed and properties were plundered. Police, who had initially supported the violence, had to use force to stop it once they realised that they could no longer control it. Martial law was announced in Istanbul. The government declared that the communists were responsible for the violence. Many people known to be leftist, were placed under police supervision. Later, it was discovered that the events had been planned by the National Intelligence Agency (MIT) and that the bomb had been planted by Oktay Engin, an MIT agent who, in 1992, was Governor of Nevsehir, a Turkish province.[6]

When we look at some of the recent attacks against the Kurds living on the west coast of Turkey, we see that the 'September 1955' violence is not an 'historical incident'. Especially at the funerals of soldiers who died in combat in Kurdistan, cities outside Kurdistan staged massive and violent anti-Kurd protests. This was not a nationwide, public response. Government officials organised these protests and still do.

Fethiye is a town on the west coast. Besides Turks, Kurds who have moved to the west live here. After a funeral in 1992, shops owned by Kurds were attacked. A newspaper journalist reported: 'Kurd hunt in Fethiye . . . The houses were identified, trucks full of people started to drive around shooting, houses were destroyed, people were forced to move . . .'[7] Human rights organisations, and the People's Labour Party organisation in Fethiye, claimed that the events had been organised by the Mayor (a Social Democrat) and other government officials.[8] 'Forty-five houses and shops belonging to Kurds were bombed and guns were fired in Alanya.'[9] Some measures were taken to force the Kurds to move from the west to the east. People were told that they would be punished if they rented houses or shops to Kurds, and that this was a decision that had been taken by the city councils in western Turkey.[10]

Various slogans were written in big letters, not only on visible places in the cities, but also in the high mountains surrounding the cities in Kurdistan – slogans such as: 'What a happiness to say that I am Turkish', 'One Turk is worth all the world', etc. Broadcasting or publishing the Kurdish language was prohibited, as was education in the Kurdish language.

Kemal's words: 'Peace in the country, peace in the world' are repeated continuously during official speeches. Yet it is generally believed that each internal enemy is supported by outsiders. Efforts to seek out this external support depend on the position of the people or groups involved within the Kemalist context, and on the attributes of the enemies. According to left-wing Kemalists, the Kurds are a problem created by Western imperialists. Muslim fundamentalism is a problem that was exported to Turkey by the reactionary Arab countries and, more recently, by Iran. According to right-wing Kemalists, Turkey is opposing a world that is against the development of Turks and Muslims and that wants Turkey to become a communist country. Both groups are governed by one feeling: 'Turks do not have any friends but Turks themselves.' The whole world is afraid of the Turks and their development. In addition to this, Turkey is surrounded by enemies. According to the Turkish press, Western European anti-racists are called 'Friends of Turkey', and racists are 'People who see Turks as their enemies'. The 'Atatürk Peace Award', which has been awarded since 1984, was awarded to Nelson Mandela in 1992 for being anti-racist and a hero. When he refused the award because of the oppression of the Kurds, he was called 'an insolent African', 'an ugly African' and 'the terrorist Mandela'.[11]

'Turan' is still a dream. But realising this dream is not so easy in the world of today. On the contrary, it is easier to aim at being the leader of the Turks in the world. The disintegration of the former USSR created great opportunities for Turkey to reach this goal. Wide-ranging campaigns have been launched to spread the feeling of being Turkish in the originally Turkish Republics of the former USSR. Prime Minister Süleyman Demirel added Alparslan Türkeş, the 'Führer' of the nationalists, to the group that visited these countries. During meetings held with the leaders of the nationalist fronts in Azerbaijan, security was provided by guards who wore T-shirts with 'Grey Wolf' pictures.[12] The 'Grey Wolves' are an armed and extreme-right group, labelled as 'Fascist' in Western Europe, and banned in several European countries (Amnesty International, 1979 and 'Nederlands Centrum Buitenlanders', 1980).

TURKISH IMMIGRANTS IN WESTERN EUROPE

During the 1960s, many Turkish people moved to Western European countries as migrant workers. Turkey was interested in these people for

two reasons. First, the currency sent back home substantially
supported the Turkish economy. Second, it wanted to make sure that
these people did not forget their nationality. The mother-tongue
education provided the means for achieving this. Special nationalist
teachers were sent to the various countries – Germany, for example –
and Turkey was able to decide who to send. Research has shown that
the teaching materials used for this mother-tongue education are no
different from those used in Turkey itself.[13] Another example of this
policy by the Turkish state involves the military service for Turkish
youths living outside Turkey. They have the choice either to accept this
service in Turkey for 16 months or to pay 10 000 German Marks and to
accept one month of military training. This training is meant to 'make
a real Turk' of the youngsters. During this month Turkish youth are
'overfed' with nationalistic slogans, like 'I am glad that I am Turkish'
and 'A Turk is worth all the world' in a way that some speak of as 'a
month of brainwashing'.[14]

Even if one of the basic goals of the Kemalist ideology is to become
'Westernized', the adaptation of people who moved to the European
countries was not seen as a positive development. Being 'Westernized'
should only be achieved by Kemalist intellectuals. This would provide
them with privileges and make them different from the rest. Thus, they
would gain rights to 'protect the others from dangers' and would act as
leaders. Various right-wing and left-wing movements began to develop
among these migrant workers. The state responded to these organisations according to its official ideology. Nationalists (left-wing and
right-wing) and the Muslim organisations controlled by the state were
supported. The state officially requested governments of the host
countries to prohibit or ban other organisations. However, they did
not succeed in going beyond the 'walls of the Western democracies'.

The National Intelligence Agency (MIT) was involved in the
organisation of the Turkish extreme right in Germany. It is known
that Enver Altayli has been an MIT agent since 1968. At the end of the
1970s, Alparslan Türkeş appointed him leader of the organisation in
Germany of the Nationalist Movement Party (MHP) with which the
'Grey Wolves' were associated (Mumcu, 1988). In the same article, by
letters written to Türkeş, the President of the Party, the author proves
that Enver Altayli was also connected with *Die Bundesnachrichten-
dienst* (German Secret Intelligence Agency). His successor was Musa
Serdar Çelebi, who was tried together with Mehmet Ali Ağca, for the
attempted assassination of Pope John II. He was found not guilty.

The Turkish right-wing extremists do not only have relations with the German Intelligence Service. The group also established close relations with the German CSU and with neo-Nazi groups. The president of the party, Alparslan Türkeş, wrote a letter on 28 July 1977 to his associates, stating:

> our party is developing in Turkey. It is required to reflect the same developments to our citizens living in Germany and to speed up the work of getting organised. In order to achieve the desired results, it is necessary to improve the relations with the *National Sozialisticher Partei Deutschlands* (the German National Socialist Party, NSPD) and to benefit from their experiences and methods.'[15]

A report published by Amnesty International (1979) indicates that the European organisations of MHP had connections with other right-wing extremist organisations outside Germany. Another example is the French *Ordre Nouveau*. From time to time, right-wing extremist Turks have been known to be organised together with Muslim fundamentalists or to be supported by people belonging to Islamic groups.

Right-wing and left-wing Turkish organisations in Europe have done everything possible to exclude or marginalise organisations that do not fit in with Kemalism. Their greatest supporters in this are the media, broadcasting in Turkish all over the continent. With respect to these organisations, two examples can be given. Professor Dr Faruk Şen, director of the Turkey Research Centre in Germany, has written (in his column in *Milliyet*) an article entitled 'Never-ending Pain, Kurdish Reality' in which he stated:

> the subject of the Kurds which we have excluded until today, has begun to take on a relatively important place in our day-to-day life here in Germany. Everyone, from the taxi driver to the German we meet in a restaurant, from our German doctor to the German postman, is reproachful about this matter.

The author asks Kurds to help to change this situation and continues his article stating:

> the Kurdish intellectual is also responsible. The approach used by Kurdish intellectuals to solve this problem by creating pressure on Turkey through German politicians, journalists and bureaucrats, but not solving it with the people with whom they live together in the same country, offends the people living in Turkey. In this matter, Kurdish intellectuals also have to take positive steps.

The director of the Turkish Research Centre is in effect asking the Kurds in Europe to remain silent about the oppression of Kurds in Turkey and not to conduct any studies in Europe related to the Kurds.

Another example of the work of Turkish organisations in Western Europe in line with Kemalism, concerns the Turkish Consultancy Council in the Netherlands. This Council, which is an institution on a level above the Turkish federations organised throughout the country, advises the Dutch government with respect to various issues. It does not accept the inclusion of Kurds and Alawiis (Şener, 1989), who are not officially recognised in Turkey but who are organised on their own throughout the Netherlands.

At the time that I decided to write this chapter, the neo-Nazi attack in Mölln had not yet occurred. The plan had been to evaluate the ideas of Turkish people living in Western Europe with respect to racist violence by analysing the Turkish press. However, the broadcasts, advertisements, official statements, etc., in the aftermath of the murders in Mölln can provide a general summary. Special attention should be paid to the *Hürriyet* newspaper, because this newspaper is read by the vast majority of the Turkish population both inside and outside Turkey (for instance, *NOS*, 1986). Both leftist and rightist people publish in this newspaper, such as the chief editor of the newspaper, Oktay Ekşi, who is also the elected president of the Turkish Press Council, and Mümtaz Soysal, who writes daily articles in this newspaper and is also a member of Parliament for the Social Democratic People's Party. Soysal also chairs delegations which represent Parliament at various international meetings in Europe.[16]

In the upper left corner of the 'liberal' *Hürriyet* there is a Turkish flag and printed above it is a picture of Atatürk. Underneath the picture is written: 'Turkey belongs to the Turks.' After the Mölln murders, *Hürriyet* (25 November 1992) published the news under the heading: 'Humanity is assassinated in Mölln. Condolences to us all.' The article invites people to send letters to Chancellor Kohl of Germany and it publishes the text for such a letter. In its edition on 27 November *Hürriyet* states: 'We are Turkish, we are not afraid, we are proud of being Turkish and we are not going anywhere.' On 29 November, almost the complete front page is dedicated to the funeral ceremonies in Germany. At the top of the front page the next headline reads: 'Magnificent Turk.' At the same time there is a warning for Turkish immigrant workers in Western Europe:

Turkish immigrant workers became the darlings of the world. This created a very favourable base in the international platform for our Turkey. Officials are warning our citizens against the 'dividers and instigators' to avoid the reversal of this situation.

The newspaper is asking the Turks to beware of the Kurds, whom it refers to as 'dividers', in order to protect the prestige of Turkey. The newspaper states that this prestige has been increasing because of the Mölln murders. There is another title next to this news: 'The divider creates an event.' It reports on a big demonstration march where Turks replied to the dividers, who had opened up PKK flags[17], by singing the Turkish national anthem. Seven people were injured during the resulting fights. In its edition on 30 November 1992, the front page has the headline: 'A message to the World.' A subtitle of the news articles, for example is: 'Turkish resistance to Nazi savageness has been a wonderful message to humanity.' At the bottom other news is given, showing a picture of how 'the dividers' who opened up PKK flags were beaten by the Turks. In Çarsamba, the Turkish town where the three bodies of the murdered women were buried, government officials gave speeches criticising racism everywhere in Europe, especially in Germany.

With respect to the events during the demonstration, *Cumhuriyet* (a left-wing Kemalist newspaper) reported on 29 November 1992 that a group, provoked by idealists (the legal name used by the 'Grey Wolves') attacked the Kurds. The event took place as follows: a group of Turks with 'Grey Wolf' rosettes and Turkish flags joined the demonstration march. When the Kurds saw this they opened the Kurdish flag, which is seen as the PKK flag by Turkish authorities, and they shouted the slogan 'Kurdistan will become the grave of Fascism.' After this, the 'Grey Wolves' provoked the others and they all started to attack the Kurds. Germans interfered and the fight was suppressed before it escalated.

After the Mölln violence, Turkey's authorities started firm diplomatic efforts to protest against Germany, and demanded that active measures be taken against racism. The Turkish Parliament also sent its own committee to Germany to investigate the events in Mölln and the increasing racist violence against Turkish people in Germany. It should be noted that, just one month earlier, a German delegation, representing the *Verein der Bundesdeutschen Anwälte* (the German Association of Lawyers) and the *Deutsche Pressegewerkschaft* (the

German Union of Journalists) had visited Turkey for two weeks to investigate the situation on human rights in Kurdistan.[18] Yet, parallel to this campaign, another effort by Turkey can be observed: the demand by Turkish authorities that Germany should prohibit the Kurdish organisations that are active in Germany. Onur Öymen, the Turkish Ambassador in Germany, visited the German Ministry of Foreign Affairs and requested the prohibition of 'these terrorist organisations, including those which were founded by Turkish people' (meaning Kurdish organisations). This request is supported by the seventeen different Turkish organisations which published an advertisement in *Tercüman* (a Turkish newspaper) on 28 November 1992. Some of these organisations are known to support the extreme Right publicly. Taking advantage of the mood, organisations working against the infringement of the human rights in Turkey are also criticized. *Milliyet* (28 November 1992) asks 'Where are you? Organizations, such as Amnesty International, which see Turks as an enemy, will be held accountable to history.' *Hürriyet* (30 November 1992) broadens this even more: 'Humanity saw the danger of the Nazis. Recognised the guilty party. Protected the Turks who are away from home. With the only exception of institutions using the label of "human rights". They have preferred to be "human injustice organisations".'

The summary of Turkey's approach to this event can be found in the statements by the Prime Minister, Süleyman Demirel: 'When portraying foreigners as enemies turns into portraying Turks as enemies, this is embarrassing, I am protesting against this' (all Turkish newspapers, 27 November 1992).

CONCLUSIONS

Turkey is the mother-country of many people living all over Europe. These people constitute minorities in their host societies and are increasingly under racist attack. With the increase of racist violence in Europe, the Turkish minorities live with a growing feeling of insecurity in everyday life. The Turkish state responds to these developments with harsh statements and strong demands on the governments of these host societies actively to fight racism and racist violence against Turks. On the other hand racist violence and racism are part of everyday life in Turkey itself. Often, this is supported, or even directly or indirectly organised, by state authorities themselves.

Minorities are portrayed as 'threats to the Turkish society' and treated correspondingly. On the same line one can also see Turkey's involvement in ethnic violence in the 'new Republics' which were created after the collapse of the former Soviet Union. Racism is prohibited in Turkey and abroad by the Turkish state. Racism is defined and portrayed as being identical to anti-Turkish sentiment. This kind of racism is combated. All other kinds of racism, especially those directed against minorities in Turkey itself, are neglected or even supported. Certainly, we may speak here of a double standard.

NOTES

1. The boundaries of this empire are determined by Turkish language and culture.
2. *Kadro* (magazine) January 1932 (first edition), and November 1932 (eleventh edition) pp. 17–18.
3. *Ayin Tarihi* (magazine) May 1930 (74th edition) pp. 6201–6215.
4. The *Suryanis* (Christians who use Syriac as a liturgical language) are still among the oppressed minorities within Turkey. In connection with this oppression and the violence against them they started a hunger strike in the Netherlands in January 1993.
5. *Nokta* (a Turkish weekly magazine), vol. 10, no 27 (4 July 1992) pp. 12–17; and an article written by Bülent Tarakçioğlu, in Nokta, 6 September 1992, pp. 46–47.
6. *Özgür Gündem*, 6–7 September 1992.
7. Ravali, A. in *Tempo* (weekly magazine) no 43, pp. 66–71.
8. *Özgür Gündem* (daily newspaper), '*Kurden Raus* in Fethiye', 5 October 1992.
9. *Milliyet* (daily newspaper) 9 November 1992.
10. *Yeni Ülke* (weekly newspaper) 1–7 November 1992, pp. 12.
11. *Milliyet, Türkiye* and *Sabah* (newspapers) 19 and 20 May 1992.
12. *Nokta* (weekly magazine) no 20, 17 May 1992.
13. See Yeşilgöz, in *NRC Handelsblad* (daily newspaper) 21 March 1989; and Aslan and Braam, in *Vrij Nederland* (weekly magazine) 24 March 1990.
14. *Casablanca* (a Dutch/Belgian monthly magazine) no 2, 1993, p. 23.
15. *2000'e Doğru* (weekly magazine) sixth year, 49th edition, 6 December 1992.
16. A professor in Constitutional Law who attended the CSCE meeting on Tolerance in Warsaw from 16 to 20 November 1992 as the Head of the Turkish Delegation and who presented an article explaining the tolerance of the Ottoman Empire and Turkey towards minorities.
17. The PKK is the Kurdish Workers Party, which is illegal in Turkey.
18. At a press conference on 16 October 1992 this delegation stated that 320 murder cases in Kurdistan had been committed, including the murder of nine journalists. See *Yeni Ülke* (weekly magazine) 18–24 October 1992.

14 Between Freedom and Persecution: Roma in Romania

Katrin Reemtsma

By Spring 1993, about 25 pogroms have been committed since the end of the Ceausescu dictatorship, mainly during the years 1990 and 1991 and in rural areas (Reemtsma, 1992, pp. 39–51). In 1992 and the first-half of 1993 there were several further but less violent attacks.

POGROMS[1]

Mihail Kogalniceanu, 9 October 1990

At the beginning of the 1950s a group of Roma was forcefully settled at the outskirts of Kogalniceanu. This was an administrative measure which neither the Roma[2] nor the villagers wanted. Over the decades conflicts evolved.

When, on 4 October 1990, a fight between an ethnic Aromune and a Rom in front of a disco broke out and the police did not intervene, tensions intensified. During the following days hints that a long-planned attack against the orthodox and xoraxane Roma who lived in a separate quarter at the outskirts of Kogalniceanu was to take place on 11 October became more frequent. On 9 October a tractor driver was beaten up by a Rom. This incident unleashed the pogrom before the intended date.

Between 9 and 10 p.m. the church bells rang as a sign to attack. About 1000 inhabitants of Kogalniceanu,[3] mainly ethnic Aromunians, gathered in front of the Catholic church. For the Roma the ringing of the church bells was the signal to run away. In addition, a Romni reports, some villagers ran to the quarter and warned the people. An old Romni describes the situation:

194

When we heard the bells and saw the torches, we ran. We had already been threatened by the villagers. We ran into the forest and only returned to look at our houses one day later. The houses were still burning when we returned. We left and stayed away for over a month (Helsinki Watch 1991, p. 55).

Thirty-five houses were burned down, eight houses were otherwise destroyed. Although there is now a reintegration programme under way, about 200 people lived for almost two years in makeshift shelters, with relatives, or left for Germany.

According to some Roma, police and mayor of the village marched in the first row of the attackers. These, however, say that they tried – without success – to prevent the villagers from attacking. A larger number of policemen arrived in Kogalniceanu only at 11p.m.; and their assignment was not to protect the Roma (who had fled already anyway) but to protect the perpetrators from supposed revenge of Roma (Helsinki Watch, 1991).

Investigations against the perpetrators came under way very slowly and only because of pressure on the part of Roma organisations and of the international attention this pogrom received. By now, almost 2½ years after the attack, twelve people will go on trial. They are charged with 'destruction of personal belongings' and 'association with purpose of doing criminal offences' acccording to articles 217 and 323 of the Romanian Penal Code.

Bolintin Deal, 7 April 1991

During Easter night, 6 to 7 April, a Romanian student was killed in an argument with a Rom. Several hours later the murderer was arrested and put on trial.

At 10 a.m. the next day the siren of the town sounded and inhabitants gathered in front of the house of the victim. Between 10 and 10.30 at least a thousand people moved towards the houses of the Roma. It was planned originally to burn the house of the murderer, but soon the action turned into an attack against all (Ursari-)Roma. Twenty-two houses were burned down and three cars were destroyed.

According to varying reports of Roma the involvement of the mayor was contradictory. One eyewitness reports:

The mayor came to the house and told us to leave because people would set fire to the houses. It was about 7.30 – 8 a.m. He came again around 10.00 – 10.30 a.m. I didn't leave until I saw houses were on fire and I was nearby when I saw the flames coming from my own house. The mayor warned us because he didn't want deaths. They just wanted to get the Gypsies out of the village (Helsinki Watch 1991, p. 60).

Although the mayor was obviously informed (he was also the only person who had the key to the Cultural Centre where the siren is) and warned the Roma, he did not call the police to prevent the attack. At the time of the pogrom, only thirteen police officers who temporarily tried to calm down the crowd were present. Only at 1 p.m. when the houses were already burnt down did a larger police unit arrive.

The Roma fled to relatives or friends. Those who had no place to stay returned on 7 April to live in the destroyed but not burnt houses. Again the siren sounded and the last five houses were burnt. This time the police prevented the Roma from being beaten up by driving them out of town in a car. The mayor and the priest, however, were actively involved in the attacks. The investigations are still going on.

Ogrezeni, 17 May 1991

On 16 May a Romanian was hurt with a knife by a Rom. A Romanian neighbour of a Roma family reports:

That night a group of youths, including the Romanian who had been stabbed, were walking through the street shouting 'fire'. It must have been about 9–9.30 p.m. Then they set fire to one house. A Gypsy living in the area reported this to the police, and the police arrived around 11.30. Nothing else happened (Helsinki Watch 1991, p. 62).

When the bells rang on the following evening another crowd gathered and became violent. According to a Romanian villager, at least six houses were burnt down. In addition adolescents destroyed further houses with tractors. Another Romanian describes the conduct of the police:

There were many police standing around. I think there were two big trucks full of police. They were here when the houses were burnt. They didn't say anything. One policeman told me that if they had an order to act, they would have restored order in 30 minutes. The police stayed in the village until [June or July], but there were no Gypsies in the village during that time (Helsinki Watch 1991, p. 63).

Fourteen houses were destroyed. The families fled to relatives or friends in other towns (including Bucharest) or to Germany. The investigations are finished. Thirty-two persons are accused and currently on trial.

Bolintin Vale, 18 May 1991

On the next day the violence spread to nearby Bolintin Vale. On Friday evening the bells rang and a crowd gathered. The police were lined up at night, but when the houses were attacked the following afternoon they did not intervene. A Romanian eyewitness reports:

> Between 1 and 2 p.m. on Saturday a crowd of villagers came down the street. We saw the whole street was full of people. Many of the neighbours here on this street were helping with the destruction. We were opposed to setting fire to the house next door because it was too close to our house. I was afraid our house would also catch fire.
>   About 1 to 2 p.m. the house next door was destroyed. No police on the street came to the house. We saw the police withdraw in the trucks. We could see some of the trucks from the house. The police could see the crowd, but they didn't intervene. By 4 p.m. everything was calm again. Since then we have police patrols in our neighbourhood (Helsinki Watch 1991, p. 65).

Seven houses were destroyed. The investigations are finished; seven people will be accused.

Valenii Lapusului, 13 August 1991

About 150 gadjikane-Roma lived in the village of Valenii Lapusului and in nearby Ponorita until 13 August 1991. On that evening – after the rape of a village woman by a Rom in the morning – all huts were burnt down or otherwise destroyed.

But it was not the rape which angered the villagers most, but rather a combination of different reasons. An old Romanian farmer explained that two Roma families which in 1939 had been admitted to the village because of pity for their poverty had by now increased to 150 people. They 'always stole', shouted a woman. 'Mainly chicken', others added.

Since the return of the collectivised land into private ownership this offence is interpreted in national terms: as an offence of a (supposedly foreign) Gypsy against a Romanian. 'None of them will ever return. This is a Romanian village,' yelled the same woman (Reemtsma, 1992, p. 50). And to Roma she offered the alternatives 'to disappear in the blocks of Baia Mare' – a deadly vision for people who live in agricultural-village traditions – or to move into the houses of emigrated Germans in the Banat.

Except for the police officer of Tirgu Lapus who, he claims, confronted the villagers with the fact that the Roma are registered inhabitants of Valenii, the authorities gave in to the anti-Roma sentiment of the villagers. It was only after the intervention of Roma from Bucharest that they slowly started acting. Investigations against the perpetrators were begun very slowly and were seriously conducted only after the rapist was caught and sentenced to 12 years. Although the construction of houses at the former segregated place – instead of reintegration – has been started, most of the families still live in makeshift shelters. The villagers still do not want the Roma families close to Valenii. Eleven of the perpetrators of violence went on trial in June 1993.

Bucharest, Piata Rahova, 3 July 1992

A member of the military police unit UM 2180 and a Rom spent the evening of 1 July drinking together. After a dispute they had a fight whereafter the soldier had to be taken to hospital. Supposedly the incident was investigated on the same evening and following day.

On 3 July, forty to fifty other members of the same unit came to the Piata around 3.30 p.m. Equipped with uniform, black head-masks, rubber truncheons, *nunchakus* (a weapon consisting of two sticks connected by a chain), chair-legs and pickaxes they split into three groups and indiscriminately attacked Roma – men, women and children – who were at the market. They wounded several people and continued beating at least one when he was already unconscious.

Another group of soldiers entered the 'Minodora' restaurant, broke furniture and threatened the visitors that next time they would come and destroy their homes.

Two traffic police officers and a unit of the Ministry of Interior were present at the time of this unprovoked attack, but did not intervene (Amnesty International, 1992).

THE PATTERN

The mechanisms of the pogroms are essentially the same. After a history of conflicts one criminal offence sets off the violence (in one case it needed not even an offence; violence simply spread to the next village). Roma, be they babies or old people, are collectively held responsible for the offence of one individual and – since the police supposedly remain inactive – vengeance is justified.

The violent and racist reactions are committed in large groups of mainly ethnic Romanians, but also by Hungarians or Aromunians, either spontaneously (although there generally must have been a willingness to use violence) or premeditated. The villagers are encouraged by passive or active participation of local state authorities (mayor, prefect, police) or priests of the Orthodox church.

The villagers organise and equip themselves with torches, clubs, explosives, tools or tractors and then move into the segregated living quarters of the Roma, where they burn or destroy the huts and other property. They must have taken deaths approvingly into consideration. In fact several people have died.[4] The aim generally was to expel all Roma.

RESPONSES OF THE ROMANIAN STATE

Since the end of the dictatorship, the situation for Roma has improved as far as individual civil rights (freedom of expression, organisation, travel, trade, culture) and a rudimentry recognition of Roma as a people with culture and history are concerned.

On the other hand, since nationalism has been an integral part of the Romanian communist system and is now openly flourishing in most circles of society, it can easily be instrumentalised by the press but also by the staff in administration and politics.

The International Labour Organisation (ILO) and the Rapporteur for Romania of the Human Rights Commission of the United Nations, both point out the dangerous role the press has played:

According to the information received, even though the members of the Gypsy community in Romania have been able to form political parties and independent cultural associations which have enhanced awareness of its civil and political rights, [the Gypsy community] is subject to defamation campaigns that sometimes take the form of public incitement to racial hatred and lead to acts of physical violence, looting and the destruction of houses (Report on the Situation of Human Rights in Romania 1991, p. 27).

While the violence against Roma is not denied in administrative, judicial and political circles, the racist aspect is ignored.

It can be difficult for the prosecution to find the main perpetrators out of groups numbering hundreds or even thousands of attackers; yet investigations have come under way only very slowly and often only under pressure of Roma organisations or international attention. While the Roma perpetrators whose crime sparked the violence have been accused and tried immediately, it is only in a few places that investigations against the attackers have been completed and a limited number of perpetrators will go to court (e.g. Kogalniceanu). They will not be tried for propagation of ethnic hatred or potential murder but for the material damages only.

Nicolae Gheorghe of the Ethnic Federation of Roma describes the dilemma as follows: 'Roma only have the choice between social peace and justice' (Reemtsma, 1992, p. 54).

It means that in many cases Roma had to make substantial compromises as far as speed, charges, punishment and number of people accused are concerned. Insisting on an adequate prosecution would have generated further hatred.

If the prosecutions of the Rom perpetrators and the *Pogromchiks* (perpetrators of pogroms) are compared (International Romani Union, 1992), it is obvious that as far as the ethnic affiliation of the perpetrators are concerned impartiality does not exist. The Law takes sides and ethnically biased justice is performed.

The same apologetic attitude towards the pogroms can be found in the political reactions. In June 1990, in a RIAS (Radio) interview in Berlin, Gelu Voican-Voiculescu, then deputy Prime Minister, called Roma 'social scum and a danger for society'.

Gabriel Gafita, advisor to the Inter-ethnic Relations Group of the Government Commission of Local Conflicts implicitly justifies the violence against Roma when he states:

Those places where conflicts have occurred are where there are many unemployed Gypsies, many black marketeers, many criminal elements. All these conflicts were caused by violent assaults by Gypsies against non-Gypsies . . . These are local conflicts which have grown in time; people will tell you a long history of theft, of children being attacked on their way to school, of women being assaulted (Helsinki Watch 1991, p. 70).

The vice-chairman of the Romanian delegation to the Minority Expert meeting of the Conference on Security and Cooperation in Europe (CSCE), which took place from 1 to 9 July 1991 in Geneva, Nicolae Dascalu, played down the attacks as follows:

Involvement of citizens belonging to various ethnicities in the conflicts with certain Roma indicates that such conflicts did not have an ethnic motivation, but a social one (Helsinki Watch 1991, p. 70).

In an Information Circular of the same delegation this argumentation is continued by presenting a distorted picture of the pogroms and by blaming Roma because of (for example): 'a history of general disorderly and antisocial conduct by the majority of the Romas of Turu Lung' (Information Circular no 2, p. 2). In another context, blame is again put on the Roma because of the 'provocative attitudes of certain Roma' and 'their ostentatious opulence acquired by illicit means' (Letter of Response of the International Romani Union, 1991).

Some individuals in administrative and political circles have become more cooperative. Several projects affiliated to the Ministries of Work and Education, and reintegration projects in Kogalniceanu and Valenii Lapusului have been initiated by Roma. Although direct state-ordered persecution does not exist, local, regional and central authorities have in varying degrees been part of the actual attacks: by actively participating, by tolerating the violence, by reactivating and transporting traditional stereotypes, by blaming Roma and by im- or explicitly justifying the violence.

CONTINUITIES

According to the German–Romanian agreement signed on 24 September 1992, citizens of either country residing illegally on the territory of the other can now be sent home when they do not have a passport.

The agreement – which does not seem to violate international standards – opens the way for more restrictions of national, legal practises. Up to now, persons who entered illegally could still request political asylum and persons who did not have a passport could not be forced to leave Germany. Since the agreement came into effect on 1 November 1992, about 5000 Romanians have been sent back.

The agreement is the first of its kind and unfolded its importance in several respects; two of them will be pointed out here.

The first aspect concerns German domestic affairs. The design of the agreement suggests that it was intended as a test for further political goals. By selecting Romania, the Minister of Interior could profit from the widespread antipathy or racism against Roma. In many places – Lebach in 1990 or Rostock in 1992 are only highlights – Roma have already been used by the local administration to escalate the conflicts. In addition, Roma are the only refugee group who meets on a traditional structure of prejudices. This led to the creation of a category 'Gypsy' perceived as below the general category of asylum seekers who so far had been at the bottom of the 'ethnical hierarchy'. 'Asylum-seekers yes, Gypsies no', was an often-heard sentence by people who have no experience at all with Roma.

Although an ethnically selective immigration policy is no longer or not yet again possible, a covert attempt is made to continue the century-old 'Gypsy' politics.

Between the middle of the last century and the First World War a strong immigration of Roma from southeastern Europe took place. They fled from 500 years of slavery which had been abolished in the old Romanian principalities of Moldavia and Wallachia in 1855/56 (Beck and Gheorghe, 1981, pp. 4–8; and Hancock, 1987, pp. 17–36), from Yugoslavian territories where national tensions were strong and the Balkan wars were fought, and they came from Hungary or Poland. Then, as now, the reasons for migration ranged from war to human rights violations, discrimination and economic motives. The German Reich reacted with a flood of decrees by which 'foreign Gypsies' should be prevented from entering the Reich (even when they fulfilled the necessary requirements such as papers and money) or – if they had already entered – should be transported back to the border. A network of resettlement agreements existed with all neighbouring states (Reemtsma, 1990, p. 7 and 1992, pp. 7–10).

While Romania is the country which the highest number of asylum-seekers is coming from, Roma make up only part of them. The intention of the agreement then goes beyond a simple anti-'Gypsy' measure. By talking about asylum-seekers from Romania and from other countries almost in general from a supposed criminal perspective[5], verbal arson is committed.

The combination of 'Gypsies', supposedly criminal asylum-seekers coming from Romania, a fairly unknown country, guaranteed that the agreement would meet only little resistance.

The *defacto* abolition of the right for political asylum, the establishment of a list of countries where there is supposedly no persecution (Romania and Turkey among others have been suggested) and a net of resettlement agreements can now be pushed through.

In Germany, a discussion about immigration regulation is necessary. But the incessant discussion in government circles about asylum-seekers for several years is used to divert attention from the failure to manage the unification process and the increasing social unrest. For internal peace a new scapegoat or enemy which unites East and West is needed.

Being indirectly involved in racist attacks in its own country and having a tradition of denying that there is racism against Roma and Sinti, silence towards – or even silent consent with – pogroms against Roma in Romania on the part of German state representatives is a consequence. 'No findings, no need for action', was the comment from one of the responsible persons on part of the Ministry of Interior when his attention was called to the attacks.

The second aspect of the agreement then is the continuation of collaboration between Germany and Romania sacrificing human and minority rights.

The most intense phase of collaboration began after Romania had joined the 'Axis Powers' in 1940. Persecution of Jews and 'Gypsies' became systematic.

Anti-Semitism, socially or religiously motivated, has been an integral part of the new Romanian state, but during the 1930s the biological version began to prevail. On 8 August 1940, a biological definition of who was a Jew, was published. In addition, marriages between Romanians and Jews were forbidden with reference to the 'Nuremberg laws'.

The organisation of the state according to the 'law of blood' (Ioanid, 1990, p. 194) also affected Roma. On 8 July 1941, the then dictator, Antonescu, demanded the annihilation of all national minorities. The fascist paper, *Eroica*, found that

> the Gypsy question is of the same importance as the Jewish question. That is why Gypsies [had] to be eliminated from all circles of social life in the state. (Kenrick and Puxon, 1980, p. 95).

Jews and Roma, be they sedentary or nomadic, were deported systematically from the Bukowina and Bessarabia to Transnistria. Of particular interest were the nomadic Roma of inner Romania. Ion Chelcea expressed the view of many Romanians in his 1944 book, *Tigani din Romania*, when he regarded them as:

> not [able] to assimilate. And even when, only God knows how, assimilation could be reached, they would severely disturb the composition of the Romanian blood (Ioanid, 1990, p. 217).

In Transnistria, the region between Dnestr and Bug under Romanian administration, Jews and Roma were killed by Romanian authorities with German support through shooting, burning, forced labour, diseases, hunger (Kenrick and Puxon 1980, pp. 95–96; Ioanid, 1990, pp.194, 213, 217). In addition they were handed over to the organisation *Todt* for forced labour or they were handed over to the German colonies to be murdered by the SS. The number of murdered Roma was around 35 000 (Kendrick and Puxon, 1980, p. 95; Reemtsma, 1992, pp. 12–15).

In socialist Romania, Roma were no longer considered from the racial aspect but as a marginal social group. Where cultural autonomy was obvious, it had to be destroyed, for example, through forced settlement of nomadic Roma, especially during the 1950s. But other measures such as resettlement, police violence and forced labour were taken. Roma, a culturally diverse people with a particular history, were suppressed or ignored in Stalinist Romania.

The Federal Republic, like many other Western states were as tolerant towards violation of human and minority rights in Romania then as the united Germany and its partners are now towards the lack of democratic development in post-communist Romania in general and the pogroms against Roma in particular.

In one of the situation reports of the Ministry of Foreign Affairs the official Romanian position is repeated:

> the violence against Roma in Bucharest (1990), Kogalniceanu, Bolintin Deal and Bolintin Vale was sparked by criminal behaviour of particular Roma groups, they were local incidents, the police did intervene to protect Roma and the Romanian state did not approve the violence. Not even indirect persecution takes place (*Auswärtiges Amt* 514–516.80/3 1991, pp. 5–8).

Neither the resettlement agreement which is combined with an economic project nor the current international consultations about refugees, such as in Berlin in October 1991 or Budapest in February

1993, were used to put pressure on the Romanians to guarantee human and minority rights.

In March 1992, it was the German government which blocked a rather far-reaching resolution of the Subcommission for the Prevention of Discrimination and the Protection of Minorities at the annual session of the United Nations Commission on Human Rights. The German delegation successfully prevented 'protection' and 'security' being explicitly accorded to Roma in the final compromise (Resolutions 1991/21, E./CN.4/1992/L72, 1992/65).

For both Romanian and German officials, the pogroms are social and local events. Their racist and structural elements and the involvement of state authorities are denied.

The function of the denial is twofold. A short-term aspect is populist and involves a diversion of attention from social and economical crisis in both countries. The long-term aspect touches the concept of the state.

Although Roma have lived for hundreds of years in, and are citizens of, the respective countries, their history – despite the integration of a number of Roma and despite phases or regions where majority and minority lived peacefully together – is one of exclusion, suppression or persecution.

Many Roma who have hoped for more structural changes since the political events of 1989 have become skeptical. The trend – not only in Romania and Germany – is national–conservative. Ethnic affiliation and citizenship are not kept separate. This means in turn that minorities – even if they are citizens of the state – or immigrants of the second or third generation will continue to be in danger of not really belonging, of not receiving adequate social and political participation, of not receiving the full protection of the state.

Again by denying the racist aspect of the violent attacks against Roma in Romania, Romanian and German governments continue to rid themselves of their responsibility towards Roma as citizens and members of a minority or as refugees.

Instead of tabooing the vital issues such as racial violence, discrimination and the socio-economic situation, it is necessary to address them and to take steps towards a more collective integration of this minority. Otherwise these will continue to be refugees. As it is now, governmental 'Gypsy' politics of denial in all countries continue to intensify the problem.

NOTES

1. The description of the pogroms is based on field research by Helsinki Watch, Amnesty International, Ethnic Federation of Roma and the author. They reconstructed the events after talks with Roma, Roma representatives, local citizens of other ethnic affiliations, and local state representatives such as prefects, mayors or policemen.
2. Roma are those 'Gypsies' who since their arrival around 1200 live primarily in eastern and southeastern European countries. Many of them have for different reasons migrated to western or northern Europe, to the Americas or Australia. Roma are a segmented society which means they tend to split and subdivide into many groups; the subgroups mentioned in this text are the Ursari, who originally lived a travelling life showing bears; the xoraxane (Turkish/Moslem), orthodox/Romanian Roma, gadjikane Roma. A large number of Roma do not affiliate with any particular group any longer but call themselves Roma or Gypsy. Rom means man, husband and human being, Romni means (Roma) woman and wife. Sinti are those 'Gypsies' who have lived in the German-speaking countries for almost 600 years. Their language is Romanes.
3. Mihail Kogalniceanu is a multi-ethnic rural community close to Constanta on the Black sea. Romanians are in the majority; the other nationalities are Turks, Macedo-Romanians or Aromunians, Roma and Germans.
4. The parents of Stefan Varga, a 2-year-old child who burned to death during an attack on 10–11 January 1990 in Lunga, have not up to now even received an answer to their complaint.
5. The Minister of Interior suggests an 99.8 per cent misuse of the right for political asylum; 70 per cent illegal entries – at the end of November his Ministry said, however, that 85 per cent of the asylum-seekers would come with a visa from the German Embassy in Bucharest; an estimated 80 per cent would come on organised tours.

15 Racist Violence and Anti-racist Reactions: A View of France

Cathie Lloyd[1]

'Racist violence' in France is closely linked to socio-economic factors and to patterns of institutionalised racial violence which developed in different ways through the collaborationist Vichy regime of the Second World War and the Algerian war. Today, these institutional patterns of racism affect the legal system and the police, but also influence behaviour in civil society. However, there is growing understanding of the existence of a 'climate' for racial violence; a tense atmosphere of anxiety about law and order and 'security'. These understandings have taken a considerable time to develop, partly because of powerful tendencies towards amnesia which surround the legacy both of Vichy and of the Algerian war. In France this has powerfully shaped the organisational responses to racial violence, including the room for manoeuvre of anti-racists. Racial violence has been a powerful factor in the mobilisation of anti-racist youth movements which, as we shall see, have themselves been coopted.

This chapter examines the theme of institutional racial violence in an historical perspective and then analyses the main categories of incidents over the past ten years in the context of *Arabacides* (Guidice, 1992).[2] It considers some of the existing research on this subject in France. The response of the state and anti-racist organisations to racial violence is then analysed in this context, in terms of symbolic protests, educational activity, support for victims and their families and the development of multi-agency responses. It is suggested that the shocked response to recent cases may be building pressure for effective and practical action.[3]

HISTORICAL PERSPECTIVE OF INSTITUTIONAL VIOLENCE

A brief historical survey shows us that similar patterns of behaviour have been repeated over many years. Within those patterns there are changes, the reason for violence against 'foreigners' may differ, the

207

groups of people who are the targets for violent acts may vary (although there are some constants, particularly anti-Semitism). Violence seems to increase at times of national crisis, war, or of economic insecurity when people become guarded against foreign competition. Noiriel (1988, p. 89) points to the link between acts of violence and government policies to restrict foreigners. Another constant seems to be the sort of act which takes place and the kind of circumstance, although a more complete study of this aspect of history is needed to reveal these details. There is a gap in our knowledge about the history of resistance to these acts.

Lequin (1988) traces the history of xenophobia back to the early sixteenth century with Italians, Dutch and Bohemians accused of enriching themselves at the expense of the French. Jewish communities were rejected because of their 'strange customs' and religion, although it is clear that different communities had quite different experiences, sometimes between regions of France. An anti-Jewish campaign is recorded in 1615 with the murder of a jeweller at Tournellerie (Lequin 1988, p. 236). In Bordeaux in 1755, after a dispute between students, a group assembled and attacked Jewish property for several days.

The Emancipation of the Jews during the Revolution was an important step forward, but there was a current of fear of foreigners during this time, emerging from struggles for the life of the Revolution itself. While in the early years some foreigners among the active Revolutionaries were given citizenship, as the wars in Europe began, foreigners became suspect.

In the nineteenth century the 'immigrant worker' emerged in popular imagery (Noiriel, 1988, pp. 87–124). With economic recession, increased foreign labour competition and the demand for the protection of 'nationals' employment became important. The main reason for anger was the fear of competition of foreign labour causing reduced wages, price increases and the acceptance of worse working conditions forced by strike-breakers.

The target of hostility varied according to the immigration to a particular area. In Northern France, Belgians were a target against whom whole local populations mobilised to drive them out. There are many examples of French workers forcing foreign competitors to return home. In 1819 and 1847 violence took place in Lille, and Belgians were forced to leave Ghent; in 1837 similar moves were made against English immigrants in Paris and Charenton. In 1819, 1830 and 1839 German tailors, carriage workers and cabinet makers were the focus of xenophobia (Lequin, 1988, p. 389).

From the late 1840s rejection focused on Belgian industrial workers. There were daily demonstrations against Belgian workers in the spring of 1848, and attacks on groups returning to, and leaving Belgium (Noiriel, 1988, p. 258). In 1848 foreign workers in Lille were threatened and public buildings (especially the railway station) were attacked. Incidents took place throughout the early summer. A 'tradition' of popular hostility emerged:

> In Paris logically the targets diversified with the ethnic variety of foreigners. In March 1848, several hundred demonstrators marched towards Noisy and Bondy along the railway line which was being built to Strasbourg, to chase away Belgians as far as Meaux. In the city, they were roughed up at the Chapelle Saint Denis, in the steel workshops, on the Ste Germain line. In the rolling-stock factories the *Savoisards* were picked upon. Troubles spread to the quarries of Orsay and as the harvest began, it [trouble] broke out in the agricultural belt nearby. In Normandy they went for the English, behind the red flag of Rouen at Sotteville. A general strike was declared at Strasbourg against foreigners, and there were demonstrations in Marseille (Lequin, 1988, p. 390).

The economic crisis of the late nineteenth century saw another period of high levels of xenophobia (Noiriel, 1988, p. 258). In 1892 at Drocourt (Pas de Calais) the population mobilised to force Belgian miners to leave without stopping to collect their belongings. In some areas (like Lievin and Lens in 1901), people were killed in manhunts. In 1910 there were attacks on the Belgian community of Montigny en Golielle (Noiriel, 1988, p. 259). It is argued that these attacks accelerated the assimilation of the Belgian population in France by encouraging them to disguise (or change) their national identity.

In Southern France the main targets for popular racism were Italians. Between 1881 and 1893 some thirty Italians were killed, and their property was regularly attacked. In Marseille there were anti-Italian riots for several days in 1881, starting in isolated incidents and escalating to organised attacks. Hundreds of Italians left town after this (Noiriel, 1988, p. 259). At Aigues-Mortes in 1893 ten Italians were killed and others forced to flee for their lives when a mob of about 300 armed with truncheons, spades and the branches of trees, attacked them. The following year a riot took place in Lyon against Italians after the assassination of Carnot. All foreigners were targets at this time, particularly during community festivals where xenophobic inhibitions were lifted by consumption of alcohol (Noiriel, 1988,

p. 261). In Toulouse in 1895, during a popular dance 4000 demonstrators marched on the Bohemian community at Saint-Cyprien and pillaged and burnt many homes. In 1897 a Municipal election theme was *Nice aux Niçois*.

The war of 1914–18 refocused hostility on Germans and Poles. Mass attacks on foreigners began again in the 1930s, still closely linked to industrial disputes (Schor, 1985). In 1931 there were repeated fights in the North between French strikers and Belgian non-strikers, with stonings and drownings in canals. A fight between French and Moroccans in Lyon left one dead and two seriously injured in 1934. In 1938 a Polish supervisor was killed by French strikers. In Valence there were attacks on Armenian strike-breakers by (CGTU) activists.

Thus, as immigration became increasingly diverse so did the targets of xenophobia. The period which followed, of the 1940s and 1950s, produced two privileged targets of racist violence; the Jews, with feelings drawn from the older current of anti-Semitism, and North Africans linked to the terrible experience of decolonisation in Algeria. During this period we can also see the emergence of state structures clearly linked to racial violence. It is to the first of these, the wartime apparatuses of Occupied and Vichy France, that we now turn.

STRUCTURES OF RACIAL VIOLENCE: THE OCCUPATION AND VICHY FRANCE

Just before 1939 there had been (apart from the period of the *Front Populaire*) a general clamp-down on foreigners in France, in terms of how they were regulated and what work they were allowed to do (Dewitte, 1986). With the Vichy regime, the panoply of state control and the administration of violence was focused on the Jewish community.

Soon after the occupation of Paris on 14 June 1940, French Fascists terrorised and attacked customers of Jewish shops,[4] and others banned Jews from entering their premises. From 15 July the Jews of Alsace-Lorraine were expelled south and on 22 July a law ordered the revision of all naturalisations since 1927 which led to 6000 Jewish people losing their citizenship. On 27 August 1940 Vichy repealed the Marchandeau Law[5] which had banned press racism, enabling a media campaign to be launched about the 'Jewish invasion'.

The first orders against the Jewish population of occupied France on 27 September 1940 imposed a religious definition of 'Jews', a census of the population, a requirement for Jewish shops and businesses to identify themselves and a ban prohibiting them from holding meetings. Jews were excluded from political office, liberal professions or media employment. Prefects in Vichy France were to intern 'foreign' Jews. Vichy was just as hostile to the Jews as the Nazis and enacted similar legislation.[6] The forced wearing of the yellow Star of David (from 29 May 1942) preceded a series of raids in which an estimated 12 884 people were taken – initially men and subsequently women and children. The most notorious one was the Vel d'Hiv raid, where some 7000 Jews (including about 4000 children) were rounded up by French police and taken by bus to a cycle stadium before being deported to extermination camps (Finger and Karel, 1992). These events showed the readiness of many French officials to go beyond what was required of them by the Germans. Klarsfeld estimates that Vichy contributed to the death of 75 000 Jews (Klarsfeld, 1992).[7] The role of Maurice Papon in Bordeaux should be noted in particular for its relation to further events.

At the end of war, despite measures against collaborators, there was a move to cover up the divisions in France, the collaboration and the true nature of the Vichy regime. Those responsible (in almost all fields of life – administrators, police, church dignitaries and so on) had not been dealt with adequately (Rousso, 1990).

THE ALGERIAN WAR: THE ESTABLISHMENT OF NEW PATTERNS

The Algerian war left a specific word to describe attacks on North Africans: *ratonnades*, literally 'rat hunts'.[8] Torture was widespread in Algeria, and even many Frenchmen are still haunted by the experience (Stora, 1991).[9] The Algerian war was a formative event in French consciousness, particularly for violence against a specific group of people. About 350 000 Algerians lived in France during the war. Roughly 130 000 of them are estimated to have supported the National Liberation Front (FLN) (Stora 1991), but they were all French citizens.

Routine identity controls by French police took place from the early 1950s, causing anti-racists to make parallels with the treatment of Jews during the war.[10] Casual *ratonnades* – many of them said to have been by off-duty police organised by the Secret Armed Organisation (OAS) – were against *bidonvilles* (shanty towns) inhabited by Algerian immigrant workers (Levine, 1985, p. 13).

There were institutional links also to the experience of the 1940s. Parts of the apparatus (including individual officials) which had sent Jews to concentration camps were still in place.

In the tense and violent atmosphere towards the end of the war, the Paris Prefect of Police, Maurice Papon,[11] announced in October 1961 a curfew on 'Algerian workers' between 8.00 p.m. and 4.20 a.m., requiring that they should not travel in small groups. There had not been such treatment of a specific category of French citizens since the war. The FLN organised a peaceful march of protest in Paris on 17 October 1961 with an estimated 30 000 people participating (*Le Monde*, 19 October 1961). The police drove demonstrators into the Seine to drown, some clubbed Algerians to death, others fired machine-guns directly into the densely packed crowds. At least 200 Algerians are known to have died and a further 11 000 were arrested and taken to be held for several days in the *Palais des Sports* and the Coubertin stadium. Sporadic raids followed. The parallel with the raids on the Jewish population in 1942, particularly the Vel d'Hiv, were evident. Other demonstrations followed (Stora, 1991, pp. 588–92), and were repressed in similar conditions. On 19 October two Algerians were killed in Colombes. On the following day, a demonstration of Algerian women at the Paris Town Hall was broken up and 530 women and 118 children were arrested (Stora 1991, p. 97).

The response in France was muted. Media reports gave the police version – that the demonstrators were terrorists. The left attempted to draw attention to the killings without success,[12] and only in recent years has more information come to light (Levine, 1985; Tristan, 1991; Assouline, 1991; Lloyd and Waters, 1991).[13]

DEVELOPMENT OF RACIAL VIOLENCE IN THE 1970S AND 1980S

Events in 1973 illustrated the enduring level of violent feelings in France against Algerians, who had become a special target for attack since the war. On 25 August Salah Bouguine, suffering from some kind of depression stabbed to death a bus driver in Marseille. The next day a violent article in the local paper, *Le Méridional*,[14] called for stringent government measures to be taken against immigration and threatened direct action. Violence, unprecedented since the end of the war in 1962, was unleashed against Algerians. A 'Marseille Defence Committee' was established with members of the extreme right *Ordre Nouveau* at its core (Guidice, 1992, p. 98). In the following week seven Algerians were killed in the Marseille area, ten in the whole of France.[15] One of the most publicised (perhaps because of his youth) was the shooting of 17-year-old Ladj Lounes, at close quarters, by a man in a car while he was playing football near his home. There were machine-gun and petrol-bomb attacks against North African cafes, hotels, *bidonvilles*, and *Sonacotra* (immigrant workers' hostel association) hostels.

Algerian workers declared strikes throughout France, supported by the main trade-union federations (Guidice, 1992, p. 102). An estimated fifty-two Algerians were either killed or badly wounded in 1973. The Algerian government suspended emigration to France (Guidice, 1992, p. 102).

The violence continued. We have already referred to the role of the extreme Right *Ordre Nouveau* (New Order) in the Marseille 'defence committee'. During the following years, the sequence of events suggests that the extreme Right's interventions prime the pump of daily acts of racism by individuals, bar-owners, clubs and public premises, with the background of the institutional racism of the police.

Bombings and organised violence against premises occupied by immigrants (North African bars, clubs, cafes and hostels) took place. More recently, cemeteries (particularly Jewish) have been a target closely associated with the daubing of Fascist imagery, swastikas and anti-Semitic slogans. In 1974 five people were injured by a bomb in an Algerian bar in Draguignan; a series of attacks against anti-racists took place in February and March 1977.[16] *Organisation Delta* claimed the killing of Laid Said in December 1977 and in the same month there was a serious attack on an immigrant hostel in the Moselle. In August 1980 Saardi Areshi was killed by a member of the *Front National* and in October a serious attack was made on the Jewish community at the Synagogue of the *Rue Copernic*.

During the Algerian war North Africans were frequently denied service in cafes and restaurants. This discrimination became part of a campaign for a Law Against Racism in the 1960s and 1970s.[17] The resentment about the presence of 'immigrants' in public places came to the fore in the form of refusals of service, arguments and violence.[18] Violence was directed at 'outsiders' who strayed into community celebrations.

Police violence has been a constant, with many cases of people killed or badly injured after police beatings and shootings of North Africans who fail to stop at identity or road checks (Bernheim and Borgese, 1992).

A new target of violence emerged in the 1980s: young people of immigrant origins. In Febuary 1980, 15-year-old Kader was killed in the *Cité des Montagnards* (Vitry, near Paris) by a housing guardian who had been watching violent Charles Bronson movies on television. He shot at a bunch of young people congregating near his flat, killing Kader.

The scenario at Vitry was repeated throughout the 1980s. Local people with shotguns were dispensing summary capital punishment for young people's nuisance and high spirits in areas which had few if any social or recreational facilities.

During the summer of 1982 resources were poured into the housing estates to prevent the 'rodeos'. Young people taken on holiday away from their home environment, experienced hostility in some areas.[19]

RESPONSES TO RACIAL VIOLENCE

There has been an official reluctance to take up the issue of racial violence in France. This may be partly explained by the *ad hoc* policy-making on immigration and the subsequent social issue of 'integration' (Wihtol de Wenden, 1988). Violence became embroiled in the debate about *insécurité* (law and order) which was exploited by the extreme Right in the 1980s. Even when Ministers promised to take initiatives they have never seriously considered doing more than enabling existing voluntary associations to take action against racism through the law courts, thereby passing on responsibility.

A recent report of the *Fédération Internationale des Droits de l'Homme* focused on three main problems in the exercise of police powers, identity controls; abuse of people during detention for questioning; and access to a lawyer.[20] Their report avoided highly publicised cases of racism to avoid controversy and to underline the insidious banality of police racism.

Other official reports have analysed 'different manifestations of racism and xenophobia'. The *Commission Nationale Consultative des Droits de l'Homme* (CNCDH) has presented figures and cases (CNCDH 1991, 1992) using monthly statistics from the *Renseignements Généraux* (RG) which have been collected since 1977. From June 1989 other government departments have collected data to improve local understanding of this type of violence.

The CNCDH emphasises the difficulty of distinguishing the motive behind violent actions. The first report of the CNCDH (1991) analyses

Ministry of the Interior figures from 1979 and comes to three main conclusions. First, since 1982 there has been a general increase in violence, linked to the upsurge in populist nationalism (in the form of the *Front National* (FN)) and the scapegoating of immigration for social ills like unemployment and 'insecurity'. Second, the main target for racial violence is the '*Maghrebien* immigrant population' (people from North Africa). Third, the documentation of violence suggests that it is of an extreme gravity with two killed and twenty-eight injured in 1987, three killed and sixty-two injured in 1988 and one killed and thirty injured in 1989. Much of this increase is attributed to skinhead activity, linked to extreme-right wing organisations, particularly the *Parti Nationaliste Français et Européen* (PNFE) who were implicated in arson attacks on *Sonacotra* immigrant hostels in south-east France.[21]

The CNCDH links anti-Maghrebien violence to events outside France (the growth of Muslim fundamentalism, particularly the *Front Islamique du Salut* (FIS) in Algeria and conflicts in the Middle East). A marked increase in racial violence in the first months of 1991 is attributed to the Gulf war (CNCDH, 1992).

Anti-Semitic attacks such as the 1980 bombing of the *Rue Copernic* synagogue and the 1982 shootings at the Goldenberg restaurant, both in Paris, and the profanation of the Carpentras cemetry in 1990, set off further incidents in the wake of media publicity which may lift social taboos against violence. The broader conduits of racism are seen as extreme racist or anti-Semitic organisations,[22] skinheads and hooligans; revisionist intellectuals; and the anti-immigrant propaganda of the *Front National* (FN) and its associated organisations.

The problem with this official view is that it removes a general responsibility from French society, regarding racial violence either originating in marginal groups (the extreme Right or pathologised social groups such as skinheads) or in external events (again, a pathologised category of international or foreign affairs). The media have a special amplifying responsibility. There is little room to move from the analysis of these official documents to social policy interventions 'on the ground'.

SOCIO ECONOMIC EXPLANATIONS

A rather different view is offered by Charles Palant (*Différences*, 1991) (Palant represented the *Mouvement Contre le Racisme et pour L'Amitié entre les Peuples*, MRAP on the CNCDH). While still focusing on the effects of the FN he attempts to explain the climate of violence in the context of social deprivation:

> The potential for racism which continues to exist in our society provides the basis for the success of the FN in these past years. They have been nourished by the little phrases and puns of Le Pen, which have sometimes contributed to appalling or dramatic acts. In a difficult social context such as that in which we live, the potential for racism turns into violence, mixing becomes promiscuity and all this nourishes hostilities in situations where mutual enrichment should be growing and expressing itself.[23]

This theme of a broader context has been used by other anti-racist organisations, in responding to racial violence. The socio-economic context of racism was raised in a television interview with Harlem Désir, then President of *SOS Racisme*, in August 1987.[24] Désir suggested that local joint committees for the prevention of racism should be established and that it was insufficient to focus on the FN leader:

> To struggle against racism, we shouldn't just shout 'Le Pen, Le Pen', but attack the inadequacies of French society . . . we should start by repairing the lifts and repainting stairwells.

In activist circles this statement was seen as opting out of the struggles against police abuses, but the theme was maintained in an interview in 1990 (*Libération*, 28/29 April 1990). Désir admitted that he had moved on from suggesting cosmetic solutions but still emphasised urban problems as a source of racism and racist violence:

> Ghettos and educational failure threaten the French melting-pot and the republican idea of a France which can integrate everyone in its territory.

The theme was maintained. In a response to the events of Vaulx en Velin MRAP analysed 'the violence of exclusion', linking discrimination to social exclusion and acts of despairing rage.[25] After the killing of Djamel by a supermarket guard, MRAP expressed the raw anger of young people while situating the death in the specific context of privatisation and reduced resources:

Djamel should never have been killed. Even if some places need surveillance, how can the presence of an armed militia be justified in public places like shopping centres, how can we not demand the respect for regulations on the carrying of arms? . . . the tragic consequences of the substitution of private companies operating for profit for the preventative role of public force, the only real guarantee of public order and social peace. Lack of space for living, meeting, activities in cities ravaged by exclusion . . . youth who are fed up with speeches and who really want their lives to have a meaning.[26]

Thus there are possibilities for action against racial violence. This stresses the value of a broad focus on the political, social and historical context of racism in contemporary society (Kushner and Lunn, 1989).

French sociologists (particularly Touraine's 'social movement' school) have analysed this context (Dubet 1987; Wieviorka, 1992; and Jazouli, 1992 and 1992a). They have focused on the growth of racism and the hopelessness of young people in suburban housing estates. Dubet (1987) studied 'the galley', the sense of aimlessness and drifting in social exclusion which accompany high unemployment and other social problems in the suburban housing estates of France. Wieviorka (1992) uncovered the subtleties of racism among ordinary people in this context, emphasising the distinction between the 'hard core' and more casual, knee-jerk reactions.

RACIAL VIOLENCE: THE MOBILISATION OF RESISTANCE

Concern about racial violence was an important mobilising factor in the youth-based anti-racist movements of the early 1980s although subsequent developments have shifted this focus to more mainstream political activity in *SOS Racisme* and *France Plus* (Jazouli, 1992a). Rock against Police (in the Paris region) and *Zaama de banlieue* (in the Lyon region) were established because of conflicts between police and young people and racist violence (Mogniss, 1982).[27]

Optimism about the new Socialist government in 1981 was short-lived. 'Rodeos' in the Lyon area during the summer highlighted the existence of complex, underlying social problems.[28] A series of racist crimes at the end of the following summer increased the feeling of insecurity and anger among young people.[29] There was considerable mobilisation of local defence committees around the specific problems of police behaviour, racist crime, housing and living conditions. When in 1982 Abdel Guemiah was killed neighbours declared a rent strike for safer housing.[30] There were similar issues in Lyon especially at *Les Minguettes* and *Venissieux*.[31]

The March 1983 *Front National* breakthrough in local elections led to further grass-roots initiatives. The *Cité Gutenberg* (where Abdel Guemiah had been killed) held an 'open-door festival'. At *Les Minguettes* a hunger strike defused tension between the police and young people. When Toumi Djaidja (one of the leaders of this hunger strike) was shot and badly injured,[32] there was an acrimonious debate about the merits of self-defence and non-violent action (Jazouli, 1972, p. 51). A group of youths led by Christian Délorme (a priest, active in the earlier hunger strike)[33] organised a march for Equality across France, drawing attention to racial violence and the everyday problems of 'the *beurs*' (the second generation of North African migrants, born in France). The March culminated on 6 December with a demonstration of some 100 000 people in the streets of Paris and a reception with President Mitterrand. The main thrust of the march had been to promote a moral message close to dominant universalist discourse in France (Lloyd, 1993, forthcoming), but it lacked either an organisational structure or subsequent programme.

The road was clear for the establishment of organisations (notably *SOS Racisme* and *France Plus*) who were stronger at national level and did not reflect the raw anger of young people on housing estates. Today, mobilisation against racist violence tends to be divided between the massive national demonstration and local committees of anti-racist and human rights organisations.

NOTES

1. I want to thank MRAP, especially Michelle Ganem, for their assistance in accomplishing this study.
2. In *Arabacides* Guidice is referring to the series of killings of 'Arabs' in France.
3. The Reims baker case, 1992.
4. *Le Monde*, 7/8 October 1940: '*Il y a cinquante ans, Vichy promulge le statut des juifs*'.
5. Of 21 April 1939.
6. The 'Statute of the Jews', ordering the census, defining Jewish status, restricting their professions, was enacted on 3 October 1940.

7. See also M. Henry, '*Il y a cinquante ans, la rafle des juifs en zone libre*', in *Libération*, 26 August 1992; '*Que faire de Vichy*' *(no spécial)*, *Esprit*, Mai 1992; and repeated attempts to secure a proper condemnation of the Vichy regime which at the same time recognises the responsibility of French officials but disclaiming responsibility because 'Vichy was not the republic', that is, abnormal, as in the Touvier verdict 1992. P. Rochette, '*Le fardeau du silence officiel sur les crimes de Vichy*', *Libération*, 11/12 Juillet 1992.

8. The Petit Robert dictionary gives the origin of *ratonnade* as around 1955 specifically to describe large attacks on North Africans.

9. The magazine, *Actuel*, published a SOFRES survey on torture in the Algerian war, emphasising the large number of French families whose members are still traumatised by the torture which they dispensed towards Algerians (January 1989). Also see Stora (1991) for an account of the numerous films which make reference to the trauma of this period, mainly from a French perspective.

10. In the early 1980s the MRAP ran a 'green star' campaign to protest at identity controls in the Metro.

11. Papon, prefect of police in Paris in 1961 had been responsible for Jewish Affairs in Bordeaux during the war, organising the deportation of Jews to death camps (Slitinsky, 1983). In the 1950s he served in the French colonial administration, including Algeria.

12. *Bulletin Municipal Officiel de la Ville de Paris*, 27 October 1961; It was difficult either to publish criticism of what was going on or to demonstrate in public against events; the brutal repression of the demonstration on 8 February 1962 against OAS atrocities was the occasion of the killing of eight demonstrators and other injuries by Papon's police.

13. Also remarks by F. Guidice during conversation 17 December 1992 with C. Lloyd.

14. By G. Domenech, on 26 August 1973, cited in Guidice, 1992, p. 93.

15. Among these were: Ladj Lounes killed in Marseille on 28 August, *Libération*, 2 November 1973, 6 January 1975; Hermahan Mebarki (died of wounds to the head), *Libération*, 2 November 1973; Ghillas Said (died of wounds from attack from an axe), *Libération*, 2 November 1973; Mouka Rachid (killed by an axe), *Libération*, 2 November 1973; Mebarki Hammou, (killed in Marseille) on 26 August, *Libération*, 2 November 1973.

16. The home of Charles Palant (Vice President of MRAP) was attacked in February and two other bombs were used against the MRAP offices in March 1977.

17. This is mentioned in the account of the campaign for the Law against Racism, MRAP 1984.

18. For instance a North African was shot dead at a dance club in Grenoble in January 1974, another killed 'because he had drunk too much' by a bar-owner in December of the same year; Belkacem Aouanmi killed by a Toulouse cafe-owner and Djellali Baghous killed by a night-club 'bouncer' in the Oise (both in August 1975); two Algerians killed during a disco fight in Aubusson (March 1976). There are countless other examples.

19. Such as *Belle Ile* in Brittany, *Searchlight*, November 1984, p. 18.

20. This report was specially commissioned by the Ministry of the Interior, partly as a result of disturbances between suburban youth and the police.
21. Four PNFE activists were convicted of these attacks, CCNDH, 1990, pp. 11, 28.
22. In 1991 and 1992 these included the *Parti Nationaliste Français et Européen* (PNFE); *Troisième Voie; Le Groupe Union Défense* (GUD); *Les Faisceaux Nationalistes Européens* (FNE); *Le Parti Nationaliste Français* (PNF); *L'Oeuvre Française* (OF).
23. Translations unless indicated otherwise are my own.
24. On the television programme, *L'Heure de Vérité*, reported in *Libération*, 20 August 1987.
25. A police intervention against a rodeo in October 1990 left three people (one a police officer) dead, *Différences*, December 1990.
26. Djamel was shot dead by a store guard at Satrouville. The chief magistrate of the town is said to have commented that the town was living through 'a mini Algerian war', MRAP Press statement 27 March 1991 and *Différences*, April 1991.
27. As the title 'Rock against Police' suggests, these young people were influenced by movements in the UK, especially Rock against Racism and the events of 1981 in Brixton and other inner-city areas, and the culture of resistance which accompanied these events.
28. *Rodeos* involved the stealing and driving at high speeds of cars which were finally set on fire.
29. On 28 September 1982 Ahmed Boutelja was shot by a neighbour in *Saint Jean de Bron* in Lyon (Guidice, 1992; *Le Monde* 30 March 1983; *Libération*, 5 December 1985); at the Gutenberg 'transit camp' at Nanterre, on 23 October 1982 Abdenbi Guemiah was mortally wounded, dying on 6 November (*Le Monde* 30 March 1983); a 21-year-old Algerian, Abdelkrim Haouette was killed at Livry-Gargan on 27 October 1982 (Guidice, 1992, p. 166); on 28 October 1982 18-year-old Wahid Hachichi was killed in Lyon by the owner of a vehicle who thought he was about to steal it (Guidice, 1992, p. 166, Jazouli 1992a, p. 44); and 41-year-old Abidou Mohammed was shot dead by the police in Lyon on 5/6 November 1982 (Guidice, 1992, p. 166).
30. Abdenbi Guemiah was a 19-year-old Moroccan who was shot on 23 October 1982 in the Gutenberg transit city (Nanterre near Paris) by a man who was aiming indiscriminately at a group of North African youths, *Le Monde* 30 March 1983.
31. C. Lloyd: interview with Tarik of IM'media 22 January 1988.
32. On 17 June 1983.
33. The CIMADE (*Comité Intergouvernemental auprès des évacues, Service oecuménique d'entréaide*) and MAN (*Mouvement d'action non-violent*).

16 A Local Response to Racial Violence

Benjamin Bowling and William Saulsbury[1]

From the limited material available on the subject of racial violence in Europe, it appears that the British government recognised the problem as a specific form of crime some time before many of its European neighbours (Evrigenis, 1985; Ford, 1990; Read and Simpson, 1991). By the time that other European countries started addressing the problem in the early 1990s, official policy had been developing in Britain for almost a decade. This is no cause for complacency on the part of British policy-makers, however. Surveys and research reports indicate that the problem is as chronic as it was at the start of the 1980s, that ethnic minority communities remain under the fear and threat of attack and that effective action to combat racial violence is still lacking (House of Commons, 1986; Home Office, 1989; Dunhill, 1989; Gordon, 1990). This is cause for concern and requires that continued attention be paid to shortcomings in the existing practice of statutory agencies.

One way central and local government, and the police have attempted to improve their response to racial violence in recent years has been to develop a coordinated approach to the problem. This chapter draws on the experience of an 'action-research' project aiming to develop a comprehensive local response to racial harassment and attacks in the East London borough of Newham between 1987 and 1991 (Saulsbury and Bowling 1991). The chapter first describes briefly the policy context of the project, focusing on the development of a coordinated or *multi-agency approach* to racial violence. It then outlines the lessons learnt from the east London project and, finally, draws out the implications of this experience for those who might consider following a similar path in other localities.[2]

THE DEVELOPMENT OF A LOCALLY COORDINATED
RESPONSE TO RACIAL VIOLENCE

Racial violence became an official policy issue at the beginning of the 1980s in Britain with the publication of the 1981 Home Office report, *Racial Attacks*. In the report, the Home Secretary announced that anxieties expressed about the 'wicked crime' of racial attacks were justified, were more common than formerly supposed and might be on the increase (Home Office, 1981, p. iii). The report and subsequent debate about what should be done about racial violence prompted the development of policies in various organisations where none had existed before. London's Metropolitan Police introduced recording and monitoring procedures in 1982 and the Greater London Council introduced a racial harassment policy into its housing department in 1983 (House of Commons, 1982; Greater London Council, 1984). Many other police forces and local councils followed their example during the 1980s (see Ginsburg, 1989; Hesse *et al.*, 1992; Bowling, 1993).

In addition to the development of policies within individual agencies, the 1980s saw the emergence of initiatives and procedures entailing *coordination* between the police, local public housing officials and other agencies. The idea that a coordinated approach was the best means to prevent and respond to particular forms of crime emerged in policing and Home Office policy documents since the 1950s (Home Office, 1982, 1991a; Weatheritt, 1986; Gordon, 1987). This approach was thought to be particularly useful for crimes such as racial harassment (Home Office 1981, 1982, p. 3). For example, the 1981 Home Office report urged authorities with a responsibility for dealing with racial attacks to make arrangements for coordination between services. This, the report suggested, would make possible a 'swift and coherent' approach coordinated between local authority officers (such as teachers and housing managers) and the police (Home Office, 1981, p. iv). As racial violence became a policy issue, coordination between agencies emerged as a key policy response. The idea of collaboration between the police and other agencies also dovetailed neatly with the recommendations arising out of Lord Scarman's report on the Brixton riots (Scarman, 1986), and the discussion of the issues surrounding policing and race relations in the 1981–2 Home Affairs Committee Report (House of Commons, 1982). Both emphasised the need for mechanisms by which the police could maintain contact with the people of the locality in which they worked and called for a framework for consultation and liaison between the police and local communities.[3]

It is evident from the literature that *ad hoc* coordination between the police and other statutory and voluntary agencies occurred from at least 1981 (London Race and Housing Forum 1982). Then, between 1984 and 1986, a specifically 'multi-agency approach' was applied to the problem of racial violence in a 'pilot study' conducted in four areas of London by the Community Relations Branch of the Metropolitan Police. This, in turn, led to the development of a policing policy of fostering and encouraging the multi-agency approach across London (Metropolitan Police, 1986; House of Commons, 1986). Local authorities, some of whom were reluctant at first to cooperate with the police (e.g. Greater London Council, 1984; Keith and Murji, 1990), began to participate in and initiate joint initiatives from around the mid-1980s (House of Commons, 1986; London Borough of Newham, 1986). Other agencies, such as Victim Support and local councils for racial equality also began to become involved actively in multi-agency initiatives from around this time (Kimber and Cooper, 1991).

By the mid-1980s a range of statutory and voluntary organisations were advocates of the multi-agency approach. It is important to note, however, that different organisations presented different rationales for their advocacy. Organisations representing ethnic minority communities, who encountered racial violence most directly, reasoned that a coordinated approach would provide a forum through which the police and other agencies could be persuaded to acknowledge the existence of the problem of racial violence and take action against perpetrators (London Race and Housing Forum, 1982; Manchester Council for Community Relations, 1986). At their most optimistic, they saw the approach as a means of combating racism and overcoming the causes of racial harassment (London Race and Housing Forum, 1982). Local government agencies tended to echo the views of community organisations, citing the benefits of multi-agency cooperation as being a means by which local organisations working in support of victims might try to make demands on the police and local authority housing departments (Greater London Council, 1984; London Borough of Newham, 1986). The police, in contrast to local authorities and community organisations, saw the benefits of the approach as 'the establishment of confidence and understanding between agencies, the establishment of common ground and the increased exchange of information' (Metropolitan Police, 1986; House of Commons, 1986, p. 29). They also reasoned that the approach would release the police from the position of sole responsibility for creating the social conditions which make racial incidents less likely (Metropolitan Police, 1986). Each of these rationales for advocating coordination may be valid, but it is important to recognise that they are not the same rationale and can be at odds with one another.

In 1986 the Commons Home Affairs Select Committee on Race Relations and Immigration made the strongest case yet for the development of a coordinated approach to racial violence. Its report concluded that:

> A multi-agency approach is not simply a way of making the police more effective and more aware of the problem, but should also promote action by other agencies and in particular a coordinated approach towards racial incidents in general and towards individual cases. . . . We regard a multi-agency approach as crucial in developing an effective response to racial incidents, and we pay tribute to those who have worked to establish such an approach (House of Commons, 1986, p. xiv).

The Committee did note that there was no guarantee that multi-agency schemes would work well and that they could be no substitute for each agency developing their own policies for tackling the problem. They also noted that in the recent past, both the police and local authorities had been critical of each other in such forums. Such problems notwithstanding, the Committee recommended that 'all police forces and local authorities whose areas contain an appreciable ethnic minority population give serious consideration to the establishment of a multi-agency approach to racial incidents' (House of Commons, 1986, p. xv).

The committee also recommended that the Home Office ensure that knowledge acquired as to the best ways of organising a multi-agency approach be disseminated, in response to which the Home Office initiated the development of an action-research project which became known as the North Plaistow Racial Harassment Project (Saulsbury and Bowling, 1991). The remainder of this chapter describes the development of the project and draws out some of the lessons learnt about multi-agency collaboration at the local level.

INITIATING THE PROJECT

In 1987, the Metropolitan Police, the London Borough of Newham, Newham Council for Racial Equality (NCRE), Victim Support Newham (VSN) and the Home Office formed a local multi-agency partnership to develop a comprehensive response to racial attacks and harassment in North Plaistow, an east London housing district.[4] The project aimed to prevent racial harassment and attacks, assist victims, identify and take action against perpetrators and tackle under-reporting by more efficient use of existing resources and through cooperation among the agencies involved. A local steering committee comprised of officers and elected members of the local authority, senior police officers and senior representatives of the other agencies was convened to direct and oversee the project's development. A working group comprised of community police officers, officers from local authority housing, social services, education and chief executives' departments and representatives of NCRE and VSN was also formed to carry out the day-to-day work of the project. A consultant (W. Saulsbury) was employed by the Home Office to organise and facilitate working relationships among the agencies involved and to participate actively in all the work of the project. A Home-Office-funded researcher (B. Bowling) assisted the consultant and undertook the evaluation.

Although the terms of reference for the project were agreed locally, a rational model to structure the work of the project known as 'problem-solving' was used as a guide (Goldstein, 1990). This involved problem description, strategy development, implementation and evaluation.

PROBLEM DESCRIPTION

As a first step, the working group produced an objective description of racial harassment and of the existing responses to it in the project area (see Saulsbury and Bowling, 1991: Appendix 4; Bowling, 1994). This description involved analysis of police records, a series of group interviews with the staff of local agencies and a victimisation survey.[5] The survey of local residents confirmed official records and local opinion that racial harassment was, and was seen as, a serious problem in the project area. Between one in five and one in six Afro-Caribbean and Asian men and women said they had suffered a racially motivated incident in an 18-month period. Racist insults, verbal abuse, threats and property damage were predominant, but stone-throwing, serious assault and arson were also mentioned. Those most fearful of racial attack were Asian women, nearly three-quarters of whom worried a 'great deal' or a 'fair amount' about themselves or a member of their family being victimised. When perpetrators were identified they were reported to be mainly groups of white males aged between 11 and 25.

In few cases was the offender known to the victim. There were some specific locations where incidents were most prevalent, though it was less easy to identify when they were most likely to occur.

Many of those surveyed thought that local agencies were not very helpful to the victims of racial harassment. Of those victims who had contacted the police or housing department, fewer than one in ten said that they were very satisfied with the way in which their case had been handled, while nearly one in five said that they were very dissatisfied. The most common reasons for dissatisfaction were that the agencies did not do enough to help, that they failed to keep the respondent informed about the progress of their case, or that they seemed not to be interested. 8 per cent of victims thought that the extent of racial harassment had declined over the past five years, just under half thought that it had stayed the same, while 28 per cent thought that it had worsened.

In the group interviews, officers from each agency pointed to weaknesses in the way in which they responded to both victims and perpetrators and offered suggestions as to how their response might be improved. In particular, officers pointed to limits in their statutory powers and a lack of communication about racial harassment cases *within* as well as between agencies.

DEVELOPING AN ACTION PLAN

The working group then began to develop a range of initiatives to address various aspects of the problems of racial harassment and attack. The project's terms of reference were intended to provide members of the working group with as much latitude to develop initiatives as they wished. However, they were constrained by existing legal and administrative definitions of racial harassment, and by a concern that resources were unlikely to be made available to translate their ideas into practice. As a consequence, working-group members – all of whom were experienced officers within their own organisation – were reluctant to recommend initiatives that went beyond the established practice of their agency, or those that required new resources. In their usual roles, working-group members would be defending their organisation's interests and operating within their limitations. They anticipated correctly that their agencies would resist new ideas. The task that faced them required them to step away from their normal practices and to confront problems with their own agency's response to racial harassment in front of officers from other departments and organisations.

Despite these constraints, an action plan was produced which included more than twenty separate initiatives (Saulsbury and Bowling, 1991, Appendix 5). The majority represented enhanced *single-agency* procedures – such as targeted patrolling and an outreach programme undertaken by the police; upgraded lighting and environmental improvements by the local authority technical services department; improvements in immediate response and follow-up by the housing department; and the introduction of recording and monitoring procedures in local schools by the education department. The joint initiatives which were developed aimed to improve communication and cooperation between agencies. These included the development of referral systems between housing, police and Victim Support and the production of an information pack for victims.

IMPLEMENTATION AND EVALUATION

The development of an appropriate evaluation strategy for the project was not at all straightforward. The project was concerned with the responses of several very different agencies working towards several distinct goals: improving communication and cooperation between agencies, preventing racial attacks and harassment, encouraging reporting, tackling perpetrators and supporting victims. The evaluation involved assessing how the initiatives were actually implemented and carried out on the ground (*process* evaluation) and assessing their effect in reducing the extent of racial harassment (*impact* evaluation).

Each agency took responsibility for implementing the initiatives in which they were involved. As the process evaluation unfolded, however, it became clear that the working and steering groups had failed to specify clearly enough how the initiatives were to be implemented. Interviews with members of both the steering and working groups suggested that changes in practices had not been communicated effectively down through their organisations. Some first-line managers had not been informed adequately of the purpose of the project or of what their responsibilities were. In turn, front-line staff who were actually to carry out the initiatives were not fully aware of what was expected of them. It became apparent that many of the initiatives had not been fully implemented and some had not been implemented at all. In the final report on the project it was concluded that the style of preventive policing, the quality of services for victims and the way in which perpetrators were dealt with remained largely unchanged from that at the start of the project (Saulsbury and Bowling, 1991, pp. 54–61).

In common with many other developmental projects, most of the lessons learnt from the North Plaistow experience are to do with over-ambitious expectations, unforeseen constraints, and mistaken assumptions. The agencies involved shared an assumption that a coordinated, multi-agency approach offered a number of significant advantages over unilateral action. However, the consensus view that 'good cannot help but come from greater coordination' hides the fact that different agencies hold different stated and unstated goals for participating in such a multi-agency effort (Blagg *et al.*, 1988). Coordination may be suggested as a means of establishing a comprehensive response, realigning cross-purposes, avoiding duplication, filling gaps in service delivery and meeting client demand for resources (Rein, 1983). As well as these stated objectives, each agency will have its own reasons for advocating multi-agency coordination which stem from their different statutory responsibilities, organisational environments, and methods of operation. It must be recognised that the goals of each agency involved may not necessarily be compatible, and may sometimes conflict with each other (Sampson *et al.*, 1988).

At one point in this project, for example, it was suggested that interviews with the parties involved in a racial incident should be conducted jointly by council and police officers. However, this initiative did not get off the ground because it was found that the legal approaches taken by each agency were at odds with one another. In preparing *civil* cases, council departments took a victim-centred approach which entailed accepting the victims' perception of events at face value and acting to some degree as their advocate. By way of contrast, the police approach was geared to the requirements of *criminal* law, and typically involved challenging victims' evidence in the same way that they would challenge that of any other witness or of the alleged perpetrator. Consequently, a shared approach could not be agreed, even in principle.

Attempting to coordinate the work of several agencies does not, of itself, lead to the solution of problems. It will not compensate for any single agency's failure to come to grips with a problem. Most certainly, it will do little to alleviate problems of coordination *within* agencies. Multi-agency coordination can only augment effective action taken by individual agencies.

The first steps for those considering multi-agency working are to decide very precisely what their common goals are and whether coordination is the best means of achieving them. Having agreed upon general goals, agencies must agree on more detailed aims, such as which aspects of their operational procedures are to be coordinated, exactly how this will be done and what they hope to achieve.

Although the multi-agency approach seeks to make a more efficient use of existing resources, the need for additional resources to develop some joint initiatives should not be overlooked. In North Plaistow, officer time had to be dedicated to the collection, analysis and interpretation of information, and to the development and implementation of joint initiatives. Some initiatives needed financial support, at least in the form of 'seed-corn' money. In this project, the task of developing new initiatives was undermined because there was no guarantee of resources to support them. For others taking this route, the financial foundation of the project should be made clear early on and shared equitably among the agencies involved.

The failure to involve community members fully was a source of disappointment throughout the project's life. The original intention was for members of the community to participate in the steering and working group of the project, but this met with little success. As a result, the project became almost exclusively agency-centred. In our final report on the project we attributed this to the use of an unduly restrictive definition of the 'local community', weakness in the mechanism for including community participation, failure to capitalise on the willingness of those who did express their desire to become involved and the formality of the 'agency-dominated committee' (Saulsbury and Bowling, 1991, p. 82). We concluded that community participation in a strategy to combat racial violence was vital, and that all possible ways to involve the community and ensure the representation of their views should be explored.

CONSTRAINTS ON IMPLEMENTING A LOCALLY COORDINATED APPROACH

The North Plaistow project, in common with many others, made a number of assumptions about the degree to which implementation of its action initiatives would be straightforward (Hope 1985; Rein 1983). It was assumed, for example, that having agreed a set of new or revised procedures, the steps necessary to mesh them with existing procedures would be readily apparent to and automatically undertaken by the representatives of the agencies involved. However, implementation was more complex and needed a greater degree of guidance than had been anticipated. For future attempts to introduce locally coordinated action, it is essential that a plan for translating policy into practice which identifies organisational constraints which could affect implementation, is agreed in advance.

Three types of constraints on implementing organisational change were identified. A range of *internal constraints* (operating within individual agencies) affected the ability to change or suspend existing policies, even in a small site for a limited period of time. Implementing new initiatives involved going through a lengthy and complex decision-making process within each organisation. For example, before the police could refer racial attacks to Victim Support a new internal procedure had to be agreed between three separate elements of the police organisation – the first response units (or 'reliefs'), the community contact team and the crime desk – each of which had separate line management and were located in different parts of the police station. Internal constraints also stemmed from the inflexibility of each organisation's structure, ideology and working practices. These factors affected the ability of officers to be critical of their organisations, to accept ideas which challenged traditional ways of looking at the problem, and therefore to develop innovative multi-agency strategies. Perhaps the greatest internal constraint concerns the services which agencies are in a position to provide. What each can offer is limited by its statutory powers and the resources that it has at its disposal. For example, a housing department's primary concern is the provision and management of public housing. While it may seek to prevent people from being harassed (using legal measures, for instance), there are strict limits on its ability to do this (FitzGerald, 1989).

Inter-agency constraints on coordination arise from differences in the priorities, ideological perspectives and practices of participating organisations. The degree to which these conflicts affected this project can be seen in the failure to agree on a definition of racial harassment for practical purposes. Even at the end of the project there was still disagreement between ground-level police and housing officers over whether a given incident was racially motivated, or merely a neighbour dispute. Multi-agency cooperation implies and requires consensus in the ideas underpinning action. Conflict, although it may be necessary to bring about change, endangers the basis for cooperation (Sampson *et al.*, 1988). In North Plaistow, this meant that initiatives for which agreement among the agencies involved seemed unlikely were avoided or, if they were suggested at all, were abandoned quickly in the belief that disagreement would undermine the principle of cooperation that brought them together.

Finally, there is a set of *external constraints* which are imposed by the procedures, practices and legal frameworks of agencies and which lie completely outside of local control. For example, some key posts such as housing department officers responsible for monitoring racial harassment cases (race equality officers) rely on central government funding. The prosecuting authorities (the Crown Prosecution Service or CPS) make the ultimate decision in prosecuting in harassment and attack cases, and obviously the outcome of any prosecution lies with the courts. The policies of the CPS, the higher tiers of police management, the courts, the probation service and central government departments influence the outcomes of legal action, the implementation of new procedures, and the allocation of resources.

IMPLICATIONS FOR OTHER EUROPEAN COUNTRIES

The key question for the purposes of this chapter is: how can the lessons learnt from this project be of benefit to those wishing to develop a local response to racial violence in other European countries?[6]

First, one should point to the *potential* of the coordinated approach. The idea that all the state and voluntary organisations who have a responsibility for tackling racial violence in a particular locality should try to work together to support victims, prosecute perpetrators and prevent attacks from occurring is an appealing one. It is one that, on the surface, may appear to be an unproblematically 'good thing' and, in theory, the idea has tremendous potential. For example, the behaviour of perpetrators of racial attacks or harassment could be challenged by probation officers, social workers, youth leaders, teachers as well as dealt with by the police, housing officials and the courts. Similarly, victims of attacks or harassment could be supported by support workers from specialist support agencies such as Victim Support, public housing authorities, community workers, tenants' associations, church groups, teachers and ordinary citizens. Who could oppose such united opposition to such a divisive and abhorrent social problem? Indeed, in certain specific circumstances, action coordinated between the police and other agencies has advantages over the actions of agencies acting alone.

While recognising the potential of such an approach, however, it is important to bear in mind its limitations. It is clear, for example, that multi-agency cooperation will not, in and of itself, solve the problems of racism and violence. Most importantly, attempts to initiate coordinated or joint action *cannot substitute for effective action by individual agencies*. The most important lesson for others going down this road, therefore, is that national and local police forces, authorities responsible for public housing, social services, education and the welfare of ethnic minorities must ensure the adequacy of their *individual* responses as well as attempting to develop coordinated policies.

It is also important to bear in mind the problems encountered in implementing a coordinated response to the problem of racial violence in North Plaistow. If the East London experience holds for other European countries, the statutory and voluntary agencies and community groups responding to 'racial violence' will conceptualise the problem differently, have competing views about the causes of the problem and, therefore, have different views about how it should be prevented or responded to. It must be recognised that by its very nature, views about what the problem is and what should be done about it will conflict. As the coverage of the 'outbreaks' of violent racism in European countries illustrates, the problem of violence directed against 'foreigners' is, tragically, as likely to be attributed to the presence of the 'foreigners' themselves as to resurgent nationalism, xenophobia or racial hatred. Obviously, the conceptualisation of the problem has profound implications for the development of its solution.

The participants in a multi-agency initiative may also have different stated and unstated goals for coordination which may well be incompatible or in conflict. For example, ethnic minority communities' goal of using the multi-agency approach to gain greater police protection, is not compatible with the desire of the police to broaden the burden of responsibility for the dealing with the problem. Even when an agreement about what is to be done is reached among decision-makers, there are further problems in implementing any coordinated strategy which has been agreed upon. The officers responsible for implementing single- or multi-agency policies may resist, ignore or subvert instructions aiming to change their working practices.

CONCLUSION

Racial violence takes many forms – from violent disorder directed against ethnic minorities of the sort witnessed in Rostock and elsewhere; sporadic arson attacks, physical violence and murder of ethnic minority individuals; to sustained campaigns of harassment on the homes of ethnic minority families. In whatever form, racial attacks and harassment are 'unquestionably the most obnoxious and destructive aspect of . . . racial discrimination'[7] and must be overcome. The question of *how* to overcome racial violence, therefore, has become one of the most pressing concerns for black and other ethnic minority communities, anti-racist activists, police and governments across Europe (Hesse *et al.*, pp. xxvi–xxvii). Most specifically, police forces, local government agencies (particularly those responsible for public housing) and organisations representing ethnic minority communities must be prepared and equipped to respond to racial violence in all its forms.

The idea that various statutory and community organisations should work in partnership to tackle this problem is an appealing one, but one that is beset with practical problems. Lack of consensus over how the problem is to be defined, explained and tackled undermines the basis for collective action. Conflict over the goals of coordination may lead to agencies working at cross-purposes. Local organisations must be clear about what they can do individually to tackle racial violence within their areas of responsibility and statutory powers. Collective action will be most effective when cooperating agencies have gone to the limit of their individual action and now seek to go further.

Finally, how 'the community' is represented in such a locally coordinated approach is of crucial importance to its effectiveness, though by no means unproblematic. Racial violence is a problem which arises from a 'community' divided against itself. It may prove to be impossible to find consensus among the inhabitants of a locality when some oppose the presence of ethnic minorities as strongly as others oppose racism and racial hatred.

The success with which central and local government agencies, the police and communities themselves resolve the problems outlined in this chapter will affect the extent to which racism and racial violence are controlled or entrenched in the coming decade.

NOTES

1. An earlier, shorter version of this paper appeared in the *Home Office Research Bulletin*, no 32 (1992).
2. Participants at the Oslo workshop questioned the extent to which it is possible to generalise from a single case study. Like any case study, there are a series of atypicalities that make it distinctive and idosyncratic (Yin, 1989). Undoubtedly, coordinated action will develop differently in other localities where other social and political factors obtain. Nonetheless, it seems likely that much of what was observed in North Plaistow will recur in many other localities. It is only by documenting such experiences that this will become clear. As Yin (1989) argues, case studies require replication no less than quantitative surveys. Indeed, evidence from North Plaistow has confirmed observations from earlier coordinated crime prevention initiatives in the UK (Hope, 1985; Weatheritt, 1986). On the basis of the North Plaistow experience, we offer pointers – suggestions where both potential for, and constraints on, effective action may lie. As Martin Rein suggests: 'social understanding . . . depends upon telling relevant stories: that is, deriving from past experience a narrative which interprets the events as they unfolded and draws a moral for future actions, suggesting, for example, how the future might unfold if certain steps were taken' (Rein, 1976 pp. 265–6).
3. Such a framework was embodied in legislation in Section 106 of the Police and Criminal Evidence Act which required Police Authorities to make arrangements 'for obtaining the views of people in that area about matters concerning the policing of the area and for obtaining their cooperation with the police in preventing crime in the area' (see also House of Commons, 1986, p. xv).
4. A few words should be said about the locality at this point. East London, of which North Plaistow is a part, has a long history of racial antipathy and exclusionism, territorial defensiveness and violence directed specifically against ethnic minorities. East London is cited as the geographical origin of the skinheads and of the term 'Paki-bashing' to describe systematic attacks on the Asian community *circa* 1969. In the mid-1970s East London localities were foci for racial violence and where explicitly racist political parties (such as the National Front) were most successful electorally (Husbands, 1983). This violence continued throughout the 1970s and 1980s with peaks in 1978–81 and again in 1985 (Hesse *et al.*, 1992). During the mid-1980s, Newham also saw numerous clashes between the police and Asian self-defence organisations. The issue of racial violence was highly politicised over this period, as evidenced by the often acrimonious debate among the police, local authority and community organisations conducted in the local press. In 1987 (at the start of the North Plaistow project) police statistics indicated that Newham had the highest rate of recorded racial incidents in Greater London (364), and that Plaistow North housing district had the highest number of recorded cases in Newham.
5. The survey was based on a random sample of 751 and a 'booster' sample of Asian respondents, giving a total sample size of 1174 drawn from residents

of the study site. 163 respondents reported being the victim of a racial incident, 114 of whom provided details of their experience.

6. It should be noted that the idea of coordinated action has long been evident elsewhere in Europe, with different experience from that in the UK (King, 1991; Cathie Lloyd, Chapter 15 in this volume). Participants in the Oslo workshop also pointed to their experience of effective locally coordinated action against racial attacks – in Brumunddal, for instance. The Norwegian Ministry of Local Government and Labour has recently made cooperation among local agencies a component of its strategy to combat racial violence.

7. Comment made by Kenneth Baker, former Home Secretary, in the foreword to the *Second Report of the Inter-Departmental Racial Attacks Group* (Home Office, 1991).

Bibliography

Amnesty International, *Turkische Rechtsextremisten in der Turkei und in Europa* (Bonn: Amnesty International, 1979).

Amnesty International, *Alleged Torture and Ill-treatment of Roma in Piata Rahova in Bucharest*. AI Index: EUR 01/04/92 (London, 1992).

Andison, F. S., T.V. Violence and viewer aggression: A culimination of study results, 1956–1976', *Public Opinion Quarterly*, 41 (1977) pp. 314–31.

Aronson, I. Michael, *Troubled Waters: The Origins of the 1881 Anti-Jewish Pogroms in Russia* (Pittsburgh, 1990).

Assoulinge, D., 'Ce jour là', *Politics* (19 September 1991).

Auswärtiges Amt/Ministry of Foreign Affairs, *Lagebericht Rumänien 514–516.80/3* (Bonn, 1991).

Barker, M., *The New Racism* (London: Junction Books, 1981).

Bayerisches Staatsministerium des Innern, *Verfassungsschutzbericht Bayern* (1991).

Bech, Sam and Nicolae Gheorghe, *From Slaves to Nationality: Political Economy and Cultural Interpretation of Gypsy Ethnicity in Romania* (Amsterdam, 1980).

Benyon, J., *A Tale of Failure: Race and Policing*, CREC policy paper, no 3 (Coventry: University of Warwick, 1986).

Benyon, J., 'Unrest and the Political Agenda', in J. Benyon and J. Solomos, *The Roots of Urban Unrest* (Oxford: Pergamon Press, 1987).

Benz, Wolfgang, *Rechtsextremismus in der Bundesrepublik* (Fischer Informationen zur Zeit, 1984).

Bernheim, J.C. and G. Borghese, *Racisme et Police en France*, Rapport Federation Internationale des Droits de l'Homme, no 51 (1992).

Beşilçi, I., *Kürtlerin Mecburi Iskani* (Ankara, Komal Publishing, 1977a).

Beşilçi, I., *Türk Tarih Tezi, Güneş-Dil Teoresi ve Kürt Sorunu* (Ankara: Komal Publishing, 1977b).

Beşilçi, I., *Cumhuriyet Halk Firkasi Programi (1931) ve Kürt Sorunu* (Ankara: Belge Publishing, 1990).

Bethnal Green and Stepney Trades Council, *Blood on the Streets: A Report on Racial Attacks in East London* (London: Bethnal Green and Stepney Trades Council, 1978).

Björgo, Tore, *Vold mot innvandrere og asylsøkere* (Oslo: NUPI-rapport nr 136, 1989).

Björgo, Tore, 'Legal Reactions to Racism: Law and Practice in Scandinavia', in Hamm (1994).

Björgo, Tore: 'Militant Neo-Nazism in Sweden', *Terrorism and Political Violence* vol. 5, no 3 (Autumn 1993).

Björgo, Tore and Daniel Heradstveit, *Politisk terrorisme* (Oslo: TANO, 1993).

Blagg, H., Pearson, G. Sampson, S. Smith, D. and Stubbs, P., 'Inter-agency Cooperation: Rhetoric and Reality', in T. Hope and M. Shaw (eds.), *Communities and Crime Reduction* (London: HMSO, 1988).

236

Bovenkerk, F., Miles, R. and Verbunt, G., 'Comparative Studies of Migration and Exclusionism on the Grounds of 'Race' and Ethnic Background in Western Europe: A Critical Appraisal', *International Migration Review*, XXV, no 2 (1990a) pp. 375–91.

Bovenkerk, F., Miles, R. and Verbunt, G., 'Racism, Migration and the State in Western Europe: A Case for Comparative Analysis', *International Sociology*, vol. 5, no 4 (1990b) pp. 475–90.

Bowling, B., *Policing Racial Violence in Britain*, paper presented to the Learned Society, University of Victoria, British Columbia, 1990.

Bowling, B. and W. Saulsbury, 'A multi-agency approach to racial harassment', *Home Office Research Bulletin*, no 32 (London: Home Office Research and Planning Unit, 1992).

Bowling, B., 'Racial Harassment in East London' in Hamm (1994).

Bowling, B., 'Racial Harassment and the Process of Victimisation: Conceptual and Methodological Implications for the Local Crime Survey', *British Journal of Criminology*, vol. 33, no 2 (Spring 1993).

Brants, C. H. and Brants, K. L. K., *De Sociale Constructie van Fraude* (Arnhem: Gouda Quint, 1990).

Bunyan, T., 'Towards an Authoritarian European State', *Race & Class*, vol. 32, no 3 (1991).

Butterwegge, Christoph and Jäger, Siegfried, *Rassismus in Europa* (Köln: Bund-Verlag, 1992).

Campaign Against Racism and Fascism (CARF) and Southall Rights, *Southall. The Birth of a Black Community* (London: CARF, 1981).

Cashmore, E. and McLaughlin, E. (eds) *Out of Order: Policing Black People*, (London: Routledge, 1991).

Cheles, Luciano *et al.* (ed.) *Neo-Fascism in Europe* (Longman, 1991).

Chicago Commission on Race Relations, *The Negro in Chicago: A Study of Race Relations and a Race Riot* (Chicago, Ill.: University of Chicago Press, 1922).

Christians, Georg, *Die Reihen fest geschlossen* (VA&G, 1990).

Coates, James, *Armed and Dangerous: The Rise of the Survivalist Right* (Hill & Wang, 1987).

Cobb, R. W. and Elder, C. D., *Participation in American Politics: The Dynamic of Agenda-Building* (Baltimore: Johns Hopkins University Press, 1983) (1st edn, 1972).

Cohen, Stanley, *Folk Devils & Moral Panics: The Creation of Mods and Rockers* (Oxford: Basil Blackwell, 1980).

'Collective', *L'Europe en chemise brune* (16 : Reflex, 1992).

Commission Nationale Consultative des Droits de l'Homme (CNCDH), *1990: La Lutte Contre le Racisme et la Xénophobie* (Paris: Documentation Française, 1991).

Commission Nationale Consultative des Droits de l'Homme (CNCDH), *1991: La Lutte Contre le Racisme et la Xénophobie* (Paris: Documentation Française, 1992).

Commission of Human Rights, *Resolutions E./CN.4/1992/L.72 and 1992/65 Protection of Roma* (Geneva, 1992).

Commission of Human Rights, *Report on the Situation of Human Rights in Romania*, submitted by Mr Joseph Voyame, Special Rapporteur appointed in Accordance with the Resolution 1989/75 of the Commission of Human Rights, E/CN.4/1991/30 (Geneva, 1991).

Commission for Racial Equality, *Learning in Terror: A Survey of Racial Harassment in Schools and Colleges in England, Scotland and Wales, 1985–1987* (London: Commission for Racial Equality, 1988).

Council of Europe, *Report on Racial Violence and Harassment in Europe*, prepared by Mr Robin Oakley (Strasbourg, 1992).

Crenshaw, Martha, 'Theories of Terrorism: Instrumental and Organizational Approaches', in D.C. Rapoport (ed.) *Inside Terrorist Organization* (New York: Columbia University Press, 1988).

Crenshaw, Martha, 'How Terrorism Declines', *Terrorism and Political Violence*, vol. 3, no 1 (Spring 1991).

De Jong, W., *Inter-etnische verhoudingen in een oude stadswijk* (Delft: Eburon, 1986).

Delegation of Romania, *Meeting of Experts on National Minorities*, Information Circular no 2 (Geneva, 1991, unpublished).

Der Bundesminister des Innern, *Schutz der Demokratie* (Bonn, 1992a).

Der Bundesminister des Innern, *Verfassungsschutzbericht* (Bonn, 1989, 1990 and 1991).

Der Bundesminister des Innern, *Aspekte der inneren Sicherheit* (Bonn, 1992b).

Der Bundesminister des Innern, *Extremismus und Fremdenfeindlichkeit*, vol. 2 (Bonn, 1992c).

Dewitte, P., 'Immigrés et Front Popu', *Différences* nos 57–8 (Juin/Juillet 1986).

Donselaar, Jaap van, *Fout na de oorlog; fascistische en racistische organisaties in Nederland 1950–1990* (Amsterdam: Bert Bakker, 1991).

Donselaar, Jaap van, 'Post-war Fascism in the Netherlands', *Crime, Law and Social Change*, vol. 19 (1993).

Dubet, F., *La galère: jeunes en survie* (Paris: Fayard, 1987).

Dudek, Peter, *Jugendliche Rechtsextremisten: Zwischen Hakenkreuz und Odalsrune, 1945 bis heute* (Cologne: Bund-Verlag, 1985).

Dunhill, C., 'Women, Racist Attacks and the Response from Anti-Racist Groups', in C. Dunhill, (ed.) *The Boys in Blue: Women's Challenge to the Police* (London: Virago, 1989).

Eijck, C. van der and W. J. P. Kok, 'Non-decisions reconsidered', *Acta Politica*, X (1975a) pp. 277–301.

Eijck, C. van der, 'Politieke Participatie; Een Overzicht van Recente Literatuur', *Acta Politica*, X (1975) pp. 341–63.

Elbers, S. and Fennema, M. *Racistische Partijen in West Europa* (Amsterdam: Stichting Burgerschapskunde, 1993).

Eroğlu, H., *Türk Devrim Tarihi* (Ankara: Council of Research for Ataturk and his Revolutions, 1974).

Ethnic Federation of Roma, *The Escalation of Racial Violence against Roma in Romania*, Statement for the International Conference on Ethnic Conflict Resolution (Institute of Peace: Washington DC, 12–14 June 1991).

European Parliament, *Untersuchungsausschluß 'Wiederaufleben der Faschismus und Rassismus in Europa'* (1985).

European Parliament, *Bericht im Namen des Untersuchungsausschluäes Rassismus und Ausländerfeindlichkeit* (1990).

Evrigenis, G. (rapporteur) *Report on the Findings of the Committee of Inquiry into the Rise of Racism and Fascism in Europe* (Strasbourg: European Parliament, 1985).

Field, Daniel, *Rebels in the Name of the Tsar* (Boston: Houghton Mifflin, 1976).

Finger, B. and N. Karel, *Opération 'Vent Printanier' 16–17 juillet 1942. La Rafle du Vel d'Hiv* (Paris: La Découverte, 1992).

FitzGerald, M., 'Legal Approaches to Racial Harassment in Council Housing: The Case for Reassessment', *New Community*, vol. 16(1) (1989) pp. 93–106.

Forbes, Duncan, *Action on Racial Harassment: Legal Remedies and Local Authorities* (London: Legal Action Group and London Housing Unit, 1988).

Ford, G. (rapporteur), *Report on the Findings of the Committee of Inquiry into Racism and Xenophobia* (Strasbourg: European Parliament, 1990).

Ford, Glyn, *Fascist Europe: The Rise of Racism and Xenophobia* (London/ Boulder: Pluto Press, 1992).

Friedman, S: *Pogromchinx: The Assassination of Simon Petlura* (New York: 16B, 1976).

Frigaard, Iver, 'Terrorism in a Nordic Perspective', in E. Ellingsen (ed.) *International Terrorism as a Political Weapon* (Oslo: The Norwegian Atlantic Committee, 1988).

Fryer, P., *Staying Power* (London: Pluto Press, 1991) (1st edn, 1984).

Fuller, William C., *Civil–Military Conflict in Imperial Russia, 1881–1914* (Princeton, Princeton University Press, 1985).

Gheorghe, Nicolae, 'Zwischen Emanzipation und Diskriminierung. Historische und aktuelle Aspekte der rumänischen Roma Frage', in *Halbjahresschrift für Südosteuropäische Geschichte, Literatur und Politik*, no 2 (Ippesheim, 1992).

Ginsburg, N., 'Racial Harassment Policy and Practice: The Denial of Citizenship', *Critical Social Policy*, no 26 (1989) pp. 66–81.

Goffman, Erving, *The Presentation of Self in Everyday Life* (New York, London: Penguin, 1959).

Goldstein, H., *Problem-Oriented Policing* (New York: McGraw-Hill, 1990).

Gordon, P., *White Law: Racism in the Police, Courts and Prisons* (London: Pluto Press, 1983).

Gordon, P., 'Racial Incidents in Britain 1988–90: A Survey', *Runnymede Bulletin*, no 254, April 1992.

Gordon, P., 'Community Policing: Towards the Local Police State? in P. Scraton (ed.) *Law, Order and the Authoritarian State* (Milton Keynes: Open University Press, 1987).

Gordon, P., *Racial Violence and Harassment* (London: The Runnymede Trust, 1990) 2nd edn (1st edn, 1986).

Graaf, H. van der and Hoppe, R. *Beleid en Politiek: Een Inleiding tot de Beleidswetenschap en de Beleidskunde* (Muiderberg: Coutinho, 1989).

Greater London Council, *Racial Harassment in London: Report of a Panel of Inquiry Set Up by the GLC Police Committee* (London: GLC, 1984).

Groenendijk, Kees, 'Verboden voor Tukkers; reacties op rellen tussen Italianen, Spanjaarden en Twentenaren in 1961', in F. Bovenkerk et al. (eds) *Wetenschap en partijdigheid* (Assen, 1990).

Guidice, F., *Arabacides* (Paris: La Découverte, 1992).

Hagendoorn, Louk, and Joseph Hraba, 'Foreign, Different, Deviant, Seclusive and Working-Class: Anchors to an Ethnic Hierarchy in The Netherlands', *Ethnic and Racial Studies*, vol. 12, no 4 (October 1989) pp. 441–68.

Hainsworth, Paul (ed.) *The Extreme Right in Europe and the USA* (London: Pinter, 1992).

Hall, S. *et al.*, *Policing the Crisis: 'Mugging', the State and Law and Order* (London: Macmillan, 1978).

Hamm, Mark S. (ed.) *Hate Crime: International Perspectives on Causes and Control* (Cincinnati: Anderson Publishing Co/Academy of Criminal Justice Sciences, 1994).

Hancock, Ian, *The Pariah Syndrome – An Account of Gypsy Slavery and Persecution* (Karoma Publishers: Ann Arbor, 1987).

Hanioğlu, M. S., *Osmanli Ittihad ve Terakki Cemiyeti ve Jön Türklük (1889–1902)* (Istanbul: Iletisim Publishing, 1985).

Heitmeyer, Wilhelm, *Rechtsextremistische Orientierungen bei Jugendlichen: Empirische Ergebnisse und Erklärungsmuster einer Untersuchung zur politischen Sozialisation* (Weinheim and Munich: Juventa Verlag, 1988, 1992a).

Heitmeyer, W., 'Wenn der Alltag fremd wird', in *Blätter für deutsche und internationale Politik*, 7 (1991) pp. 851–2.

Heitmeyer, Wilhelm, *Rechtsextremismus: 'Warum handeln Menschen gegen ihre eigenen Interessen?': Materialien zur Auseinandersetzung mit Ursachen* (Cologne: Bund-Verlag, 1992a).

Heitmeyer, Wilhelm (1992b) 'Die Widerspiegelung von Modernisierungsrückständen im Rechtsextremismus', in Karl-Heinz Heinemann and Wilfried Schubarth (eds) *Der antifaschistische Staat entläßt seine Kinder: Jugend und Rechtsextremismus in Ostdeutschland* (Cologne: Papy Rossa Verlag, 1992b) pp. 100–15.

Helsinki Watch, *Destroying Ethnic Identity: The Persecution of Gypsies in Romania* (New York, 1991).

Heradstveit, Daniel and Tore Björgo, *Politisk kommunikasjon* (Oslo: TANO, 1992).

Hernes, Gudmund and Knudsen, Knud, *Svart på hvitt: Norske reaksjoner på flyktninger, asylsøkere og innvandrere* (Oslo: FAFO-rapport no 109, 1990).

Hesse, B., Rai, D. K. Bennett, C. and McGilchrist, P. *Beneath the Surface: Racial Harassment* (Aldershot: Avebury, 1992).

Hewitt, Christopher, 'Public's Perspectives', in Paletz and Schmid (1992).

Hill, Ray with Bell, Andrew, *The Other Face of Terror: Inside Europe's Neo-Nazi Network* (Grafton: Collins, 1988).

Hiro, D., *Black British White British* (London: Paladin, 1992) (1st edn, 1971).

Hirsch, Kurt, *Rechts von der Union - Personen, Organisationen, Parteien seit 1945* (Knesebeck & Schuler, 1989).

Home Affairs Committee, *Racial Attacks and Harassment* (London: HMSO, 1986).

Home Affairs Committee, *Racial Attacks and Harassment* (London: HMSO, 1989).

Home Department, Secretary of State for the, *Racial Attacks and Harassment: Government Reply to the Home Affairs Committee* (London: HMSO, 1986).

Home Office, *Racial Attacks: Report of a Home Office Study* (London: Home Office, 1981).

Home Office, *Crime Prevention: A Co-ordinated Approach*, proceedings of a Seminar on Crime Prevention, Police Staff College, Bramshill House, 26–29 September 1982 (London: Home Office, 1982).

Home Office, *The Response to Racial Attacks and Harassment: Guidance for the Statutory Agencies*. Report of the Inter-Departmental Racial Attacks Group (London: Home Office, 1989).

Home Office, *Safer Communities: The Local Delivery of Crime Prevention through the Partnership Approach*, Report of the Home Office Standing Conference on Crime Prevention (London: Home Office, 1991a).

Home Office, *The Response to Racial Attacks and Harassment: Sustaining the Momentum*, 2nd Report of the Inter-Departmental Racial Attacks Group (London: Home Office, 1991b).

Hope, T., *Implementing Crime Prevention Measures*, Home Office Research Study no 86 (London: HMSO, 1985).

House of Commons, *Racial Attacks*, Second Report from the Home Affairs Committee, Session 1981–82, HC106 (London: HMSO, 1982).

House of Commons, *Racial Attacks and Harassment*, Third Report from the Home Affairs Committee, Session 1985–86, HC409 (London: HMSO, 1986).

Hunte, J., *Nigger Hunting in England?* (London: West Indian Standing Conference, 1965).

Husbands, Christopher T., *Racial Exclusionism and the City: The Urban Support of the National Front* (London: Allen & Unwin, 1983).

Husbands, Christopher T., 'Racial Attacks: the Persistence of Racial Harassment in British Cities', in Tony Kushner and Kenneth Lunn (eds) *Traditions of Intolerance: Historical Perspectives on Fascism and Race Discourse in Britain* (Manchester: Manchester University Press, 1989) pp. 91–115.

Husbands, Christopher T., 'Militant Neo-Nazism in the Federal Republic of Germany in the 1980s', in Luciano Cheles, Ronald Ferguson and Michalina Vaughan (eds.) *Neo-Fascism in Europe* (Harlow: Longman, 1991a) pp. 86–119.

Husbands, Christopher T., 'Neo-Nazis in East Germany: The New Danger?', *Patterns of Prejudice*, vol. 25, no 1 (Summer 1991b) pp. 1–15.

ID-Archiv, *Drahtzieher in Braunen Netz* (Edn ID-Archiv, 1992).

Innenministerium/Ministry of Interior, *Presserklärung zum Rückübernahmeabkommen mit Rumänien* (Bucharest/Bonn, September 1992).

Institute of Race Relations, *Police Against Black People* (London: Institute of Race Relations, 1979).

Institute of Race Relations, *Policing Against Black People* (London: IRR, 1987).

Institute of Race Relations, *Deadly Silence: Black Deaths in Custody* (London, 1991).

Inter-Departmental Racial Attacks Group, *The Response to Racial Attacks and Harassment: Guidance for the Statutory Agencies* (London: Home Office, 1989).

International Labour Organisation, *Report of the Commission of Inquiry Appointed under article 26 of the International Labour Organisation (ILO) to Examine the Observance by Romania of the Discrimination (Employment and Occupation) Convention*, 1958, no 111 (Geneva, 1991).

International Romani Union and Ethnic Federation of Roma in Romania, *Prosecuting and Preventing Violence and Intolerance against Romanies-Gypsies in the CSCE Countries: The case of Roma in Romania.* Draft Report prepared for the CSCE Seminar on 'Human Dimension of Tolerance' Discussion Group no 3, Legal Issues and Law Enforcement (Warsaw, 16–20 November 1992).

Ioanid, Radu, *The Sword of the Archangel: Fascist Ideology in Romania* (New York, 1990).

Jansma, L. and Veenman, J., 'De Schiedamse rel', *Mens en Maatschappij,* 2 (1977).

Jazouli, A., *Rapport sur observations dans six quartiers,* Délégation interministrielle à la ville, Délégation interministrielle à l'insertion de Jeunes, le FAS, la Caisse des Depots & Commissariat general du Plan (Institut Banlieuscopies, 1992).

Jazouli, A., *Les Années Banlieues* (Paris: Seuil, 1992a).

Jenkins, S. and Randall, V., *Here to Live: A Study of Race Relations in an English Town* (London: Runnymede Trust, 1970).

Joint Committee Against Racialism, *Racial Violence in England* (London: Joint Committee Against Racialism, 1980).

Judge, Edward H., *Easter in Kishinev: Anatomy of a Pogrom* (New York and London: New York University Press, 1992).

Judge, Edward H., *Plehve: Repression and Reform in Imperial Russia, 1902–1904* (Syracuse, NY: Syracuse University Press, 1983).

Keith, M. and Murji, K., 'Reifying Crime, Legitimising Racism: Policing, Local Authorities and Left Realism', in W. Ball and J. Solomos, *Race and Local Politics* (London: Macmillan, 1990).

Kenez, Peter, *Civil War in South Russia, 1919–1920* (Berkeley, 1977).

Kenrick, Donald and Puxon, Grattan, *Sinti und Roma: Die Vernichtung eines Volkes im NS-Staat* (Göttingen: Pogrom, 1980).

Kimber, J. and Cooper, L., *Victim Support Racial Harassment Project* (London: Community Research and Advisory Centre, The Polytechnic of North London, 1991).

King. M., 'The Political Construction of Crime Prevention: A Contrast between the Frence and British Experience.' in K. Stenson and D. Cowell (eds) *The Politics of Crime Control* (London: Sage, 1991).

Kirfel, Martina and Oswalt, Walter (ed.) *Die Rückkehr der Führer – Modernisierter Rechtsradikalismus in Westeuropa* (Europaverlag, 1989).

Klarsfeld, S. *Le rôle de Vichy dans la solution finale de la question juive en France* (Paris: Fayard, 1992).

Klier, John D., 'The Russian Press and the Anti-Jewish Pogroms of 1881', *Canadian–American Slavic Studies,* XVII, 1 (1983).

Klier, John D. and Lambroza, Shlomo (eds) *Pogroms: Anti-Jewish Violence in Modern Russian History* (Cambridge, 1991).

Klug, F., *Racist Attacks* (London: Runnymede Trust, 1982).

Krabbe, Mette and Lundgren, Malin, *Nynazism i kvällspressen: En studie av hur nynazism framställts i Aftonbladet och Expressen* (Gothenburg: University of Gothenburg, Spring 1992).

Kühnen, Michael, *Unser Weg – Geschichte des Nationalsozialismus* (Das Deutsche Reich, 1986).

Kushner, T. and C. Lunn (eds) *Traditions of Intolerance. Historical Perspectives on Fascism and Race Discourse in Britain* (Manchester: Manchester University Press, 1984).

Ladurie, Emmanuel LeRoy, *Carnival in Romans* (New York: Braziller, 1979).

Lambroza, Shlomo, 'Jewish Self-Defence during the Russian Pogroms of 1903–06', *Jewish Journal of Sociology* (1981) pp. 123–34.

Lambroza, Shlomo, 'Pleve, Kishinev and the Jewish Question: A Reappraisal', *Nationalities Papers*, XII, 1 (1984).

Landesamt für Verfassungsschutz Baden-Württemberg, *Verfassungsschutzbericht Baden-Württemberg* (1991).

Landesamt für Verfassungsschutz Baden-Württemberg, *Rechtsexstremismus in der Bundesrepublik Deutschland* (1992).

Landesamt für Verfassungsschutz Baden-Württemberg, *Skinheads* (1992).

Landeszentrale für Politische Bildung Schleswig-Holstein, *Rechtsexstremismus in Schleswig-Holstein 1945–1990* (1990).

Laqueur, Walter, *The Age of Terrorism* (London: Weidenfeld & Nicolson, 1987).

Larsson, Janerik, *Ustasja* (Copenhagen: Samleren, 1972).

Lequin, Y., *La Mosaïque France: Histoire des Etrangers et de l'Immigration*, Larousse, 1988).

Levine, M., *Les Ratonnades d'Octobre, un meutre collectif à Paris in 1961* (Paris: Ramsay, 1985).

Lieven, Dominic, 'The Security Police, Civil Rights and the Fate of the Russian Empire (1855–1917)', in Olga Crisp and Linda Edmundson (eds) *Civil Rights in Imperial Russia* (Oxford, 1989).

Lindquist, Hans, *Fascism idag; Förtrupper eller eftersläntare?* (Stockholm: Federativ, 1979).

Lloyd, C. and H. Waters, 'France: One Culture, One People? *Race & Class*, vol. 32, no 3 (Jan–March 1991).

Lloyd, C., 'Universalism and Difference: The Crisis of Anti-Racism in Britain and France', in A. Rattansi and S. Westwood, *On the Western Front: Studies in Racism, Modernity and Identity* (Cambridge: Polity, 1993).

Lodenius, Anna-Lena and Larsson, Stieg, *Extremhögern* (Stockholm: Tiden, 1991).

Lodenius, Anna-Lena and Tamas, Gellert, 'Fyllegrejor och pojkstrek?', *Metallarbeten* no 6 (1992).

London Race and Housing Forum, *Racial Harassment on Local Authority Housing Estates, (London: Commission for Racial Equality, 1982).*

London Borough of Newham, *Memorandum Submitted by the London Borough of Newham to the 1986 Home Affairs Sub-Committee on Race Relations and Immigration* (printed as an appendix to House of Commons, 1986).

Lööw, Heléne, 'Rasism och rasistiska organisationer i Sverige: En historisk översikt', *Rasism och rättsmedel i Norden* (Uppsala: Seminarrapport, Autumn 1988).

Lööw, Heléne, 'Från nassar till seriösa patrioter', *Tvärsnitt*, no 3 (1991).

Lööw, Heléne, 'Tant Brun – män och kvinnor i 'Vit Makt världen' and 'De Nationella leden' 1920–1992', *Historisk Tidskrift*, no 4 (1992).

Lööw, Heléne, 'Hundra år av svensk antisemitism', *Ord & Bild*, no 3 (1992).

Lööw, Heléne, 'Vår tids nationalsocialism', in Charles Westin (ed.) *Skolan, Hjärtat och Världen* (1992).

Manchester Council for Community Relation, *Racial Harassment in Manchester and the Response of the Police, 1980-1985. (Manchester: Manchester CCR, 1986)*.

Marshall, George, *Spirit of '69 – A Skinhead Bible* (S.T. Publishing, 1991).

Merkl, Peter H., 'Rollerball or Neo-Nazi Violence?', in Merkl (ed.) *Political Violence and Terror: Motifs and Motivations* (Berkeley: University of California Press, 1986).

Metropolitan Police, *Recording and Monitoring Racial Incidents Guidelines* (London: Metropolitan Police Community Relations Branch; printed as an appendix to House of Commons, 1986).

Miles, R., 'The Riots of 1958: Notes on the Ideological Construction of 'Race Relations' in Britain', *Immigrants and Minorities*, 3, 3 (1984) pp. 252–75.

Miles, R., *Racism* (London: Routledge, 1989).

Mogniss, A, 'Interview de "Rock against Police"', *Jeunes Hors les Murs*, Questions Clefs no 2 (Paris: EDI, 1982).

Mouvement Contre le Racisme et Pour l'Amitié entre les Peuples, *Cronique du flagrant racisme* (Paris: La Découverte, 1984).

Mumcu, U., 'Milliyetçi Hareket Partisi', in *Sosyalizm ve Toplumsal Mücadeleler Ansiklopedisi*, vol.7 (Istanbul: Iletisim Publishing, 1988) p. 2357.

Nederl and Omroep-Stichting (NOS), *Media en Minderheden* (Amsterdam: NOS, 1986).

Nederlands Centrum Buitenlanders (NCB), *De Grijze Wolf en de Halve Maan* (Utrecht: NCB, 1980).

Newham Monitoring Project & CARF, *Newham: The Forging of a Black Community* (London: NMP/CARF, 1991).

Noiriel, G., *Le Creuset Français* (Paris: Seuil, 1988).

O'Maoláin, Ciarán, *The Radical Right: A World Dictionary* (Longman, 1987).

Paletz, David L. and Schmid, Alex P. (eds) *Terrorism and the Media* (Newbury Park: Sage Publications, 1992).

Peyrot, M., 'La 'boulangère de Reims acquittée par la cour d'assises de la Marne', *Le Monde* (15/16 November 1992).

Pilkington, E., *Beyond the Mothercountry* (London: IB Taurice & Co.Ltd., 1988).

Read, M. and Simpson, A., *Against a Rising Tide: Racism, Europe and 1992* (Nottingham: Spokesman/Nottingham Racial Equality Council and European Labour Forum, 1991).

Reemtsma, Katrin, *Minderheit ohne Zukunft? Roma in Jugoslawien*, Menschenrechtsreport der Gesellschaft für bedrohte Völker (Göttingen, 1990).

Reemtsma, Katrin, *Roma in Rumänien*. Menschenrechtsreport der Gesellschaft für bedrohte Völker (Göttingen, 1992).

Rein, M., *Social Science and Public Policy* (Harmondsworth: Penguin, 1976).

Rein, M., *From Policy to Practice* (London: Macmillan, 1983).

Rikspolisstyrelsen: *Racism ock främlingsfiendtlighet* (Stockholm: RPS–Rapport, 1988).

Rogger, H., 'The Jewish Policy of Late Tsarism: A Reappraisal', in *Jewish Policies and Right Wing Politics in Imperial Russia* (London, 1986).

Romani International Union, *Letter of Response to Information Circular Numbers 2 and 3 and to the Remarks of the Romanian Delegation on the Situation of Roma in Romania* (Geneva, 1991).

Rousso, H., *Le Syndrome de Vichy de 1944 à nos jours* (Paris: Seuil, 1990).

Runnymede Trust, *Bulletin*, no 149, November 1982.

Säkerhetspolisen, *Verksamhetsåret 1991/92* (Stockholm: 1992).

Säkerhetspolisen, *Kartläggning av främlingsfiendtliga angrepp: 1992* (Stockholm: 1993).

Sampson, A., Stubbs, P., Smith, D., Pearson G. and Blagg, H., 'Crime, localities and the Multi-agency Approach', *British Journal of Criminology*, vol. 28, no 4 (Autumn 1988).

Sampson, A. and Phillips, C., *Multiple Victimisation: Racial Attacks on an East London Housing Estate* (London: Home Office Police Research Group, 1992).

Saulsbury, William and Benjamin Bowling, *The Multi-agency Approach in Practice: The North Plaistow Racial Harassment Project*, Home Office Research and Planning Unit Paper (1991).

Scarman, Lord, *The Scarman Report: The Brixton Disorders 10-12 April 1981* (Harmondsworth: Penguin, 1986).

Schmid, Alex P. and Graaf, Janny de, *Violence as Communication* (London and Beverly Hills: Sage, 1982).

Schmid, Alex P. and Jongmann Albert J. (*et al.*) *Political Terrorism* (Amsterdam: North-Holland Publishing Company, 1989).

Schor, R., *L'opinion française et les étrangers, 1919-1939* (Publications de la Sorbonne, 1985).

Schröder, Burkhard, *Rechte Kerle, Skinheads, Faschos, Hooligans* (Rowohlt, 1992).

Şener, C., *Alevilik Olayi* (Istanbul: Yön Publishing, 1989).

Slitinsky, M., *L'Affaire Popon* (Paris: A. Moreau, 1983).

Smith, D. and Gray, J., *Police and People in London* (Aldershot: Gower, 1983).

Soytemiz, I., 'Hitler Faşizminin Yarattiği Hareket ve Bağimsizliğin Yitirilişi', in *Sosyalizm ve Toplumsal Mücadeleler Ansiklopedisi*, vol. 7 (Istanbul: Iletisim Publishing, 1988) pp. 2220–1.

Sprinzak, Ehud, 'The Process of Delegitimization: Towards a Linkage Theory of Political Terrorism', *Terrorism and Political Violence*, vol. 3, no 1 (spring 1991).

Statens innvandrarvärk, *Flyktingförläggningar anmälda hot och attacker under perioden 90.01.12–91.01.15* (1991).

Stora, B., *Histoire politique de l'immigration Algérienne en France* (Thèse d'état, 1991).

Stora, B., *La Gangrène et l'oubli, La mémoire de la guerre d'Algérie* (Paris: La Découverte, 1991).

Stuurman, S., *Kapitalisme en Burgerlijke Staat: Een Inleiding in de Marxistische Politieke Theorie* (Amsterdam, SUA, 1978) (3rd edn, 1981).

Stuurman, S., *De Labyrintische Staat: Over Politiek, Ideologie en Moderniteit* (Amsterdam, SUA, 1985).

Subcommission on Prevention of Discrimination and Protection of Minorities, *Resolution 1991/21* (Geneva, 1992).

Tamas, Gellert and Lodenius, Anna-Lena, 'Därfor kastar snälla pojkar bomber', *Röda Korset*, 3 (1991).

Tristan, A., *Le silence du fleuve* (Au nom de la mémoire, 1991).

Tunaya, T. A., *Türkiyede Politik Partiler* (Istanbul: Hürriyet Vakfi Publishing, 1984).

Tuttle, William M., Jr., *Race Riot: Chicago in the Red Summer of 1919* (New York: Atheneum, 1970).

Viard, P., 'Les Crimes Racistes en France', *Les Temps Modernes*, XXXX, no 452–4 (1984) pp. 1942–52.

Weatheritt, M., *Innovations in Policing* (London: The Police Foundation, 1986).

Weinberg, Robert, 'The Pogrom of 1905 in Odessa: A Case Study', in Kliev and Lambrozen (1991).

Weissman, Neil, 'Regular Police in Tsarist Russia, 1900–1914', *The Russian Review*, LXIV, 1 (1985).

Wieviorka, M., *La France Raciste* (Paris: La Découverte, 1992).

Wihtol de Wenden, C., *Les Immigrés et la Politique* (Paris: Presses de la Fondation Nationale des Science Politiques, 1988).

Wilkinson, Paul, *The New Fascists* (Pan, 1983).

William, Philip, *Puppet Masters – The Political Use of Terrorism in Italy* (Constable, 1991).

Witte, Rob B. J., 'De onbegrepen verkiezingsuitslag voor Extreem – Rechts' *Acta Politica*, no 4 (October 1991) pp. 449–470.

Witte, Rob B. J., 'Comparing State Responses to Racist Violence in Europe: A Model for International Comparative Analysis', in Hamm (1944).

WODC, *Politie en Openbaar ministerie tegen rassendiscriminatie* (Arnheim: Gouda Quint, 1993).

Wynn, Charters, *Workers, Strikers, and Pogroms: The Donbass–Dnepr Bend in Late Imperial Russia, 1870–1905* (Princeton, 1992).

Yin, R. K., *Case Study Research: Design and Methods* (London: Sage, 1989).

Index